Scotland in the Age of the Disruption

Edited by

STEWART J. BROWN

and

MICHAEL FRY

EDINBURGH UNIVERSITY PRESS

© Edinburgh University Press, 1993

Edinburgh University Press Ltd
22 George Square, Edinburgh

Typeset in Linotron Baskerville
by ROM-Data Corporation Ltd, Falmouth,
and printed and bound in Great Britain by
The University Press, Cambridge

A CIP record for this book is available from
the British Library

I S B N 0 7486 0433 2

The Publisher wishes to acknowledge
subsidy from the Scottish Arts Council
towards the publication of this volume

Contents

Preface

BETWEEN FOUR AND FIVE IN THE MORNING, on 18 May 1843, spectators filled
the galleries at the St Andrew's church in Edinburgh in order to witness the
opening session of the annual General Assembly of the Church of Scotland.
As the morning progressed, thousands more gathered outside the church;
their presence confirmed the widespread expectation that this day would
mark a decisive moment for the Scottish Church and society. By the time
the commissioners to the General Assembly began taking their places shortly
after noon, the pressure of the crowd had already become suffocating. At
about half past two in the afternoon, the Royal Commissioner entered the
church at the head of a procession of dignitaries, and the retiring Moderator, the Revd Dr David Welsh, Professor of Ecclesiastical History at the
University of Edinburgh, led the Assembly in opening prayer. Then, at the
point where it was customary to read out the roll of new commissioners, the
Moderator rose and solemnly addressed the Assembly, amid a 'breathless
silence'. 'There had been an infringement', he said, 'on the Constitution of
the Church – an infringement so great, that they could not constitute its
General Assembly'.[1] Instead, Welsh proceeded to read a long document,
protesting against attacks made on the traditional liberties of the Scottish
Church and nation by the civil authorities in the British parliamentary state
– attacks which touched on even the headship of Christ in his Church. As a
result, it had become impossible for those who believed in the spiritual
independence of the national Church to remain in the existing Establishment. He then laid the protest on the table, 'turned and bowed respectfully
to the Royal Commissioner, left the chair, and proceeded along the aisle to
the door of the Church'.[2] He was followed in solemn procession by the
Evangelical leaders of the Church, Thomas Chalmers, Robert Gordon,
Patrick MacFarlan, and then by row after row of commissioners, until the
left – or Evangelical – side of the church was nearly empty.

   Outside, cheers rose from the crowd as the first of the outgoing commissioners came out of the church, but these were soon silenced as they were
deemed unseemly for the occasion. There had been no plan to form a

procession outside the church, but the crush of the crowd was so great that
the outgoing commissioners were forced to walk in column, three or four
abreast, as they made their way to the Tanfield Hall in Canonmills, which
had been fitted out to receive them. As they processed, the outgoing
commissioners were joined by hundreds of other ministers who were also
pledged to leave the Established Church. Some in the crowd jeered the
procession, but many more wept or bowed their heads. Upon reaching the
Tanfield Hall, the commissioners constituted themselves as the Free Protesting Church of Scotland, and over 450 ministers signed the Deed of Demission, giving up their churches, manses and incomes as ministers of the
Establishment, and facing an insecure future.

'Well, what do you think of it?', someone asked the Whig judge and
journalist Francis Jeffrey, who had remained in his home during the dramatic events of the afternoon. 'More than four hundred of them are actually
out'. 'I'm proud of my country', Jeffrey replied. 'There is not another
country on earth where such a deed could have been done.'[3] It was an
impressive sacrifice, and many of those going out placed not only themselves, but also their families, at risk. This sacrifice, observed Lord Cockburn
a few days after the event, formed 'the most honourable fact' in the 'whole
history' of Scotland.[4] For the Evangelical journalist Hugh Miller, the outgoing ministers were the direct heirs of the Covenanting martyrs, who had
fallen during the persecutions of the later seventeenth century:

> Then, as now, the religious principles which they maintained were
> those of the country. They were principles that had laid fast hold of
> the national mind, and the fires of persecution served only to render
> their impress ineradicable. Is it not strange how utterly the great
> lessons of history have failed to impress the mean and wretched rulers
> of our country in this the day of their visitation?[5]

Across the country, congregations of the new Free Church were formed,
often against the strenuous opposition of local landowners and employers.
Those who went out of the Establishment perceived of themselves as standing for the sacred principle of the spiritual independence of the Church and
the traditional liberties of the Scottish nation. Those who remained in the
Establishment viewed the seceders as little more than rebels and fanatics,
threatening the destruction of the ancient constitution of Church and state
and challenging the traditional social hierarchy. In some areas, particularly
in the Highlands, entire communities joined the Free Church. In most of
the country, however, communities and families were divided, often bitterly
so, and the divisions and ill-feeling would continue into the twentieth
century. In all, nearly 40 per cent of the clergy and perhaps half the lay
membership of the Established Church of Scotland left to form the Free
Church at the great Disruption of 1843.

The Disruption was the most important domestic event in Scotland
during the nineteenth century. Scarcely a Scot, at home or overseas, can
have been unaware of it, and many were profoundly affected in their daily
lives. The course of Scottish history was permanently altered, while the

ramifications spread through the United Kingdom and the British empire. For decades, the Disruption formed the subject of intense, almost obsessive, debate among the Scottish people. It was seen as a struggle over principles that were fundamental to the idea of a Christian state and to Scotland's national identity, and that involved the very nature of Christ's sovereignty in the national Church of Scotland.

The fires of the Disruption have now grown cold, and it has become difficult to understand how the principles involved in the conflict could have aroused such passion and such sacrifices. This is not for lack of accounts of the Disruption. The literature of the Disruption is voluminous – dense histories, pious memoirs, legions of pamphlets, reports of Court of Session decisions, parliamentary debates and Assembly deliberations, and lengthy articles in the newspapers and journals of the day. But most of these accounts, written during the last century, are heavy with tortuous arguments, archaic language and a tendentious tone that renders them largely inaccessible to the modern reader. While there have been some recent studies by ecclesiastical historians, there is no rounded modern account of the Disruption that takes account of its social, political and cultural effects.

The purpose of this volume is to breathe life back into these past struggles, to recapture some of the fervour and enthusiasm, and to direct attention to the crucial importance of religion in early and mid-nineteenth-century Scottish politics and society. The Disruption was a watershed in the history of Scotland, one which profoundly affected a number of changes occurring at the time in Scottish society, politics and culture. The age of the Disruption was one which witnessed the radical revision of Scottish philosophy and theology, the collapse of Scotland's historic political constitution, the rise of urban-industrial society and the coming of the railways, the commercialisation of agriculture and the Highland Clearances, and the adoption by Scots of a fresh sense of mission to the world. It was an age of revolution in Scotland, more far-reaching in its impact than that surrounding the Union of 1707, and the Disruption crystallised and symbolised the transformations being unleashed on the nation.

This volume does not pretend to provide a detailed narrative account of the Disruption or of Scotland in the age of the Disruption. Rather, the authors have sought to convey a sense of the broader national and international context of the Disruption through an interdisciplinary collection of essays exploring different aspects of Scottish politics, society and culture. The study of nineteenth-century Scotland is a growth area, and yet one where much still has to be discovered and understood. The job in hand is to provide a forum for new interpretations in the light of recent scholarship, to recover a sense of the importance of religion in modern Scottish history, and to set agendas for further research.

After an introductory chapter by Professor Stewart J. Brown, which sets out the present state of knowledge about the course of the Disruption and its direct consequences, the book is divided into three sections. The first deals with what might be called the secular side of the Disruption – its impact on the political and social foundations of Scottish society. Michael Fry concentrates on the political aspects, showing how the breakup of the national Church also represented a far-reaching constitutional shift which gave the Union of Scotland and England a wholly new shape. Dr Peter Hillis demonstrates the complexity of the way in which Highland, rural Lowland and urban communities split at the Disruption. While the splits often followed divisions along the lines of social class, this was by no means invariably the case, and his chapter demonstrates the continuing importance of ideals and religious beliefs in Victorian Scotland. Professor Donald Macleod explores the period's daunting social problems, those associated with rapid industrialisation and urbanisation, and shows how the efforts of Evangelicals such as Thomas Chalmers to respond to the social suffering proved inadequate, and undermined confidence in the ability of a national religious Establishment to provide basic social welfare.

In the second section, we examine the impact of the Disruption on the cultural life of Scotland. To a considerable extent, the cultural achievements of the Scottish Enlightenment were sustained into the early decades of the nineteenth century – largely through the connection of the national Church, the national universities and the parish schools. The Scotland of what might be termed the 'silver age' of the Enlightenment remained very much a Calvinist culture, even if many of the enlightened literati were intent on curbing religious enthusiasm. Certainly the institutional connection of Church and university conserved a sense of unity in the creative and fertile culture of the early nineteenth century. By breaking up the national Church, the Disruption removed an important institutional foundation of Scottish culture, helping to bring an end to the Scottish Enlightenment and opening the way for the increasing provincialisation of Scottish culture. Mr Donald Withrington explores this process through a study of Scottish education in the aftermath of the Disruption, in particular the attempts of the new Free Church to create a national system of schools and colleges during the 1840s. The Free Church, however, lacked the resources and perhaps also the will to recreate the unity of Church and education on a national level, and the educational disputes and failures nearly shattered the unity of the new Church within ten years after the Disruption. Dr Paul Baxter describes one of the major issues of the day – the growing disparity between the teachings of natural theology and the discoveries of science – and notes that the Disruption came at a time when it was becoming increasingly difficult for Scottish Christian thinkers to sustain the connection of natural and revealed theology that had played such an important role in the Enlightenment achievement. In his study of literature and the Disruption, Professor Angus Calder shows how religious division and doubt played their part in the weakness of Scottish fiction, a weakness not decisively reversed until the early twentieth century.

In the final section, we turn to a theme neglected not only in the previous accounts of the Disruption but until recently also in Scottish historiography in general – that is, Scotland's links with the empire and Europe, and its sense of national mission. It is now being recognised that Scotland was not simply the junior partner in the Union, but that Scotland continued to cultivate its own links with the larger world and to share in European movements. By 1843, there was a large Scottish diaspora in the British colonies, especially Canada, Australia and New Zealand, and Professor Barbara Murison surveys the very significant impact of the Disruption on the religion and identity of the Scots overseas. The Revd Dr Andrew Ross turns to the effects of the Disruption upon the considerable Scottish missionary outreach in the nineteenth century, exploring in particular the profound and lasting influence of the distinctive Free Church piety upon the Dutch Reformed Church in South Africa. Finally, the Revd Dr Friedhelm Voges brings the story back to Europe, showing how the Scottish Disruption was in a sense just one example of a general restructuring in relations between Church and state that took place in a number of European countries in the aftermath of the French Revolution and Napoleonic Wars, heralding the breakdown of the connection of throne and altar, the waning of the confessional state and the advent of a more secular order.

Michael Fry and Stewart J. Brown

NOTES

1. *Witness*, 20 May 1843.
2. W. Hanna, *Memoirs of Dr. Chalmers*, 4 vols (Edinburgh, 1849–52), vol. iv, p. 338.
3. Ibid., p. 339.
4. H. Cockburn, *Journal of Henry Cockburn*, 2 vols (Edinburgh, 1874), vol. ii, p. 32.
5. *Witness*, 20 May 1843.

Notes on the Disruption Cartoons

The eight cartoons reproduced in this volume are part of the collection of Disruption cartoons in the possession of New College Library of the University of Edinburgh, and are included with the permission of the Library. There are a total of twenty-six lithograph cartoons in the New College collection, produced by two unknown artists between 1840 and 1845, and reflecting on the controversies surrounding the Disruption. Drawn with considerable wit and skill, the cartoons approach the subject from a detached point of view – taking a light-hearted look at the presbyterian Dissenters, the Moderates and the Evangelical non-intrusionists, but directing most of their humour at four Edinburgh-based non-intrusionist clergymen, Thomas Chalmers (1780–1847), Robert Gordon (1786–1853), William Cunningham (1805–61) and Robert Smith Candlish (1806–73). The Disruption represented profound issues of Church and state, religion and national identity; at the same time, the cartoons remind us that the humour, humanity and impatience with high pretensions that had earlier characterised the poetry of Robert Burns and the novels of John Galt remained a potent force during the controversies of the 1840s.

PLATE 1   *The Famous Stalking Horse Non-Intrusion*
The suggestion in this cartoon is that the non-intrusion issue – the effort to protect against the 'intrusion' of unsuitable parish ministers in the Church of Scotland by granting a popular voice in the selection of ministers – had been a mere stalking horse, a sham issue, behind which Evangelical Church leaders pursued their real aim of preserving and extending the Established Church of Scotland against the efforts of the 'Voluntaries' or Dissenters, to disestablish the Church. Through 'non-intrusion', the cartoonist suggests, the clergy believed they could gain popular support for Church defence, while at the same time preserving most of the patronage system intact. However, by the late 1830s, as a result of a series of decisions in the civil courts, the stalking horse has come to life and has broken out of control. It now threatens the disruption of the Church, despite the efforts of the

diminutive Candlish to ride the beast, and of Cunningham to hold its reins. Meanwhile Chalmers looks on in perplexity, and wishes he had restricted his efforts to Church Extension and never dabbled with the vexed issues of patronage and popular rights.

PLATE 2 *Pope Thomas I Issueth his Bull*
Here Thomas Chalmers, in the guise of Pope Thomas I, unleashes the 'bullish' and truculent young non-intrusionist, William Cunningham, who by his extreme public statements proves a danger to friend and foe alike. While some believed that Chalmers was being driven to extreme positions in the non-intrusionist controversy by clumsy younger ministers such as Cunningham, the cartoonist here clearly suggests that Chalmers was using the zeal of his young followers to further his own aims, while he assumed the position of an authoritative leader standing aloof and issuing decrees from on high. The cartoon reflects the widespread belief that, in his insistence on the independence of the Church from civil law, Chalmers was seeking to establish an ecclesiastical tyranny in Scotland. There may also be an allusion here to Chalmers's well-known support for Catholic Emancipation in 1829.

PLATE 3 *Clerical Suspension*
The cartoon deals with the notorious Strathbogie affair, in which the Moderate majority of the presbytery of Strathbogie defied the instructions of their ecclesiastical superior, the General Assembly, and prepared to ordain an unpopular patron's candidate minister of Marnoch, at the command of the civil Court of Session. In response, the Commission of the General Assembly suspended the seven insubordinate ministers from their charges in February 1839, and sent ministers to preach in their place. Here we see the seven Moderates literally suspended above their pulpits, their bibles under lock and key, while the ministers sent by the Assembly attempt to preach in their place. The seven suspended ministers show little respect for the authority of the General Assembly, while the clerical agents of the Assembly are portrayed as uncooth agitators.

PLATE 4 *Modern Martyrs*
In response to the General Assembly's suspension of the seven Moderate ministers of Strathbogie presbytery, the Court of Session issued interdicts in December 1839 and February 1840, with the second interdict forbidding any minister of the Church of Scotland from entering the parishes of the seven without their permission for the purpose of preaching. For the non-intrusionists, this was unacceptable interference by the civil authorities in a matter of ecclesiastical discipline, and many leading non-intrusionists proceeded to Strathbogie to defy the interdict, courting arrest and martyrdom. Here the cartoonist imagines four of the leading non-intrusionists – Chalmers, Cunningham, Gordon and Candlish – as modern martyrs, being led to imprisonment. Dr John Ritchie of the United Secession church, a

leader of the disestablishment movement in Scotland, plays the fiddle and clearly enjoys the discomfort of the Church. While Candlish strikes a dramatic pose, the older Gordon, minister of St Giles in Edinburgh, is portrayed as less than enthusiastic for martyrdom.

PLATE 5 *The Reel of Bogie!! A Clerical Dance*
Probably the best known of the Disruption cartoons, this drawing expressed the growing confusion of the Scottish public over the Strathbogiè affair. The four non-intrusionist leaders are engaged in the whirling reel. Chalmers is in the centre, bearing a banner blazoned with a public statement he had made in the heat of debate announcing his refusal ever to back down to the Court of Session (and now leaving him with little room for compromise). Candlish evidently enjoys the reel, but Cunningham has to help the venerable Gordon, who admits he is having considerable difficulty with the dance (Strathbogie affair). Ritchie plays the fiddle, and the picture of Rome burning on the wall beside him bears the caption, 'Nero'. The figure about to strike Chalmers with the sword of the civil law is Charles Hope, Lord President of the Court of Session, while Ritchie goads him on. 'He's got no friends,' Ritchie calls out, a reference to Chalmers's lack of political support at Westminster.

PLATE 6 Untitled (Thomas Chalmers and friends in the bog)
Chalmers, Candlish, Cunningham and Gordon are trapped and sinking in the bog of the non-intrusionist controversy, while a crowd looks on, unable to help and clearly divided in its sympathies. The figure on the left, Lord President Charles Hope, observes that he had warned them what it would come to, 'the farther in the deeper', while behind him the home secretary, Sir James Graham, announces that 'pon my soul I cannot interfere in the matter'. Chalmers pleads for a lifeline from the United Secession leader John Ritchie, who answers that his Voluntary principles will not allow him to assist an Established Churchman. Candlish pledges that if he ever escapes, he will join the Dissenters, while his friend 'Cunnie' [Cunningham], has sunk too deep to utter anything.

PLATE 7 *The Disruption!*
The solemn procession out of the General Assembly on 18 May 1843 is here reduced to a carnival parade, led by the Voluntary John Ritchie (with his now familiar fiddle). While Candlish, Cunningham and other younger non-intrusionists are portrayed as enthusiastic for the Disruption, Chalmers is weighed down with a sense of personal responsibility and his 'no retraction' banner droops, while Gordon is literally being dragged along at the end of a rope. All the outgoing ministers are loaded down with loaves and fishes, reflecting the popular perception that most would be well provided for by the outgoing congregations. George Cook and the other leading Moderates look on sternly from the windows of the 'Constitutional Assembly', and above them the dove of peace alights for the first time in many years.

PLATE 8   *'Send Back the Money'*
Following the Disruption, the newly formed Free Church sent deputations
to North America to gather funds and international support. The cartoon
refers to the public controversy surrounding the decision of the Free Church
to accept financial contributions, amounting to about £3,000, from churches
in the slave-holding states of the American South. A cigar-smoking slave-
owner hands the bundle of money to Cunningham, who accepts the bargain
and welcomes the slave-owner into 'our *Free* Communion'. Candlish presses
'Willy' to hurry with the exchange, but it is too late. A deputation from the
American Anti-Slavery Society – Henry C. Wright, James N. Buffin and the
celebrated Black American Abolitionist, Frederick Douglass – have witnessed the deed and resolve to force the Free Church to send back the
money. 'Is that the *Free* Church?' asks a surprised Douglass. While the
controversy created a crisis of conscience within the Free Church, the bitter
attacks from their Abolitionist opponents soon brought Free Church members to rally behind their leaders. The money was not sent back.

Stewart J. Brown

Notes on Contributors

PAUL BAXTER, M.A., Ph.D., is Head of Central Services, British Library Science, Reference and Information Service. A scholar of the interactions of science and belief in Victorian Scotland, his publications include 'Brewster, Evangelism and the Disruption of the Church of Scotland', in E. D. Morrison-Low and J. R. R. Christie (eds), *Martyr of Science: Sir David Brewster* (Edinburgh, 1984).

STEWART J. BROWN, B.A., M.A., Ph.D., has been Professor of Ecclesiastical History at the University of Edinburgh since 1988. He is the author of *Thomas Chalmers and the Godly Commonwealth in Scotland* (Oxford, 1982) – awarded the Saltire Society History Prize – and is joint editor of the *Scottish Historical Review.*

ANGUS CALDER, M.A., D. Phil., has taught at the Universities of Nairobi, Malawi and Zimbabwe, and is currently Reader in Arts at the Open University in Scotland. His books include: *The People's War: Britain 1939–45* (London, 1969), *Revolutionary Empire: The Rise of the English-Speaking Empires from the Fifteenth Century to the 1780s* (London, 1981), and *The Myth of the Blitz* (London, 1991).

MICHAEL FRY, M.A., is a freelance writer and journalist based in Edinburgh. His books include *Patronage and Principle: A Political History of Modern Scotland* (Aberdeen, 1987) and *The Dundas Despotism* (Edinburgh, 1992).

PETER L. M. HILLIS, M.A., Ph.D., is Head of the Social Sciences Division and History Section at Jordanhill College in Glasgow. Among his articles are 'Presbyterianism and Social Class in Mid-Nineteenth Century Glasgow', in *Journal of Ecclesiastical History* (1990), and 'Education and Evangelisation: Presbyterian Missions in Mid-Victorian Glasgow', in *Scottish Historical Review* (1987).

DONALD MACLEOD, M.A., is Professor of Systematic Theology at the Free Church College in Edinburgh. He served as editor of the *Monthly Record* from 1977 to 1990, and his books include *The Spirit of Promise* (Tain, 1986), *Shared Life* (London, 1987) and *Behold your God* (Tain, 1988).

BARBARA C. MURISON, M.A., Ph.D., a native of Scotland, now teaches in the Department of History of the University of Western Ontario. She was a visiting fellow at the Centre of Canadian Studies at the University of Edinburgh from 1984–5, and she has published articles in the *British Journal of Canadian Studies* and the *Journal of Imperial and Commonwealth History*.

ANDREW C. ROSS, M.A., B.D., S.T.M., Ph.D., is Senior Lecturer in the History of Missions at the University of Edinburgh. He has served as Visiting Professor at the Federal Theological Seminary, South Africa (1976), the University of the Witwatersrand (1984) and Dartmouth College in the United States (1992). His publications include: *John Philip: Missions, Race and Politics in South Africa* (Aberdeen, 1986).

FRIEDHELM VOGES, Mag.Theol., Dr.Theol., a minister in Stade, Germany, is the author of *Das Denken von Thomas Chalmers in Kirchen- und Sozialgeschichtlichen Kontext* (Frankfurt, 1984), and 'Moderate and Evangelical Thinking in the Later Eighteenth Century', in *Records of the Scottish Church History Society* (1985).

DONALD J. WITHRINGTON, M.A., M.Ed., F.R.Hist.S., is Senior Lecturer in Scottish History at the University of Aberdeen. He has served as Director of the Centre for Scottish Studies at the University of Aberdeen (1970–81), joint editor of the *Scottish Historical Review* (1972–81) and editor of *Northern Scotland* (1972–80). Widely published on the religious and educational history of Scotland since the Reformation, he served as general editor of *Sir John Sinclair's Statistical Account of Scotland, 1791–99*, in 20 volumes (Wakefield, 1973–83).

   The Disruption of the Church of Scotland was the most important event in the history of nineteenth-century Scotland. The events of 1843 shattered one of the major institutional foundations of Scottish identity, divided the Scottish nation, and contributed significantly to the process of assimilation into a larger British parliamentary state that was increasingly secular in orientation. The Disruption was not only the break-up of the national religious Establishment; it was also a disruption in Scottish identity, a radical break from its Reformation and Covenanting past, and a turning-away from the vision of the unified godly commonwealth. The Disruption undermined the Presbyterian nationalism that had shaped early modern Scotland, with its ideal of the democratic intellect preserved in parish schools, kirk sessions and presbyteries. 'In the early 'forties', observed Walter Elliot, 'everything changed in Scotland at once. The distinctively Scottish tradition was broken.' 'The Disruption', Elliot added, 'was more than a quarrel about church government. It was the fall of a regime. The democratic intellectualism which had lasted for so many centuries was challenged in its own house.'[4]

I

The 'Ten Years' Conflict' that would culminate in the Disruption began in 1833, in the aftermath of constitutional changes that transformed the religious nature of the British state. Until the early nineteenth century, the British state was essentially a divine-right monarchy; its political institutions and social hierarchy were perceived as divinely ordained, reflecting not only the order of nature but also the direct interventions of God.[5] Fundamental to the constitutional order was the Protestant Establishment, preserved by providence at the Glorious Revolution of 1688, which provided religious and moral instruction to the population, fostered higher learning in the universities and represented the religious nature of the state. While religious Dissent was tolerated, full political rights were restricted to members of the Established Church. The Established Churches of England and of Ireland were Episcopalian in polity, their doctrine represented by the Thirty-nine Articles. The Established Church of Scotland was Presbyterian, with doctrinal orthodoxy based on the Calvinist Westminster Confession of Faith. Despite their differences, all three Established Churches had similar roles, representing the Christian conscience of the state, and providing religious ordinances to the nation through a parochial organisation.

   Between 1828 and 1832, Parliament enacted three major reforms which transformed the nature of the monarchial state, bringing a sudden, almost revolutionary end to what the historian J. C. D. Clark has described as Britain's *ancien régime*.[6] First, in 1828, following a prolonged campaign by Protestant Dissenters, Parliament repealed the Test and Corporation Acts, ending the political disabilities suffered by Dissenters and granting them full civil and political rights. Dissenters were no longer to be treated as a tolerated, but suspect, minority, and Parliament could no longer be regarded as in any sense restricted to members of the Established Churches. Secondly, in 1829, in response to large-scale popular agitation among the

CHAPTER ONE

The Ten Years' Conflict and the Disruption of 1843

STEWART J. BROWN

IN MAY 1843, the religious Establishment of Scotland was broken up as over a third of the ministers and perhaps half the lay members left the national Church to form the Free Protesting Church of Scotland.[1] Most of the outgoing ministers gave up secure incomes, comfortable manses and respectable social status for an uncertain future. They were prepared to sacrifice their worldly interests for a principle – that of the spiritual independence of the Church. Equally impressive were the achievements of the Free Church in erecting new churches, schools, colleges and manses, and in supporting a vigorous home and overseas mission. Within a few years, the Free Church had created an alternative national Church, with parochial churches and schools covering nearly the whole of Scotland. For many who left the Establishment, the Disruption was a deliverance: those going out were compared to the Israelites leaving the bondage of Egypt and trusting God to bring them to a better land.[2] For most of the outgoing ministers and lay members, however, there was also a sense of loss – the break-up of the national Church, the parting of friends and a waning sense of Scotland as a unified Christian commonwealth.

Those remaining in the Established Church of Scotland also experienced trials. While some welcomed the secession as a means of ridding the Church of disturbers of the existing order, many more experienced pain at the loss of so many able clergymen and committed lay members.[3] Some of those who remained had been allied with the outgoing ministers in the causes of Church Extension and Church Defence, but at the Disruption felt conscience-bound to stay at their posts within the historic Church which their ancestors had suffered to preserve and which God had called them to serve. Others simply did not believe that the spiritual independence of the Church of Scotland was under threat. Those remaining within the Church of Scotland endured taunts and accusations of being self-serving or cowardly, of having betrayed the national Church for the state's gold. In turn, they often grew suspicious and defensive. Friendships were severed, families divided, and bitterness would continue for generations.

Roman Catholic majority in Ireland, Parliament passed the Catholic Emancipation Act, granting English Catholics the right to vote in parliamentary elections, and British and Irish Catholics the right to sit in Parliament and hold most state offices. Finally, the Reform Act of 1832 swept away some 140 proprietary parliamentary seats, increased parliamentary representation in the new centres of population and granted the franchise to much of the commercial and industrial middle class. The Reform Act reduced the political influence of the Crown and the aristocracy, and made Parliament more representative of the politically articulate classes. It represented the transfer of real sovereignty from the Crown-in-Parliament to Parliament alone – and to a Parliament which now included Dissenters and Roman Catholics as a matter of statutory right.

In this new political order, the existence of the Established Churches was soon challenged. Dissenters, Irish Catholics and philosophic radicals argued that there was no justification for the state to maintain a religious Establishment or favour in any way one Christian communion over others. The Established Churches were portrayed as privileged corporations, unnecessary and wasteful of wealth that rightfully belonged to the nation.[7] In 1831, Catholic communities in Ireland began refusing to pay tithes to the minority Protestant Establishment, resisting tithe collectors and government troops by force. The tithe war created widespread rural disorder and crippled the Established Church of Ireland. In response to this unrest, and to growing criticism of the wealth and size of the Protestant Irish Establishment in a predominantly Catholic country, Parliament in 1833 passed the Church Temporalities (Ireland) Act, which made sweeping reforms in the Church of Ireland, including the suppression of ten Irish bishoprics and the suspension of a number of parishes. The money thus saved was vested in an Ecclesiastical Commission created by Parliament and charged to redistribute the revenues in order to increase the efficiency of the Irish Establishment. A clause in the Act calling for the diversion of Church revenues to education and poor-relief was only narrowly defeated, raising fears in the Establishment that disendowment would eventually follow.[8]

In England the constitutional changes of 1828–32 also stimulated criticism of the Anglican Establishment from Dissenters and radicals. During the crisis over parliamentary reform, popular hostility to the Church had been enhanced by the opposition of Anglican bishops to the Reform Bill. Parliament's suppression of the Irish bishoprics raised fears in the Church of England that it would suffer a similar fate, with reform by Parliamentary Commission eventually leading to the diversion of ecclesiastical endowments to education and poor-relief. With the existence of the Church apparently under threat, Anglicans responded with a variety of proposals for Church reform – such as the scheme proposed by the liberal Anglican, Thomas Arnold, for drawing most Trinitarian Dissenters into a comprehensive Establishment that would permit a wide diversity of liturgical practices and doctrinal beliefs. For Arnold, only such a radical reform could save the Established Church.[9] A very different call for reform was sounded in July

1833, when John Keble, Professor of Poetry at Oxford University, delivered his Assize Day sermon on 'National Apostasy', calling on the nation to rally to the defence of the historic Church of England and the ideal of national religion. Following the sermon, a group of Oxford clerics, including R. Hurrell Froude, Arthur P. Perceval and John Henry Newman, organised a movement to assert the national authority and spiritual independence of the Church. Petitions bearing the names of some 7,000 clergymen and 230,000 lay members were presented to the Archbishop of Canterbury. More significantly, the Oxford divines began issuing a series of 'Tracts for the Times', calling public attention to the dangers facing the national Church and asserting the apostolic and catholic nature of the Church of England.[10] The Church of England was not simply a religious Establishment subject to the will of parliamentary majorities; it was a true branch of the Church Catholic, under the sole headship of Christ and reflecting the purity of the primitive apostolic Church. During the 1830s, the energy and charisma of Newman, Froude and the scholar-priest, E. B. Pusey, helped to transform the Oxford Movement into a national force for the regeneration of the Anglican Establishment. The efforts of the Oxford divines to define Anglican identity, however, also created divisions in the English Church, with Evangelicals and Liberal Anglicans accusing the Oxford Movement of drawing the national Church in the direction of Rome.

In Scotland, Protestant Dissenters opened a campaign to disestablish and disendow the Established Presbyterian Church. The 'Voluntary controversy' began in April 1829 with a sermon in Glasgow by Andrew Marshall, a leading minister of the United Secession Church, who argued that religion was purest and most effective when it was 'voluntary', and that Establishments necessarily corrupted religion by connecting it with the coercive power of the state. It was unfair for the state to select one Church for privileges and endowments, and to force non-members of that Church to contribute to its support.[11] By the early 1830s, Voluntary Church associations were organised in the major towns and cities of Scotland, uniting Scottish Dissenters and radicals in a disestablishment campaign. In 1833, Voluntaries organised a campaign of non-payment of Church rates in Edinburgh, which created serious financial difficulties for the Established Church.[12]

In 1834, with the Scottish Establishment under threat from Voluntaries and radical reformers, the Evangelical party emerged to the leadership of the Church of Scotland, breaking the dominance which the Moderate party, the party of polite learning and manners and support for the status quo in Church and state, had maintained since the mid-eighteenth century. The Evangelicals claimed to be the only party that could preserve the Scottish Establishment and the principle of national religion in a revolutionary age. While they would have disowned any comparison with the High Anglican Oxford Movement, the Church of Scotland Evangelicals had much in common with Newman, Keble, Pusey and their circle. Both groups were prepared to respond aggressively to the challenges from religious Voluntaries and to defend the principle of a national Establishment. Both groups,

moreover, appealed to the idea that the national Churches were not cre-
ations of the state, but rather were branches of the Universal Catholic
Church, possessing independence from the state in matters of doctrine and
ecclesiastical discipline.

II

The Evangelical party in the Church of Scotland had its roots in the
eighteenth-century Popular party, which had stood for Calvinist orthodoxy,
a direct, emotional preaching, commitment to the parish ministry and
concern for Christian discipline. With their emphasis on the parish ministry,
Popular party ministers and elders had worked to assert the rights of
parishioners in the selection of parish ministers, and had opposed the right
of patrons (landowners, the Crown and corporations) to present candidates
to parish livings within their gift.[13] During the 1790s, the Popular party was
increasingly influenced by the thriving Evangelical movement in England,
especially its fervour for overseas missions and its effective use of the press
and voluntary societies.[14] The Popular party became known as the Evangelical party and Scottish Evangelicals were increasingly integrated into larger
Evangelical missionary and educational networks in a transatlantic context.
After 1810, Scottish Evangelicals devoted attention to strengthening the
parish ministry by ending pluralities and reasserting the traditional authority
of the parish church over poor-relief, education and communal discipline
– especially in the rapidly expanding industrial towns and cities. The leading
figure in this movement was Thomas Chalmers, a celebrated Evangelical
preacher who developed innovative parish programmes while serving as a
minister in Glasgow between 1815 and 1823. Chalmers became convinced
that only a revived parish system could preserve the social fabric in the new
industrial cities and permanently improve the condition of the labouring
orders by encouraging self-help, later marriages (and thus smaller families),
thrift and communal charity. Leaving the parish ministry for an academic
chair, Chalmers became an impassioned advocate of the parochial national
Establishment, basing his arguments on political economy as well as Scriptural imperatives. After the death of the Evangelical leader Andrew Thomson in 1831, Chalmers became generally recognised as leader of the
Evangelical party in the Church of Scotland. Between 1831 and 1833, the
Evangelicals led the effort to suppress both liberal theological speculations
and charismatic teachings, deposing several leading clergymen for heretical
doctrine. Perceiving dogma to be an essential mark of the Church, Scottish
Evangelicals worked to commit the Church firmly to the letter of the
Westminster Confession of Faith.[15]

As part of their effort to increase the independence of the national
Church, the Evangelical party revived the campaign for the abolition or
restriction of Church patronage. Patronage had existed in the Scottish
Church from the formation of the parish system in the twelfth century. It was
a property right, which empowered the possessor to present a candidate to a
parish living. Virtually every parish in Scotland had its legal patron, with about

a third of the patronages owned by the Crown, nearly two-thirds owned by the landed aristocracy and gentry, and a small number owned by burgh councils or universities. Although the First Book of Discipline of 1560 had abolished patronage and given congregations the right to elect their minister, patronage was revived after 1567. The Second Book of Discipline of 1581 had described patronage as a grievance and for the next century Presbyterians opposed patronage as giving the Crown and nobles undue power over the Church. In 1690, following the Glorious Revolution and the re-establishment of Presbyterianism in the Church of Scotland, the Church had reformed patronage and placed the selection of ministers in the hands of kirk sessions and heritors. In 1712, however, as a Tory ministry raised the cry of 'the Church in danger' in England, the recently created British Parliament restored the law of patronage in Scotland – in spite of assurances in the Act of Union of 1707 that Parliament would not interfere with the Scottish religious Establishment.[16] According to the Patronage Act of 1712, a patron had the right to present either an ordained minister or licensed probationary minister to a church living within his gift. The presentation was to be accompanied by a 'call' signed by the male heads of family in the parish, signifying their willingness to have the presentee as their minister. If the presentee was an ordained minister, the local presbytery would admit him to the charge. If the presentee was not ordained, the presbytery would take him on trials and, if satisfied with his morals, education and doctrinal orthodoxy, it would ordain him and induct him into the charge. In the Church of Scotland, candidates were not ordained until inducted into their first ministerial charge.

During the eighteenth century, the popular 'call' became viewed as a mere formality by the dominant Moderate party in the Church. Deferring to the power and influence of the gentry and aristocracy, the Church courts upheld patronage and intruded unpopular presentees into parish livings, often against the violent opposition of parishioners. Patronage became a symbol of the subordination of the Church to the upper social orders, especially the landed interest. After 1733, hostility to patronage was a major factor in the decision of tens of thousands of Presbyterians to leave the Church of Scotland and join one of the growing Presbyterian secession Churches. The large majority of those Dissenters agitating for the disestablishment of the Church of Scotland in the early 1830s were descended from Presbyterians who had seceded over the issue of patronage.

In 1834, the Evangelical party gained a majority in the General Assembly of the Church of Scotland, breaking the ascendancy which the Moderate party had maintained since the 1750s. Under Evangelical dominance, the Assembly proceeded to three major enactments, commencing a new era of reform and expansion for the Church. First, the Assembly passed the 'Veto Act', which restricted the operation of patronage and provided a greater voice to popular opinion in the selection of ministers. The Veto Act was a compromise measure, a middle path between the demands of the extreme anti-patronage group, who wanted abolition of patronage, and the desires of Moderates and conservative Evangelicals, who saw some benefits in patronage and respected it as a property right. The Veto Act gave male heads of family in communion with the Church the right to veto a patron's presentation if they felt that the candidate would not be effective as their minister. The individual heads of family were not obliged to give reasons for their decision, but they were to affirm that they had not been influenced by factious or malicious intentions. If the presentee was vetoed, the patron would be obliged either to make another presentation or allow the heads of family to select their own candidate. Although the House of Commons had appointed a Select Committee in February 1834 to look into the issue of Scottish patronage, the majority in the General Assembly saw no need to wait on the results of that inquiry, or to go to Parliament for legislation to legalise the veto.[17] Evangelical leaders in the Church had sought legal advice from the leading Whig lawyers, including Lord Jeffrey and Lord Moncrieff, and were assured that the Veto Act was not only legal, but was the most effective means of reforming patronage.[18] To Evangelical leaders, the Veto Act was simply a means of restoring the popular 'call' to its lawful place in the settlement of ministers; it was not so much a new legislative act, as a return to the spirit of the existing law governing settlements.[19] The Evangelical leadership hoped that the Veto Act would satisfy the popular spirit of reform, while at the same time preserving the benefits of patronage, including the attachment of the landed interest to the Church.[20]

Secondly, the General Assembly of 1834 passed the Chapels Act. The early nineteenth-century Church was suffering from a serious deficiency of parish churches, particularly in the new urban areas. Very few new parishes had been created in Scotland since the Reformation, largely because of legal complications involving the property rights of heritors and the responsibilities for poor-relief and parish education.[21] The new churches that had been built were almost exclusively chapels-of-ease, built in overcrowded parishes to ease the pressure of numbers on the parish church, but lacking parochial authority and representation in the Church courts. There were also approximately forty churches built in the Highlands by a parliamentary grant made in 1818, and these churches also lacked representation and parochial jurisdictions. By the Chapels Act of 1834, the General Assembly gave chapels-of-ease status as *quoad sacra* parish churches – that is, churches with spiritual jurisdiction over defined territorial districts. The civil laws respecting poor-relief and the provision of parish schools would not apply in the new parishes, but in spiritual matters, including kirk-session discipline and religious instruction, the Church now recognised *quoad sacra* parishes as territorial jurisdictions. Further, ministers and elders of the *quoad sacra* parishes could serve as commissioners in the Presbyterian courts of the Church of Scotland, including the General Assembly. The Assembly believed that the Chapels Act would regularise the position of the forty parliamentary churches in the Highlands, stimulate new church building, and encourage Presbyterian secession congregations to return to the Established Church as *quoad sacra* parish churches (especially now that the abuses of patronage had been curbed by the Veto Act).[22]

Finally, the General Assembly of 1834 created a Church Extension Committee, which was to co-ordinate a national campaign for building new *quoad sacra* parish churches under the terms of the Chapels Act. Under the convenership of the Evangelical leader, Thomas Chalmers, the Church Extension Committee proposed to build hundreds of new churches, and to organise the entire population of Scotland into small parish communities of no more than 2,000 inhabitants each, in which parish churches would reassert control over religious instruction, moral discipline, poor-relief and education. The new parish communities were to be modelled on Chalmers's parochial ministry in Glasgow, and especially his St John's experiment of 1819–23, with its innovative programmes of regular household visitations by minister and elders, neighbourhood Sabbath schools, parish schools, and communal charity directed by the visiting deacons to replace legal poor-relief. By restoring Christian values and communal benevolence, the Church would elevate the moral and material condition of the population, and eliminate the need for legal poor-relief. The Church Extension Committee planned to raise the money for building the new parish churches and schools through voluntary contributions. However, the Committee also approached the Whig government for a grant of public money to provide partial endowments for the new churches. Only endowed churches, they argued, could reach the 'sunken population' in the new industrial districts – those who were unable to contribute much to church support. In short, the new churches were not to be voluntary chapels, attracting comfortable middle-class congregations, but were to be full parochial charges endowed by the nation.[23]

Under Chalmers's energetic leadership, the Church Extension Committee created a national organisation with a hierarchy of local and provincial committees. The Committee invited contributions from people of all social ranks, including penny-a-week subscriptions from the poor. The intention was not only to build churches and schools, but to arouse national support for the principle of an Established Church. The Evangelical Church Extensionists had considerable success. Between 1834 and 1841, the Church Extension campaign erected over 220 new *quoad sacra* parish churches, increasing the size of the Established Church by over 20 per cent.[24] Further, under Evangelical leadership, the entire Church was revived and popularised, and contributions increased dramatically for a variety of philanthropic and religious causes. Between 1834 and 1841, the General Assembly created standing Committees to oversee what became known as the five great schemes of the Church: Church Extension, Education, Foreign Missions, Colonial Churches and the Mission to the Jews. Voluntary contributions to support the missionary and philanthropic work of the Church of Scotland increased fourteen-fold from 1834 to 1839.[25] An increasing number of Evangelicals entered the Church of Scotland ministry, many of them as ministers of the new *quoad sacra* parish churches (in which male heads of family were usually permitted to elect their ministers). Further, patrons became more sensitive to popular feeling in parishes, and increasingly presented Evangelical candidates. Parish churches enlarged their kirk sessions, and elders became more zealous in the work of house-to-house visiting and the supervision of moral discipline. In 1838, as the Evangelicals celebrated the two-hundredth anniversary of the signing of the National Covenant, it seemed that Scotland was returning to the seventeenth-century ideal of the covenanted nation. The upwardly mobile middle classes – small manufacturers, retailers, commission agents – particularly embraced this revival of puritan idealism.

Not everyone in Scotland, however, looked favourably on the Evangelical ascendancy. Among the older landed, mercantile and professional élites of Scotland – those groups which had dominated the eighteenth-century Establishment – many were uncomfortable with the Evangelical regime in the Church, which seemed to combine a seventeenth-century religious enthusiasm with the new spirit of democracy. The distance between middle-class Evangelical reformers and the Moderate or Episcopalian landed classes grew particularly marked. While the Evangelicals in the Church of Scotland marked the bicentenary of the signing of the National Covenant in 1838, members of the landed aristocracy and gentry celebrated a very different social ideal in 1839 with the jousting tournament at Eglinton – part of the revival of the aristocratic ideal of chivalry.[26] While Evangelicals gained their view of Scottish history from the stern Calvinist, Thomas McCrie, the landed and professional élites usually preferred the historical romances of the Tory and Episcopalian, Sir Walter Scott. Within the Church of Scotland, moreover, many Moderate clergymen opposed the enthusiasms of the prevailing Evangelical party, with their expectation that all ministers should engage in regular house-to-house visiting, organise parish prayer meetings, missionary societies, Sunday schools and Church Extension societies, and adopt an emotional, conversionist preaching.

In 1838, the Church of Scotland Evangelicals suffered a major reverse over Church Extension. The Church Extension Committee, it will be recalled, had requested a state subsidy for each of the new *quoad sacra* churches built by voluntary contributions. Not surprisingly, the Voluntaries had vigorously opposed the Church Extension campaign. For them, efforts to revive the parish system represented a fundamental threat to the religious and civil liberties of Dissenters. During the mid-1830s, Scotland became torn by the struggle between Church Extensionists and Voluntaries, with bitter debates conducted through newspapers, pamphlets and public meetings throughout the country.[27] The Scottish Voluntaries managed to convince the Whig government to question the Establishment's case for new churches – arguing that if Dissenting churches were taken into account, there was already sufficient accommodation. In 1835 the government appointed a Royal Commission of Inquiry to investigate church accommodation in Scotland, and invited Dissenters to give evidence. The implication was that in the eyes of the government, it made no difference whether church accommodation was provided by the Established Church or Dissenters. In March 1838, following the initial reports of the Commission, the Whig government announced that it would not provide endowment grants for new Establishment churches. 'Gentlemen,' a sympathetic Duke of Wellington informed a deputation of the Church Extension Committee in an interview on 21 March 1838,

> you will get nothing… . I am sorry for it; but so you will find it. You have two parties against you – the Radicals, with Lord Brougham at their head; and the Government, who are really as much opposed to you as the Radicals.[28]

The Church Extensionists felt betrayed by the state. They had collected money for building new churches on the principle that only endowed churches could be effective as parish churches and on the virtual promise of state endowments. After 1838, contributions for Church Extension rapidly dried up, and the vision of a godly commonwealth of small, close-knit parish communities began to fade.[29] While the failure of Church Extension thwarted the Church's effort to respond to the needs of a growing population, another conflict was developing between Church and state, which threatened the Church's spiritual independence.

III

The Church's Veto Act on the whole had worked effectively after 1834 to ensure peaceful settlements of ministers. Heads of family in parishes acted with restraint in exercising their right of veto, while patrons evidently became more sensitive to parish opinion. Of 150 settlements of new ministers in the Church of Scotland between 1834 and 1839, only 10 presentations were vetoed.[30] Yet difficulties emerged when a few candidates appealed against the parish veto – difficulties which grew to involve the nature and location of sovereignty within the British state.

The first serious appeal against a veto decision occurred in the Perthshire parish of Auchterarder. In October 1834, Robert Young, a probationer minister, was presented to the parish living by the patron, the earl of Kinnoull. After hearing Young preach, however, the male heads of family in the parish vetoed the presentation by a vote of 286 to 2, and the presbytery declined to take him on trials for ordination to the ministry of Auchterarder. Young appealed against the presbytery's decision in the ecclesiastical courts, but on 30 May 1835, the General Assembly upheld the veto.[31] Young was now approached by John Hope, the Dean of Faculty and son of the Lord President of the Court of Session. As a member of the Assembly of 1834, Hope had formally dissented from the passage of the Veto Act and he now intended to test its legality. On Hope's advice, Young appealed his case from the ecclesiastical to the civil courts, where Hope, as his counsel, argued that the veto was an illegal encroachment on the civil rights of both Young and the patron.[32] The case opened before the Court of Session on 21 November 1837. On 8 March 1838, the Court of Session found in Young's favour by a vote of eight to five, and decided that the Veto Act had no existence in law. Following the decision, Young raised an action to have the local presbytery take him on the customary trials, and, if it found him sound in morals, education and doctrine, to ordain him minister of Auchterarder. Further, he submitted a notarial protest, holding the individual members of the presbytery liable to him for damages.[33]

The Court of Session's Auchterarder decision was taken up at the meeting of the General Assembly of the Church in May 1838. The decision had been unexpected and the Assembly was divided on how to respond. The Moderate party leadership argued that the Church had no choice but to defer to the decision of the Court of Session and set the Veto Act aside. Evangelical speakers, however, took the position that the Church had acted within her province in passing the Veto Act, as the ordination and installation of ministers were spiritual functions. By a vote of 183 to 142, the Assembly supported the Evangelical position and approved a motion asserting the spiritual independence of the Church of Scotland. The Assembly also agreed to appeal to the House of Lords, the supreme civil court of the British state, for a judgement on the respective jurisdictions of the ecclesiastical and civil courts concerning settlements of ministers.

On 4 May 1839, the House of Lords gave its judgement on the appeal, deciding in favour of Young and the patron, and declaring the Church's Veto Act to be illegal. In delivering his judicial opinion, the mercurial Lord Brougham (who in July 1834 had congratulated the General Assembly in the House of Lords for having passed the Veto Act) now saw no grounds whatsoever for the Church's appeal.[34] The 'call' of the parishioners, he argued, had always been a mere formality – comparable to the actions of the champion's horse at the coronation ceremony; the opinion of the parishio-ners, whether expressed through a call or a veto, could have no effect on the patron's rights or the obligation of the Church to ordain a licensed presentee. Further, the House of Lords denied the Church's claim to spiritual independence. As an Established Church, its courts were described as subordinate to the civil courts, and members of Church courts were held to be liable to the imposition of damages by the civil courts for their actions.[35]

While the Auchterarder case was being pursued in the courts, another dispute involving patronage had developed in the Perthshire parish of Lethendy – which further polarised Church and state in Scotland. In 1835, Thomas Clark, a probationary minister, was appointed assistant and succes-sor to the infirm minister of Lethendy by the Crown, the patron of the parish. After hearing Clark preach, however, 53 of the 89 male heads of family vetoed his presentation. Clark appealed against the veto in the ecclesiastical courts, but in June 1836, the Commission of the General Assembly upheld the veto. The Whig government had previously announced that it would respect the veto in all Crown patronage. The Crown accordingly withdrew its presentation of Clark, and in January 1837 it presented a second candi-date, Andrew Kessen, who was acceptable to the overwhelming majority of male heads of family. However, encouraged by the Auchterarder case, Clark appealed to the civil courts against the veto of his presentation. The Court of Session issued an interdict, forbidding the presbytery of Dunkeld to proceed to the ordination of Kessen, the Crown's second presentee, until the Court of Session had ruled on Clark's appeal. In May 1838, the presbytery of Dunkeld referred the matter to the General Assembly, which instructed the presbytery to proceed at once to Kessen's trials and ordination. The presbytery obeyed its ecclesiastical superior and in September 1838 ordained Kessen minister of Lethendy.

Clark now initiated civil action against the presbytery for breach of interdict, and in June 1839 the Court of Session found in Clark's favour and summoned the presbytery of Dunkeld before it for sentencing. Five of the thirteen judges on the Court were prepared to imprison the entire presbytery for their defiance of its authority. In the event, the Court of Session did not imprison, but its sentence was harsh. It admonished and imposed heavy court costs upon the individual members of the presbytery. Further, it issued a solemn warning that future acts of disobedience by ecclesiastical courts would be met by imprisonment and fines.[36] In delivering the judgement, Lord President Charles Hope insisted that ministers who were unable to acknowledge the authority of the civil law over the Established Church would have to demit their charges: 'It is impossible that they should remain ministers of the Established Church, and yet reject the law by which they have become an Established Church.'[37]

With the Auchterarder and Lethendy cases, two distinct positions on the relations of Church and state in Scotland had taken shape. First, according to the judgements of the Court of Session and the House of Lords, and the arguments of the Dean of Faculty, John Hope, the Church of Scotland, as an Established Church, was a creation of statute law. At the Scottish Reformation in 1560, the medieval Roman Catholic Church had been swept away and a new national religious Establishment had been created by the state to provide religious instruction and administer the sacraments to the people of Scotland. The state had given the Established Church certain privileges, including the privilege of managing its internal affairs. But the Established Church possessed no independent jurisdiction and no inherent rights. It was not outside the civil law, nor could it encroach on civil rights as defined by the state. Once the civil courts had declared the Veto Act to be an illegal encroachment on the civil rights of patrons and presentees, it had become incumbent on the Church to set the veto aside. Behind this line of argument was the idea of a unitary sovereignty. There could be only one sovereign power in the state, that of the Crown in Parliament, and this power could not alienate its sovereignty by recognising any independent jurisdictions.[38]

Opposed to this was the view of what was coming to be called the 'Non-intrusionist' party in Church – so called, because of its resistance to the 'intrusions' of patron's candidates into churches against the will of the parishioners. The Non-intrusionist party contained most, though not all, of the Evangelical party and was led by Thomas Chalmers. Appealing to the history of the Church of Scotland, especially the Second Book of Discipline of 1581, they insisted on the doctrine of the 'two kingdoms'. Church and state, they maintained, each had a separate province. The one was spiritual and the other temporal; the one was under the sole headship of Christ, the other under the sovereignty of the Crown in Parliament. The Church of Scotland was part of the universal Church established by Christ. The Church had reformed itself at the Reformation and then had voluntarily entered into a compact with the state, by which the Church had agreed to provide religious instruction to the people of Scotland, and the state had agreed to protect the property of the Church. But in entering into this compact, the Church had not surrendered the sovereignty of Christ in spiritual matters; for that would have been to relinquish its character as a Christian Church. The Church's spiritual independence included power to regulate both the ordination of ministers and ecclesiastical discipline. It could not agree that because the ordination of ministers or enforcement of ecclesiastical discipline might affect civil rights, the state therefore had authority over these spiritual functions.[39] It was difficult to see how the prevailing views in the civil and ecclesiastical courts could be reconciled. Either the Church had spiritual independence, including the power over ordination and discipline, or it was subordinate to the authority of the state; either the commonwealth consisted of two kingdoms, spiritual and temporal, with separate jurisdictions, or there was only one sovereign power. Unfortunately, the Scottish Reformation was a sufficiently muddy territory to enable both sides to claim historical justification.

The Evangelical Non-intrusionists, for their part, were in no mood to compromise on the issue of the Church's spiritual independence. Their intransigence was strengthened by what they perceived as Parliament's short-sighted and unreasonable response to Church Extension in March 1838. By refusing to provide the funds needed by the Church to expand its parish system in response to the growing and urbanised population in industrial society, the state seemed to be condemning the Established Church to a diminished social influence and authority. After 1838, the Non-intrusionist party was increasingly influenced by younger enthusiasts, including Robert Smith Candlish, William Cunningham, Thomas Guthrie and James Begg, who took a high view of the Church's spiritual independence and Reformed dogmas and who pressed Chalmers and other older Evangelical leaders not to compromise on fundamental principles. If the state was not prepared to honour its part in the compact between Church and state in Scotland, it might be time for that compact to be dissolved.

At the General Assembly of May 1839, Chalmers, as leader of the Non-intrusionist majority, raised the prospect of a disruption of the connection of Church and state in Scotland if the civil courts were permitted to override the Church courts in matters of ordination and ecclesiastical discipline. On Chalmers's motion, the Assembly appointed a standing Non-intrusion Committee, which was to co-ordinate the defence of the Church's spiritual independence and confer with both parties in Parliament about how to 'end the collision between the civil and ecclesiastical authorities'.[40] The Evangelical Non-intrusionists had hoped that the Committee would be representative of the whole Church, and thus present a united front in any negotiations with Parliament. However, George Cook, leader of the Moderate party, refused to serve on the Committee, and he made it clear that the Moderates would not co-operate with the Evangelicals in approaching Parliament.[41]

For the Moderates, the Church had no alternative but to accept the law as defined by the civil courts, and therefore it must set aside the Veto Act. Cook and most Moderates did not support the argument that the Church of Scotland was a creation of the state, and they maintained that the Church was independent in spiritual matters. However, they also maintained that when there was a conflict between the civil and ecclesiastical courts concerning the limits of their respective jurisdictions, it must be left to the civil courts of a Christian state to interpret the law and determine the limits of the ecclesiastical jurisdiction. In May 1839, the House of Lords, as the supreme court of the land, had decided that, in passing the Veto Act, the Church had exceeded its powers. The Church must now accept that decision. It was not for the Church alone to determine the limits of its authority or to claim an exclusive power to interpret the law of the land.[42] Beyond the constitutional arguments, the Moderates also supported patronage as a means of attaching the landed interest to the Church and of settling Moderate men in the parish charges. The patronage crisis had revived their fortunes in the Church and promised to undermine the ascendancy of their Evangelical opponents. These growing divisions within the Church were ominous for any negotiations between the Church and Parliament. The complex events surrounding a third patronage case, meanwhile, made a legislative solution still more dubious.

In 1837, there was a vacancy in the Aberdeenshire parish living of Marnoch, and a firm of lawyers representing the Earl of Fife, patron of the parish, presented John Edwards to the living. Edwards had previously been assistant minister at Marnoch and had been so unpopular that he had been dismissed at the request of the parishioners. His presentation was vetoed by a vote of 261 to 1. The patron then made a second presentation, which was satisfactory to the heads of family in the parish. Edwards, however, appealed to the Court of Session, which in June 1839 issued an interdict against the ordination of the second presentee. The Commission of the General Assembly instructed the local presbytery of Strathbogie to suspend proceedings, while the Church negotiated with Parliament for a legislative solution. But the Court of Session would recognise no truce, and in July 1839 it instructed the Strathbogie presbytery to take Edwards on trials immediately. In the event, the presbytery of Strathbogie had a Moderate majority, and this majority decided to obey the command of the Court of Session. Ignoring the instructions from their superior ecclesiastical court, the seven Moderate ministers of Strathbogie presbytery resolved to take Edwards on his trials.[43]

In December 1839, the Commission of the General Assembly suspended the seven Moderate ministers from the Church of Scotland ministry – both in response to their ecclesiastical insubordination and in order to stop them from ordaining Edwards. The Commission sent ministers to Strathbogie in order to announce the suspensions and carry on religious services in the churches of the suspended ministers. The seven Strathbogie ministers appealed for help to the Court of Session, which on 26 December issued an interdict forbidding any minister from entering the churches of the seven without their permission. The clerical agents of the General Assembly respected the interdict and did not enter the church buildings; instead, they announced the suspensions and conducted services in the open air. On 14 February 1840, the Court of Session responded with the notorious 'extended interdict', by which ministers of the Established Church were forbidden to enter even the parishes of the seven suspended ministers to preach or administer the sacraments. The Commission of the General Assembly condemned the 'extended interdict' as an unacceptable intrusion on the Church's spiritual independence, and Chalmers and a number of other Non-intrusionist ministers went to Strathbogie in defiance of the interdict to preach in the open air. For the Non-intrusionists, their open-air meetings recalled the resistance of the later Covenanters, when congregations had worshipped in hiding from Royalist troops on hillsides and in remote glens.[44]

While much of the public was bewildered or bemused by what was being caricatured as the 'reel of Bogie', Non-intrusionists believed that the Strathbogie affair had brought the real intentions of the Court of Session into the open. In forbidding the Church to enforce internal discipline and even to preach in part of the country, its aim seemed to be to reduce the Church to a department of the state. Many within the Church agreed with them that the Court of Session had gone too far. During 1840, petitions bearing over 265,000 signatures were laid before Parliament in support of Non-intrusion and spiritual independence, while opponents to the Non-intrusionist claims collected only 4,000 signatures.[45] In the summer of 1839, meanwhile, a religious revival had begun in Kilsyth – with the growing conflict between Church and state contributing to the sense of impending crisis and expectation. The revival spread to Dundee by the autumn of 1839, and during 1840 there were local revivals in the counties of Angus, Aberdeenshire and Ross-shire. The movement was associated with prayer meetings and millenarian expectations surrounding the mission to the Jews. Those affected by the revival often separated themselves from the unconverted and sat ever more lightly in the Established Church.[46] The revival cast light on the real differences in piety and doctrine that separated Evangelicals and Moderates, and brought many Evangelicals to look more favourably on the idea of a gathered Church of true believers, bound by shared emphasis on conversion and Reformed doctrine, and enjoying independence from an increasingly secular state and society.

IV

The efforts of the Non-intrusion Committee, formed in May 1839, to secure a Parliamentary solution, found little initial encouragement. The Whig government of Viscount Melbourne was dependent on the votes of Dissenters, who had little interest in saving the Established Church of Scotland, while the urbane Melbourne had a personal dislike for Chalmers, whom he described as a 'madman'.[47] Further, there was little understanding of

Scotland's religious settlement at Westminster, and little sympathy for the Non-intrusionists' claims of spiritual independence. The Established Church of England recognised the Crown in Parliament as governor of the Church, and Anglicans could not see that this had compromised their Church as a spiritual institution. For English Whigs, moreover, Parliament was the safeguard of civil and religious liberties, the force that had withstood the efforts of Stewart monarchs to impose absolutist rule or to revive the 'tyranny' of the Roman Catholic Church. To them, it seemed absurd for Scottish Non-intrusionists to insist that the Established Church of Scotland must be outside the sovereignty of Parliament in order to secure its liberty. Although Melbourne's Government did not rule out action in support of the Veto, there seemed little hope of Whig legislation.

In late 1839, the Tory Earl of Aberdeen announced that he would attempt to frame a bill that would satisfy all parties and save the unity of the Church. Aberdeen was a loyal member of the Church of Scotland, with a leading place in the new Tory party which had been shaped during the 1830s by Sir Robert Peel. Chalmers, who was a Tory and an admirer of Peel, was initially delighted with Aberdeen's intervention. He corresponded with Aberdeen, describing in detail the positions of the Non-intrusionist party. Unknown to Chalmers, however, Aberdeen preferred to listen to the counsels of Chalmers's foe, John Hope, the Tory Dean of Faculty. Aberdeen's bill, as it took shape in the early weeks of 1840, offered some protection against the settlement of unsuitable ministers. Male heads of families would retain the right to veto a presentee, though they were now to be obliged to give the reasons for their decision, which would be judged by the presbytery courts. This might have been acceptable to the Non-intrusionists. However, Aberdeen's bill rejected what was for the Non-intrusionists the fundamental principle of the spiritual independence of the Church. It made presbytery decisions in patronage disputes subject to review and revision by the civil courts – which would have empowered the Court of Session to impose unrestricted patronage. When the bill was introduced early in May 1840, Chalmers vigorously opposed it in the General Assembly, adding that Aberdeen had deceived him in their correspondence about the content of the bill. Aberdeen was forced to withdraw his bill, and he answered Chalmers's charges of deception and dishonesty with counter charges. The affair was disastrous for the Non-intrusionist cause. The Whig government now made it clear that as the Non-intrusionists evidently preferred to deal with the Tory party, the Whigs would do nothing. Aberdeen became one of the most bitter opponents of the Evangelical Non-intrusionists in the Church, and Aberdeen exercised considerable influence upon Peel.[48]

The prospect of a legislative solution became still more remote as the Strathbogie affair proceeded. In January 1841, in obedience to instructions from the Court of Session, the seven suspended ministers of the presbytery of Strathbogie ordained John Edwards minister of Marnoch. The ordination took place among highly emotive scenes, with the congregation filing out of the church before the ceremony and conducting worship in the snow, while an angry crowd in the galleries, apparently drawn from outside the parish, disrupted the ordination proceedings with snowballs. The 'Marnoch intrusion' stiffened the resolve of the Non-intrusionists, and in its wake the Non-intrusionist Committee sent out speakers to put their case at public meetings. Non-intrusionist societies were formed in many parishes, and the sum of £8,000 was collected to build a new church for the congregation at Marnoch.[49]

The seven suspended ministers had openly defied the sentence of the General Assembly, arguing that its decisions were not binding when over-ridden by the superior authority of the Court of Session. If unchallenged, this position would have undermined the authority of the Church courts in matters of discipline, and made the Court of Session the supreme authority over the Church. The Non-intrusionist majority in the General Assembly sought a conference with the seven suspended ministers, but when their representatives travelled to Aberdeen for the agreed meeting, they were met only by the lawyers for the seven, who informed them that the suspended ministers did not recognise the authority of the Assembly to take any disciplinary action against them. Following this rebuff, the Non-intrusionist majority in the General Assembly in May 1841 ignored an interdict served on it from the Court of Session and deposed the seven suspended ministers of Strathbogie.

But the 'reel of Bogie' continued. The Moderate party now refused to recognise the depositions and rallied behind the deposed ministers, whom they portrayed as victims of Non-intrusionist tyranny. A 'Moderate League' had been formed in July 1840, and members of this League, including James Bryce and James Robertson of Ellon, expressed solidarity with the seven deposed ministers and called on the government for punitive action against the Non-intrusionists. Members of the Moderate League travelled to Strathbogie to assist the seven in public worship and the sacrament of communion, while public meetings were held in Edinburgh and Glasgow to express support for the seven 'martyrs for law'.[50] In August 1841, the Commission of the Assembly issued a 'solemn remonstrance and warning' to the Moderate clergymen who openly ignored the deposition of the seven. George Cook, the Moderate leader, responded with a declaration of dissent, stating that the Moderates would now look to the state to determine whether they or their Non-intrusionist opponents were to constitute the Established Church.[51]

The general election in the summer of 1841 resulted in a Conservative majority in the Commons and Sir Robert Peel formed a government. The Non-intrusionists on the whole had not pressed their cause in the election. While national issues were at stake, few ministers were prepared to lead a lay political movement or appeal to national sentiment.[52] With the formation of the Peel government, any remaining hopes for a legislative solution faded. The government would not support more than a slightly modified version of Aberdeen's bill, and this was not acceptable to the Non-intrusionist Committee. Further, Peel insisted that the Church must restore the deposed

Strathbogie ministers before the government would consider any legislation. The government's firm stand seemed to bear fruit when in March 1842,
a 'Middle Party' of about forty ministers was formed among the Non-
Intrusionist clergy in the synod of Glasgow and Ayr. Withdrawing their
allegiance from the Non-intrusionist leadership, the Middle Party expressed
themselves satisfied with Aberdeen's bill.[53] To the government, it seemed
that the Non-intrusionist party was breaking up, and that the majority would
be prepared to recognise the rule of civil law.[54]

At the General Assembly of May 1842, however, the Non-intrusionist
majority responded with a renewed expression of its resolve when it adopted
the 'Claim of Right', an assertion of the principles of non-intrusion and
spiritual independence, drafted by the talented Non-intrusionist lawyer,
Alexander Dunlop. In language reminiscent of the National Covenant of
1638, the Claim of Right maintained that the Church had consistently
recognised the 'sole Headship of Christ over the Church' and that prior to
the Union of 1707 the state had recognised the Church's spiritual independence in a number of statutes and judgements. The document protested at
the breaking of the pledges to preserve the Scottish religious settlement
which were made at the Union of 1707. While it recognised the power of
the state to deprive the Church of its endowments and buildings, it insisted
that the Church could not recognise the power of the state over ordination
and ecclesiastical discipline without giving up its identity as a Church of
Christ. Despite the opposition of the Moderates, the Assembly approved the
'Claim of Right' as a final appeal to the state by an overwhelming majority
of 241 to 110.[55]

While the Non-intrusionists waited for Parliament's response to the Claim
of Right, the Court of Session struck another blow at the Church's spiritual
independence when in August 1842 it delivered its judgement in what was
termed the Second Auchterarder case. This involved the action raised by
Robert Young, the presentee, and the earl of Kinnoull, the patron, for
damages against the presbytery of Auchterarder for its refusal to ordain
Young minister of Auchterarder on the instructions of the Court of Session
in 1838. The Court of Session, not surprisingly, found in favour of the
presentee and patron, and awarded them a massive £15,000 in damages,
with members of the presbytery individually responsible for payment and
subject to imprisonment if they could not pay. The Non-intrusionists made
a national appeal to collect the funds to pay the damages, but they could
not continue to pay such crippling costs.[56] There were now thirty-nine
patronage cases in the courts, and the large award to Young and Kinnoull
would no doubt encourage further claims for damages from disappointed
presentees and patrons. It was clear that unless Parliament intervened, the
Court of Session, with the support of the Moderate party, would force the
Non-intrusionists out of the Church.

It was also clear, however, that Parliament would not intervene. In
mid-June 1842, Peel announced in the House of Commons that 'Her
Majesty's Government had abandoned all hope of settling the question in a

satisfactory manner or of effecting any good by introducing a measure relative to it.'[57] By the autumn, the Non-intrusionist leaders had become resigned to the inevitability of a Disruption. From 17 to 24 November 1842, they held a Convocation in Edinburgh, in which only ministers believed to hold Non-intrusionist principles were invited to attend. In the event, 465 ministers attended and they were informed of preparations for the coming break. Chalmers presented a plan for financing the creation and mainte-nance of a national Presbyterian Church through voluntary contributions alone. Money would be collected by local congregations according to their ability to pay, and redistributed according to need. Despite the sanguine reports of Chalmers, Candlish and other leaders, not everyone present was convinced of the need to go out. There were disagreements and angry exchanges. Of the 465 ministers present, only 354 signed a pledge to demit their charges if Parliament should reject the Claim of Right.[58]

On 4 January 1843, the Church finally received the government's response to its Claim of Right. Dismissing the Church's Claim as 'unreasonable', the government announced that it 'could not advise her majesty to acquiesce in these demands'.[59] This was followed by a further blow from the Court of Session. On 20 January 1843, in a decision involving the parish of Stewarton, the Court of Session declared the Church's Chapels Act to be illegal, and ordered that all *quoad sacra* parish churches be deprived of representation in the Church courts.[60] As the great majority of the *quoad sacra* churches had been erected during the Church Extension campaign and were largely filled by Evangelical ministers, this decision assured that the Non-intrusionists would not have a majority in the coming General Assembly.

The question now was how many would go out. John Hope assured Government ministers that the number would be very small, and there was much reason to expect this would be the case.[61] The press was overwhelm-ingly hostile to the Non-intrusionists: of sixty-three newspapers published in Scotland, only eight supported the Non-intrusionist cause, and newspaper attacks on the Non-intrusionists increased following the November Convo-cation.[62] Non-intrusionist resolve had seemed to be dissolving at the Convo-cation, while the Stewarton decision had broken the Non-intrusionist majority in the Church. And yet, as the inevitability of Disruption became clear in the weeks following the Convocation, a considerable number of Scots began to rally around the Non-intrusionist cause, attending meetings and joining local associations. The leaders of the Non-intrusionist move-ment, who included some of the most eminent ministers in the Church – Thomas Chalmers, Robert Gordon, David Welsh, Henry Dunlop – remained firm in their attachment to the principle of spiritual independence, and their example made a strong impression. Popular support for Non-intrusion was bound up with other factors – the spread of the religious revival after 1839, the antagonism of many crofters and tenant farmers to the landowning (and patron) class, the desire of an entrepreneurial middle class to break the dominance of older professional and commercial élites, and even

Scottish national sentiment directed against a British Parliament that had originally imposed the Patronage Act on Scotland and that now seemed remote and indifferent to the conflict that was destroying the Scottish national Establishment.[63] To an extent, the Non-intrusionist cause attracted democratic elements in the Church against a perceived attempt to reimpose the dominance of the traditional social élites over Church and society. But for many of those now preparing to go out, there was also heart-felt conviction that the Church of Scotland was a spiritual institution, under the sole headship of Christ, which could not accept civil control of ordination and ecclesiastical discipline.

On 7–8 March 1843, the House of Commons held its most extensive debate on the Scottish Church question when on the motion of the Scottish Whig MP, Fox Maule, a Committee of the whole House discussed the Church's petition for a consideration of its Claim of Right. In speaking for the government, Sir James Graham, the Home Secretary, acknowledged that predictions of a small secession had been wrong and that the government now expected a large number to go out, including many of the most able and zealous ministers in the Church.

'Nothing in my public life', Graham observed,

> has grieved me so much as this unhappy dispute. I think it more peculiarly unfortunate on this ground, that it arose precisely at a moment when the influence of this Church was extending itself – its usefulness was fully approved, and when it shone with the purest and brightest light.[64]

It was a tragedy, and he expressed the highest respect for those who were bound by their consciences to leave the Establishment. However, the government could see no way to satisfy the Non-intrusionist claims. While recognising the Church's claim to independence in its spiritual realm, it could not acknowledge that the Church possessed an exclusive right to determine the extent of its spiritual jurisdiction. That would open the door to ecclesiastical tyranny. In the case of disputed jurisdictions, it was the House of Lords, as supreme court of appeal, which must make the final judgement on the law, and an Established Church must accept that authority. Speaking later in the debate, Peel also emphasised this point:

> the question is, where and by whom the boundaries of civil and ecclesiastical questions are to be defined? It seems to me, that the power to determine in such a matter rests with the tribunal appointed by parliament, which is the house of lords.[65]

With a thinly veiled reference to the controversial Oxford Movement, Peel noted that if Parliament did legislate to recognise the principles of spiritual independence claimed by the Scottish Non-intrusionists, it would in consistency have to do the same for the Church of England.[66] On 8 March, the Commons rejected the Church's petition by a vote of 211 to 76. The Scottish MPs, however, voted by 25 to 12 in favour of the petition, with 10 Scottish MPs who had previously voted against Non-Intrusion now abstaining.[67]

V

On 18 May 1843, the Non-Intrusionists finally broke their connection with the Established Church. Deprived of their majority in the Assembly by the Stewarton decision, they decided they would depart at the opening session, rather than put their case to the Assembly for a vote. The General Assembly met in St Andrew's church in Edinburgh's New Town and large crowds had gathered since the early morning to witness the event. As the Assembly opened that afternoon, the retiring Moderator, the Revd David Welsh, Professor of Ecclesiastical History at Edinburgh University, read a lengthy protest and then, row by row, some two hundred Evangelical Non-Intrusionists rose and departed from the church. Joined by supporters gathered outside, the outgoing ministers and elders were forced by the crush of the crowd to walk in a narrow procession to Tanfield Hall in Canonmills. There the outgoing commissioners constituted themselves the Free Protesting Church of Scotland. Some 454 ministers now signed the Deed of Demission, surrendering stipends worth approximately £100,000 per annum, along with their churches, manses and social status, all for an uncertain future. The number signing the Demission was shortly increased to 474 ministers out of a total of 1,195 in the Church of Scotland, or nearly 40 per cent. They were joined by perhaps half the lay membership of the Church. It was an impressive act of sacrifice for a principle, that of the spiritual independence of the Church. 'I know no parallel to it', observed the Court of Session judge, Lord Cockburn, several days after the event.

> Whatever may be thought of their cause, there can be no doubt or coldness in the admiration with which all candid men must applaud their heroism. They have abandoned that public station which was the ambition of their lives, and have descended from certainty to precariousness, and most of them from comfort to destitution, solely for their principles.

'The truth is', he added, 'that these men would all have gone to the scaffold with the same serenity.'[68]

The new Free Church claimed to be the true national Church of Scotland – the historic Church of the Scottish people, the Church of the Reformation and the martyrs of the Covenant – a claim they based in part on their willingness to sacrifice for the 'Crown Rights of the Redeemer'.[69] The Disruption, in their view, was not a secession; it was a severing of the true Church of Scotland from its connection with an Erastian state, which had broken its compact to preserve and protect the Church as a spiritual institution for the religious benefit of the Scottish people. The outgoing members continued to hold to the principle of a national establishment, and they proposed to create a territorial Church that would provide Christian instruction and ordinances for the whole population of Scotland. It was a heroic aim, but one which seemed utopian. While drawing support from throughout the country, the main areas of Free Church strength were in the urban areas, especially among the commercial and manufacturing middle

classes, and in the Scottish Highlands.[70] Many of the new urban Free Church
congregations were prosperous, but outside the towns and cities, congregations were often small and/or impoverished. Opponents predicted that
popular support, especially among the middle classes, would fall away as the
Free Church failed to collect sufficient funds. 'People will wonder at the
anxiety they at first felt', John Hope had assured Aberdeen a few days before
the Disruption, 'and will laugh at the secession and its wooden churches.'[71]
Free Church difficulties in the rural areas were complicated by harassment
and intimidation. Many landowners, such as the Dukes of Sutherland and
Buccleuch, pursued a policy of denying sites and building materials for the
erection of Free churches. Several hundred Free Church tenants suffered
eviction at the expiration of their leases and Free Church labourers and
servants were dismissed. Behind such acts of intimidation was the belief that
the Free Church was a subversive force, which challenged both the rule of
law and the social hierarchy.[72]

Despite the difficulties, the Free Church rapidly created a national
institution through voluntary contributions. By 1847, the Free Church had
erected over 730 places of worship, spread throughout the country and
organised on a parochial system. Most were unpretentious structures, later
replaced by more permanent stone and mortar buildings. The continued
refusal of some landlords to provide sites resulted in some unusual structures, such as the iron 'floating church' moored for nearly thirty years on
Loch Sunart.[73] On a plan devised by Thomas Chalmers, the Free Church
Assembly provided stipends to its ministers through the Sustentation Fund,
by which wealthier congregations paid an agreed sum into a central fund,
which was then distributed to ensure an adequate stipend for every minister.
By 1846, the Sustentation Fund was paying a minimum stipend of £122 to
each minister, a modest sum, but one which compared favourably to the
minimum stipend of £150 paid to Church of Scotland ministers on the eve
of the Disruption. After paying their 'fair share' into the Sustentation Fund,
wealthier congregations were permitted to pay higher stipends to their own
ministers, and some urban Free Church ministers received larger incomes
than they had before the Disruption. In May 1845, moreover, the General
Assembly began a national manse fund, which built over 400 manses during
the next three years. The Free Church developed a national system of
schools, initially because of the dismissal of a considerable number of school
teachers for their Free Church adherence. By 1847, the Free Church was
supporting 513 teachers, while over 44,000 children attended Free Church
schools – nearly equal to the number attending the endowed Church of
Scotland schools. Immediately after the Disruption, the Free Church also
created a college for the education of ministers. In 1846, the foundation
stone was laid for the impressive set of buildings on the Mound in Edinburgh, designed by the celebrated architect, William Playfair.[74] In the mid-
1850s, additional Free Church colleges were established in Aberdeen and
Glasgow.

With the exception of one woman, all of the Church of Scotland overseas

missionaries had joined the Free Church, which not only assumed the cost
of their support, but also had to provide new churches, schools and resi-
dences, as existing buildings – such as the school and library at Calcutta –
were seized by agents of the Established Church. While contributions to
overseas missions had averaged £16,359 per annum during the five years
before the Disruption, this increased to £40,469 per annum in the Free
Church during the five years after the Disruption.[75] Further, through
Chalmers's efforts, the Free Church began a home mission campaign in the
cities, which sought to 'reclaim' the churchless populations in deprived
areas through the creation of territorial churches and schools. The aim was
to form working-class Christian communities that would encourage independence and communal concern. By 1870 some sixty new territorial
churches and schools had been created.[76]

The building of the Free Church was one of the most impressive achievements of nineteenth-century Britain. Large sums were collected, over
£334,000 in the fiscal year 1844–5 alone. Much of the money came from
contributions from the new commercial and manufacturing middle and
upper classes – and the Free Church success reflects the prosperity of these
classes in early Victorian Scotland. Money also came, however, from the
contributions of tenant farmers, artisans and labourers – those striving for
respectability and independence, and resentful of the paternalism of the
older landed and mercantile élites. Free Church collectors were criticised
by their opponents for placing too much pressure on the labouring poor for
contributions, and some poorer members were driven by the financial
demands to return to the Established Church. The success of congregations
was frequently measured by the size of their contributions to the central
funds, while individuals contributing significant amounts sometimes developed a sense of self-righteousness, a tendency to view their Free Church
membership as a badge of their election.[77] Others, however, especially
among skilled artisans and the crofters, found in Free Church membership
a sense of independence and self-respect.[78] The Free Church not only proved
able to consolidate itself and to inspire sustained giving, long after the fires
of the Ten Years' Conflict had cooled; it was also the most dynamic Church
in Scotland through the nineteenth century.

'The best ministers and the best portion of our people have gone',
lamented the Church of Scotland minister, Norman Macleod, at the time
of the Disruption.[79] Although it retained most of the clergy and laity at the
Disruption, the Established Church lacked direction and purpose. Under
the leadership of George Cook and the extreme Moderates, the Established
Assembly of 1843 acknowledged the subordination of the Church to the civil
courts, setting aside the Veto Act and Chapels Act and repealing many of
the reforms of the Evangelical era. The dominant mood was one of reaction,
and a closing of ranks against the Free Church. While Parliament passed an
act for the regulation of patronage based on Aberdeen's bill in the summer
of 1843, the Moderate leadership was unenthusiastic. However, not all of
those remaining in the old Church were reactionary Moderates. Probably

the most prominent radical Presbyterian clergyman, the Revd Patrick Brewster of Paisley, remained in the Church of Scotland in 1843, believing that it would be less dominated by the middle classes and more sympathetic to state action to improve working-class conditions.[80] Other liberal clergymen and lay members were put off by the theological conservatism of the Free Church. During the 1850s, as Cook and the older Moderates passed from the scene, the Established Church of Scotland began a period of dramatic recovery. Inspired by the vision of a new generation of leaders, including James Robertson, Norman Macleod and John Tulloch, the Established Church revived its home mission, and embraced a liberal approach to doctrine, which contrasted with the rigid Calvinism of many Free Church adherents. It was revived as a national Church, able to compete in the increasingly pluralistic religious environment.

The Disruption, however, marked the end of the religious Establishment in Scotland. After 1843, the state moved in to assume control over areas of social life previously left, at least in theory, to the Established Church. The break-up of the Establishment was followed by the Scottish Poor Law Act of 1845, which transferred authority over poor-relief from parish churches to elected poor-law boards. The power of kirk sessions to exert authority over moral behaviour in parishes largely collapsed. After 1843 primary education was provided by a variety of denominational and private schools, until most came under state control with the Education Act of 1872. Religious tests for all but theological chairs in the Scottish universities were abolished in 1852.[81] It has been argued that the Disruption marked a radical break in the inheritance of the democratic intellect, as the bitter interdenominational divisions undermined the parish school ideal and ended the national consensus that supported the generalist tradition in Scottish philosophy.[82] The Establishment, and the *ancien régime* it had represented, came to a dramatic end in Scotland in 1843. In its place, two national Churches, the Church of Scotland and the Free Church, competed with numerous other denominations in a religiously pluralistic, and also increasingly urban and secular, society.[83]

The break-up of the national religious Establishment in Scotland had in one sense been a tragedy – dividing families and communities, embittering the religious life of the nation for generations, and weakening the influence of the Church in national life. The Disruption had marked the end of a regime, and the waning of the godly commonwealth ideal in Scotland. It had, however, also been a glorious moment in the history of the Scottish people. Those who had gone out in 1843 had delivered powerful messages to the British parliamentary state – that the sovereignty of the state, even of a democratic state, must not be regarded as absolute, that the Union of 1707 and the Industrial Revolution had not brought an end to a distinctive Scottish national identity, and above all that a Church could not recognise the authority of the state over its spiritual functions and still remain a Christian Church. The Disruption had broken up the Establishment, and Scottish culture lost a powerful institutional foundation. But from the

tragedy of the Disruption there also emerged a freer, more egalitarian and √
more pluralistic Scotland. The principle of the Church's spiritual independence, moreover, was vindicated and this principle would form a fundamental part in the eventual reunion of the majority of Scottish Presbyterians in
1929.

NOTES

1   The Disruption has inspired an extensive literature, with authors from the
    three main parties in the conflict producing apologetic accounts shortly after
    the event. The Evangelical Non-intrusionist perspective was expressed in R.
    Buchanan, *The Ten Years' Conflict*, 2 vols (Glasgow, 1852); the Moderate
    perspective in J. Bryce, *Ten Years of the Church of Scotland*, 2 vols (Edinburgh,
    1850); and the Middle Party perspective in A. Turner, *The Scottish Secession of
    1843* (Edinburgh, 1859). More recent extended accounts include H. Watt,
    Thomas Chalmers and the Disruption (Edinburgh, 1943), G. D. Henderson,
    Heritage: A Study of the Disruption (Edinburgh, 1943) and S. J. Brown, *Thomas
    Chalmers and the Godly Commonwealth in Scotland* (Oxford, 1982).
2   [J. Hamilton], *Farewell to Egypt: or, the Departure of the Free Church of Scotland out
    of the Erastian Establishment* (London, 1843); W. Gibson, *The Flock in the
    Wilderness; or the Secession of 1843* (Belfast, 1843).
3   D. Macleod, *Memoir of Norman Macleod*, 2 vols (London, 1876), vol. i, pp.
    196–203.
4   Walter Elliot, *A Scotsman's Heritage*, cited in G. Davie, *The Democratic Intellect*
    (Edinburgh, 1961), p. 286.
5   For a recent discussion of the idea of the eighteenth-century Establishment
    in England, see J. C. D. Clark, *English Society 1688–1832* (Cambridge, 1985),
    pp. 199–276. For the idea of the Establishment in eighteenth-century Scot-
    land, see especially R. B. Sher, *Church and University in the Scottish Enlightenment*
    (Princeton, NJ, 1985), pp. 120–47, 175–212.
6   Clark, *English Society 1688–1832*, pp. 408–20; G. F. A. Best, 'The Constitutional
    Revolution, 1828–32', *Theology*, 62 (1959), 226–34.
7   O. J. Brose, *Church and Parliament: The Reshaping of the Church of England
    1828–1860* (London, 1959), pp. 22–42.
8   O. J. Brose, 'The Irish Precedent for English Church Reform: The Church
    Temporalities Act of 1833', *Journal of Ecclesiastical History*, 7 (1956), 204–25.
9   G. F. A. Best, *Temporal Pillars* (Cambridge, 1964), pp. 273–95; T. Arnold,
    Principles of Church Reform (London, 1833).
10 R. W. Church, *The Oxford Movement* (London, 1891), pp. 92–126.
11 A. B. Montgomery, 'The Voluntary Controversy in the Church of Scotland,
    1829–1843', Ph.D. Thesis, (Edinburgh Univ. – New College, 1953), pp. 1–16.
12 Ibid. pp. 16–80; J. McKerrow, *History of the Secession Church* (Edinburgh, 1854),
    pp. 724–34.
13 J. MacInnes, *The Evangelical Movement in the Highlands of Scotland* (Aberdeen,
    1951), esp. pp. 79–196; A. Fawcett, *The Cambuslang Revival: The Scottish
    Evangelical Revival in the Eighteenth Century* (London, 1971), pp. 182–209; J. R.
    McIntosh, 'The Popular Party in the Church of Scotland 1740–1800', Ph.D.
    Thesis (Univ. of Glasgow, 1989), pp. 100–233.
14 D. A. Currie, 'The Growth of Evangelicalism in the Church of Scotland,
    1793–1843', Ph.D. Thesis (St Andrews Univ., 1990), pp. 12–50, 145–88.
15 A. L. Drummond and J. Bulloch, *The Scottish Church 1688–1843* (Edinburgh,
    1973), pp. 193–219; J. Tulloch, *Movements of Religious Thought in Britain during
    the Nineteenth Century* (London, 1885), pp. 125–68.
16 R. Sher and A. Murdoch, 'Patronage and Party in the Church of Scotland,
    1750–1800', in N. Macdougall (ed.), *Church, Politics and Society: Scotland
    1408–1929* (Edinburgh, 1983), pp. 200, 203–5.
17 G. I. T. Machin, *Politics and the Churches in Great Britain 1832 to 1868* (Oxford,
    1977), p. 121.

18 W. Hanna, *Memoirs of Dr. Chalmers*, 4 vols (Edinburgh, 1849–52), vol. iii, pp. 351–4; Turner, *The Scottish Secession*, pp. 169–72; J. Moncrieff to H. Brougham, 3 Mar. and 22 May 1833 (Brougham Papers, University College, London, fos 33, 269 and 43, 653).

19 Buchanan, *The Ten Years' Conflict*, vol. i, pp. 258–61.

20 Turner, *The Scottish Secession*, pp. 159–68.

21 I. F. Maciver, 'The General Assembly of the Church, the State and Society in Scotland', M.Phil. Thesis, (Univ. of Edinburgh, 1976), pp. 160–4

22 Buchanan, *The Ten Years' Conflict*, vol. i, pp. 269–96.

23 Brown, *Thomas Chalmers*, pp. 234–43.

24 Hanna, *Memoirs of Dr. Chalmers*, vol. iv, p. 87.

25 Buchanan, *The Ten Years' Conflict*, vol. i, p. 230.

26 M. Girouard, *The Return to Camelot: Chivalry and the English Gentleman* (London, 1981), pp. 87–110. For the discomfort of conservatives with the bicentenary commemorations of the National Covenant, see Bryce, *Ten Years of the Church of Scotland*, vol. i, pp. 81–2.

27 R. Rainy and J. Mackenzie, *Life of William Cunningham* (London, 1871), pp. 86–90; Montgomery, 'The Voluntary Controversy', pp. 40–80; D. Chambers, 'The Church of Scotland's Parochial Extension Scheme and the Scottish Disruption', *Journal of Church and State*, xvi (1974), 263–86.

28 N. L. Walker, *Robert Buchanan: An Ecclesiastical Biography* (London, 1867), pp. 76–7.

29 Brown, *Thomas Chalmers*, pp. 273–5.

30 Hanna, *Memoirs of Dr. Chalmers*, vol. iv, p. 116.

31 Buchanan, *The Ten Years' Conflict*, vol. i, pp. 340–50.

32 F. Lyall, *Of Presbyters and Kings: Church and State in the Law of Scotland* (Aberdeen, 1980), pp. 30–1.

33 Buchanan, *The Ten Years' Conflict*, vol. i, p. 401; Lyall, *Of Presbyters and Kings*, pp. 31–2.

34 For Brougham's support of the veto in 1833, see Turner, *The Scottish Secession*, pp. 170–1.

35 Buchanan, *The Ten Years' Conflict*, vol. i, pp. 421–33.

36 Ibid., vol. ii, pp. 1–17; Watt, *Thomas Chalmers*, pp. 183–91; Lyall, *Of Presbyters and Kings*, pp. 35–6.

37 Watt, *Thomas Chalmers*, p. 190.

38 H. J. Laski, *Studies in the Problem of Sovereignty* (London, 1917), pp. 51–6; A. Taylor Innes, *The Law of Creeds in Scotland* (Edinburgh, 1902), pp. 73–9.

39 Hanna, *Memoirs of Dr. Chalmers*, vol. iv, pp. 104–14; Laski, *Studies in the Problem of Sovereignty*, pp. 38–51.

40 Hanna, *Memoirs of Dr. Chalmers*, vol. iv, pp. 106–7.

41 Buchanan, *The Ten Years' Conflict*, vol. i, p. 467.

42 R. W. Vaudry, 'The Constitutional Party in the Church of Scotland 1834–1843', *Scottish Historical Review*, 62 (1983), 35–46; Bryce, *Ten Years of the Church of Scotland*, vol. i, pp. 61–6; Laski, *Studies in the Problem of Sovereignty*, pp. 57–8.

43 Buchanan, *The Ten Years' Conflict*, vol. ii, pp. 18–21; Watt, *Thomas Chalmers*, pp. 206–10.

44 Hanna, *Memoirs of Dr. Chalmers*, vol. iv, pp. 145–50; *Journal of Henry Cockburn*, 2 vols (Edinburgh, 1874), vol. i, pp. 252–5; G. J. C. Duncan, *Memoir of Henry Duncan* (Edinburgh, 1848), pp. 273–80.

45 Buchanan, *The Ten Years' Conflict*, vol. ii, p. 121.

46 A. A. Bonar, *Memoir and Remains of R. M. McCheyne* (London, 1892), pp. 108–40; T. Brown, *Annals of the Disruption*, 2nd edn (Edinburgh, 1893), pp. 7–19; Currie, 'The Growth of Evangelicalism', pp. 362–86.

47 Machin, *Politics and the Churches*, p. 125.

48 Buchanan, *The Ten Years' Conflict*, vol. ii, pp. 72–125; Hanna, *Memoirs of Dr. Chalmers*, vol. iv, pp. 151–74.

49 *Witness*, 27 Jan. 1841; *Scottish Guardian*, 26 Jan. and 2 Feb. 1841.

50 *Journal of Henry Cockburn*, vol. ii, p. 32; *Scottish Guardian*, 4 and 11 June 1841; Vaudry, 'The Constitutional Party', pp. 36–7.

51 Hanna, *Memoirs of Dr. Chalmers*, vol. iv, pp. 232–3.
52 Machin, *Politics and the Churches*, p. 131.
53 J. F. Leishman, *Matthew Leishman of Govan and the Middle Party of 1843* (Paisley, 1924), pp. 110–42; Turner, *The Scottish Secession*, pp. 269–84.
54 Machin, *Politics and the Churches*, pp. 138–9.
55 Buchanan, *The Ten Years' Conflict*, vol. ii, pp. 357–80, 471–85.
56 Lyall, *Of Presbyters and Kings*, pp. 32–4; Hanna, *Memoirs of Dr. Chalmers*, vol. iv, pp. 302–4; *Journal of Henry Cockburn*, vol. i, p. 334.
57 Hanna, *Memoirs of Dr. Chalmers*, vol. iv, p. 302.
58 W. Wilson, *Memorials of R. S. Candlish* (Edinburgh, 1880), pp. 219–59; D. Aitken to the Earl of Minto, 13 Dec. 1842 (National Library of Scotland, Minto Papers, MS11802, fol. 201).
59 Buchanan, *The Ten Years' Conflict*, vol. ii, pp. 412–13.
60 Lyalls, *Of Presbyters and Kings*, pp. 43–5; Hanna, *Memoirs of Dr. Chalmers*, vol. iv, pp. 320–9; *Journal of Henry Cockburn*, vol. i, pp. 341–9.
61 Machin, *Politics and the Churches*, pp. 140–1.
62 Brown, *Annals of the Disruption*, p. 61.
63 For an example of the national element, see Brown, *Annals of the Disruption*, pp. 68–9.
64 Hansard, 3rd ser, vol. lxvii, p. 381.
65 Buchanan, *The Ten Years' Conflict*, vol. ii, p. 426.
66 Machin, *Politics and the Churches*, p. 142.
67 Ibid.
68 *Journal of Henry Cockburn*, vol. ii, pp. 30–1, 32.
69 G. Lewis, *Church Principles, Illustrated by Scottish Church History* (Dundee, 1843), p. 24; Gibson, *The Flock in the Wilderness*, pp. 18–24.
70 A. A. MacLaren, *Religion and Social Class: The Disruption Years in Aberdeen* (London, 1974), pp. 29–30.
71 Machin, *Politics and the Churches*, p. 143.
72 Brown, *Annals of the Disruption*, pp. 353–449; *Reports of the Select Committee of the House of Commons on the Refusal of Sites, First Report*, PP, xiii (1847: 237), 1; *Second Report*, xiii (1847: 311), 119; *Third Report*, xiii (1847: 613), 267.
73 L. A. Ritchie, 'The Floating Church of Loch Sunart', *Records of the Scottish Church History Society*, 22 (1985), 159–73.
74 Brown, *Thomas Chalmers*, pp. 337–44.
75 G. Smith, *The Life of Alexander Duff*, 2 vols (London, 1879), vol. ii, pp. 31–45; Brown, *Annals of the Disruption*, pp. 501–13.
76 S. J. Brown, 'Thomas Chalmers and the Communal Ideal in Victorian Scotland', in T. C. Smout (ed.), *Victorian Values* (Oxford, 1992), pp. 68–74.
77 MacLaren, *Religion and Social Class*, pp. 100–43; C. Brown, *The Social History of Religion in Scotland since 1730* (London, 1987), p. 40.
78 P. L. M. Hillis, 'Presbyterianism and Social Class in Mid-Nineteenth Century Glasgow', Ph.D. Thesis (Univ. of Glasgow, 1978) pp. 171–9; Brown, *The Social History of Religion in Scotland*, pp. 125–7, 151–2.
79 J. R. Fleming, *The Church in Scotland 1843–1874* (Edinburgh, 1927), p. 38.
80 D. C. Smith, *Passive Obedience and Prophetic Protest: Social Criticism in the Scottish Church 1830–1945* (New York, 1987), pp. 175–86.
81 Ibid., p. 53.
82 Davie, *The Democratic Intellect*, pp. 286–9.
83 C. G. Brown, 'Religion, Class and Church Growth', in W. H. Fraser and R. J. Morris (eds), *People and Society in Scotland*, 3 vols (Edinburgh, 1988–91), vol. ii, pp. 316–29.

PART ONE

The Disruption, Politics and Society

CHAPTER TWO

The Disruption and the Union

MICHAEL FRY

THE DISRUPTION SELDOM FIGURES among the historical episodes fondly
recalled by Scots of their recalcitrance towards the British state in which a
unionist destiny has placed them. It was doubtless not bloody or proletarian
enough for modern political taste. Yet it turned out to be one occasion when
hundreds of thousands of ordinary men and women in Scotland challenged
the authority set over them. And unlike other Scottish rebellions, it succeeded, up to a point. It created a Church, enjoying the allegiance of a large
section of the people, which denied the assertion by the British state that
religion, along with everything else, was subject to its absolute parliamentary
sovereignty.

Yet the challenge also failed in a major respect. The Free Church was
visibly not a continuation of the old Kirk, a Church of Scotland entire. It was
rather a secession, much like previous secessions in nature if not in scale,
and that soon came to be reflected in its outlook and actions. Some of its
leaders had hoped that the whole Church, or nearly the whole Church,
would break with the state, which might then be forced to deal with it on its
own terms. But that did not happen. If the state was shocked at the outcome,
it was not shaken into changing its ecclesiastical views or policies. And if it
came to regret the Disruption, it finally felt able to put the affair down to
the fissile nature of Presbyterianism, something to be counted therefore as
of no wider importance.

All this helps to explain why the Disruption had so little obvious secular
effect. It might have united Scotland in a political sense, against the Conservative government in 1843, but the Whig opposition was wary of taking sides,
and real religious partisans were found mostly on the radical fringe. The
conflict could thus not readily take on a political colour. Scotland might
have been united also in a nationalist sense, against English abuses of the
Treaty of Union. During the Ten Years' Struggle the spirits of Wallace and
Bruce were from time to time evoked and the cry of 'Scotland for ever!' had
been heard.[1] But, because of the domestic disunity, sharp lines were hard to
draw between Scottish and English interests, and the conflict could thus not

readily take on a nationalist colour either. Instead, it would be turned inwards, into bitter sectarianism within Scotland, and cease to cloud relations with England.

Yet the Disruption did alter the constitutional relations of the two countries. In other words, it altered the Union and probably gave us a different Union from the one we would otherwise have had. It brought to an end a key element of the compact of 1707, designed to preserve a semi-independent Scotland. In effect, it devised a new compact, with terms that would allow Westminster to become the centre of Scottish affairs. Since the turn of the century Scotland had anyway been subjected to ever greater pressure, internal and external, to be assimilated into the rest of Britain under centralising government in London.[2] But the formal nature of the assimilation remained open till it was decided by events, of which the Disruption was the greatest.

The most independent part of that semi-independent Scotland had been the Kirk. It held a peculiar constitutional position, essentially an inheritance from the Middle Ages, from the prevalent theory then that there were present in every polity two kingdoms, two types of sovereignty: the temporal and the spiritual, neither superior to the other, each supreme in its own sphere. In England any such idea had been indignantly repudiated during the Reformation. But John Calvin and John Knox had in this respect innovated conservatively, and bequeathed to Scotland what they conceived as a purified version of the medieval system.

Scottish historical experience had given it a still more federal character. In the temporal kingdom, the Crown shared even the seat of justice with its greater subjects, the holders of heritable jurisdictions, and did so for forty years after the Union. It might be argued that this was just a case of deficiency, of failure by any central authority to establish its power, for which English intervention through a joint sovereignty was a remedy which could never have been supplied by the Scots alone. But when administration of the law was then concentrated in Edinburgh, for the rest of the eighteenth century the Court of Session acted much as the Supreme Court acts in the United States today. It was not itself much interfered with by the Parliament at Westminster, since the volume of statute law was small. Rather the court itself met changing conditions by reinterpreting, reshaping, reforming the law, and this in no authoritarian spirit but usually with reference to the parties concerned, a coherent framework for the whole being maintained by the institutional writers. The law thus developed in line with national traditions and kept Anglicising influences at bay.[3] That was in varying degrees true of the other secular institutions perpetually guaranteed by the Treaty of Union.

In the spiritual kingdom, too, Presbyterianism diffused authority in a hierarchy of courts. But the Kirk's real constitutional peculiarity lay in its enjoying a guarantee more special than the rest: the Act of Security antecedent to the Treaty, passed by both Parliaments as a precondition of the United Kingdom. If, in the novel environment of the Union, it was to rely on secular legislation, that did not amount to an admission by it of civil supremacy, any more than to an assertion of its supremacy over the state. The admission was rather by the state, at the moment of its birth, that it accepted the Kirk's view of its own situation. On this the Scots Parliament and the English Parliament alike seem to have believed themselves to be laying down a fundamental law with as much solemnity as they could muster.[4] A Treaty resting on that basis could not be an expression of absolute parliamentary sovereignty. It stipulated that wherever else this sovereignty might extend, in Scotland the sphere of religion, morals and welfare was to be yielded to the Church. There was of course bound to be some argument about the delimitation of the two kingdoms. It arose, however, not out of assertions of supremacy by one over the other, but rather out of the problems of co-ordinating them.

Semi-independence thus extended over most internal affairs. English indifference to them was natural, indeed welcome, for it handed to Scots the prime responsibility for maintaining the delicate balance by which the settlement of 1707, with its many silences and lacunae, was made to work. The achievement looked the more remarkable because the Union's formal guarantees started to break down almost at once, notably with the Patronage Act of 1712. Scots still argued they were real. Robert Dundas of Arniston, later Lord President of the Court of Session, called the articles of the Union 'unalterable' in the 1720s, even while recognising he could do little to prevent alteration of them. Thus the heritable jurisdictions were to be abolished in 1747, though in a reform this time at least negotiated and paid for. Arniston's son, Henry Dundas, sought as Scottish manager in 1785 the King's express permission to reorganise the Court of Session, a device which might have set a useful precedent but in fact did not. The government was still asserting in the 1820s that the royal burghs' constitutions rested on chartered rights placed by the Treaty beyond the reach even of the royal prerogative.[5] By now, however, the institutions preserved in 1707 were coming under severe strain, stretched on a Procrustes' bed of an emergent industrial society. Even so, many Scots refused to concede that this was reason enough to submit them to parliamentary regulation. The Claim of Right by the General Assembly in 1842 asserted that the Kirk's constitution was 'reserved from the cognizance and power of the federal legislature'[6] created by the Treaty.

The Scottish tradition behind the Claim of Right was logical and consistent in itself. To be sure, its stream had not run unsullied since 1707, and logical consistency had at several points yielded to political expediency. The result was not its negation, though, rather a state of affairs where nobody could be quite certain if it was constitutionally proper to regard the Treaty as just another Act of Parliament, amendable at will, or if there was indeed something federal about the British constitution, at least by virtue of its comprehending Scotland. Scots holding the latter view were by no means unusual or eccentric. It was understandable, as the crisis in the Kirk deepened, that men soon to be branded Presbyterian fanatics should hold it. That it should be held by a man like Sir George Clerk of Penicuik – a pillar of the old Scots Tory establishment, a friend of Sir Robert Peel since their days together at the university of Oxford and by 1843 a minister in his government – was not easy to explain except on grounds of his genuine conviction, formed by assessment of Scotland's true constitutional position. Sir George was no natural rebel and would remain loyal to his party and to the old Kirk. Yet in 1839 he had declared plainly to the House of Commons: 'The Church of Scotland does not refuse to render unto Caesar the things that are Caesar's, but it will not allow of an interference with its spiritual and ecclesiastical right.'[7] His view stood close to that of the high Presbyterians. He was in effect denying the doctrine of absolute parliamentary sovereignty.

Again, the Moderate party in the Kirk found itself often pilloried as servile to the state. Yet the Revd George Cook, its leader in 1843, explicitly held with the theory of the two kingdoms. He spoke of 'a great and sacred corporation, possessing ample power for its own internal government, but restrained from exercising that power to the prejudice of the community, or in excess of its appropriate jurisdiction'. His qualification here was that disputes between the two kingdoms had to be justiciable, and in practice could only be so in the courts: 'When any law is declared by the competent authorities to affect civil right, the Church cannot set aside such a law ... So to do would be to declare ourselves superior to the law of the land.' Yet

> such cases would never have occurred but for the false pretensions which the church courts have put forward ... The jurisdiction of the civil courts has been invoked to meet claims before unheard of, and when such claims are abandoned all such interference will immediately cease.[8]

There he put his finger on the weakness in the Evangelicals' argument, that they were bent on restoring to pristine purity an ecclesiastical constitution in reality profaned by time and events, rather than defending an actual constitution. But in any case the basic question was the same, whether Parliament had jurisdiction over everything.

It was a momentous question on which hinged the performance of a formidable task, and one might ask why Scots felt the exertion so compelling. An obvious reason was that the means of restoration were to hand, after an era in which they had been wanting, by virtue of an Evangelical majority appearing in the General Assembly from 1832. The deeper reason was that the Kirk felt called to apply these means to a much greater end than mere manipulation of majorities, to the redemption of the new society rising round it. The Revd Thomas Chalmers tried to put all this over to the English in the series of lectures he was invited to give in London in 1838. Already a renowned churchman, he was able to draw a distinguished audience including many peers of the realm and the young William Gladstone. It was also a conservative audience, expecting from Chalmers a conservative theory of Church and state. What it heard instead must have struck it as a bizarre brew indeed, composed of a medieval theory (that of the two kingdoms) and an almost radical concern for modern problems (those of the Industrial Revolution).

Chalmers meant to show how these disparate notions were connected by arguing for the continued necessity of an established religion, which had been coming under attack from sundry political and religious quarters. He argued that the best way for modern society to fulfil its Christian duty and show compassion for suffering humanity was through a national Church. It was not yet generally thought a duty of the state to offer such succour, and the dominant secular ideology of political economy decreed that it ought not to be. Nor could the voluntary exertions of competing sects ever suffice. Parliament had to choose one Church or another – and he naturally expected the choice to fall on a protestant one – as the vehicle for promoting the spiritual and material well-being of society as a whole. This need not be uncongenial to the secular ideology, at least if the Scottish model was adopted: 'There might be an entire dependence on the state in things temporal, without even the shadow of a dependence upon it in things ecclesiastical.' Such freedom was preferable from the Church's point of view too, just so that it could be at its most effective in its own kingdom.[9] The thesis was clearly meant to challenge Englishmen, and not only with the notion that Jesus Christ rather than Queen Victoria was head of the Church, but also with a call to reflection on how else the ends Chalmers had set out were to be achieved, if not by the means he specified. Gladstone, at any rate, was so shocked that he went home and sat straight down to write his own tract on Church and state, vindicating the English view.[10]

This episode proved significant in showing that, if the Kirk was to be renewed, then the so far indifferent English would have to be enlightened about the Scottish doctrines concerning it.

> 'I have never yet met an Englishman who could understand, or even conceive, that idea of the relation between Church and State which was embedded in the constitution of Scotland. John Bull, with all his qualities, is a very parochial creature.'[11]

This was with justice written by the young Marquis of Lorne, a Whig nobleman who would exert himself in vain to avert the crisis. Indeed, whatever Englishmen may have thought of the empirical evidence for the theory of two kingdoms adduced from Scottish history, they certainly disliked the argument for it from first principles. What would really annoy Chalmers was their reluctance, after the Auchterarder case had turned the tensions into conflict, to accept that he had a valid point at all:

> 'The question of whether each court might not have its own proper and certain limits prescribed in the constitution, or whether these limits might not possibly, yea, have been actually transgressed – this is a question which they have not looked at, and will not listen to.'[12]

It was hardly the best start for a trial of whether the problem of relations between Church and state was to be resolved by an English or a Scottish interpretation of the constitution. If Englishmen had conceptual difficulty with any other model of established religion than the Anglican one, this was because England remained in essence an absolute monarchy. It had been so since 1534 when the Act of Supremacy swept away the two kingdoms and made the Crown the sole fount of sovereignty in a unitary state. While the Glorious Revolution of 1688 had rendered the monarchy less absolute, it did not create a constitution federal in the Scottish sense. It merely specified that the sovereignty should be exercised constitutionally, with the advice and consent of the Crown's subjects represented in Parliament. This expression of the doctrine of parliamentary sovereignty was thus beyond doubt recent. Contrary to English assumptions, it owed little to an ancient constitution, and embodied political notions quite the opposite of medieval ones.[13]

Still, just as the Scots tradition was somewhat sullied, so before 1843 the exercise of Westminster's sovereignty had never been absolute in practice, but modified through choice or necessity by English pragmatism. For more than a century England had, after all, put up with special arrangements in the same state for a Scotland of alien constitutional principles. Meanwhile, the muddy self-seeking of politics in the eighteenth century had left Parliament ill-equipped for the first serious test of its sovereignty, the revolt of America, a test that it miserably failed. As late as 1832 it was granting a Reform Act more in terror at the prospect of revolution than out of serene exercise of its sovereignty. In the aftermath, nobody pondered how Scotland might fit into what in effect was a new constitution, a question of no triviality when Scottish resistance to reform rested on defence of the settlement of 1707. The English jurist, William Blackstone, had already been wondering in the 1770s if its guarantees possessed any meaning under a doctrine of absolute parliamentary sovereignty. The answer was that they had meaning so long as they lasted in practice, and they did last till the 1830s and 1840s. The full doctrine would really come into its own only as a reinvention of the high Victorians, reflecting their confidence in their state.

The Disruption was formative in the reinvention and, if nothing else, answered the question of how Scotland would fit in with the new constitution, which was to say, by complete abandonment of her old one. Up to that point, though, English politicians did not impress with the quality of the ideas they advanced in answer to the points raised by the Scots. On the contrary, they were plainly unsure of the ground in their bemused search for a workable solution. Sir James Graham, Home Secretary in 1843, had earlier told Gladstone how he hoped the antagonists might 'without a sacrifice of principle, have devised some middle term'. In the same correspondence, Gladstone wrote to say that the difficulty was caused 'by principles really embodied in the presbyterian polity, though disclosed and valued in very various degrees at various periods … If the postulates of presbyterianism be granted the right is not all on our side.'[14]

While such men wanted to uphold Established religion, they had never reckoned with the Established religion now confronting them in Scotland. It insisted that for the sake of renewal the Kirk should be enabled to set priorities different from, even at odds with, secular ones, a far cry from the deference to the state of the old Moderate regime or of the Anglicans. Conservatives had already induced in themselves a thoroughgoing pessimism about the politics of the future. Now it seemed they must do the same with religion. Graham wrote in 1840: 'I am not blind to the political consequences of this struggle. I foresee its fatal effect on the peace of Scotland.' He forecast that religious radicals would come together with their political counterparts in a potentially revolutionary alliance: 'Scotland will be convulsed; and the issue no man can confidently predict.'[15]

Politicians regarding the times as so dangerous were unlikely to be absolutists. And it is not clear that their leader, Peel, asserted absolute parliamentary sovereignty in the modern form. He did distinguish between an Established and a Voluntary Church:

> 'If a Church chooses to have the advantage of an establishment and to
> hold those privileges which the law confers – that Church, whether it
> be the Church of Rome, or the Church of England, or the Presbyterian
> Church of Scotland, must conform to the law.'

Consequently it could not set the limits of its own jurisdiction, which might only be done in 'the tribunal appointed by Parliament, which is the House of Lords'.[16] His theory was, then, that while a Voluntary Church might possess the rights claimed by the Kirk, an Established Church surrendered them. If dissatisfied with the results, it could only break with the state.

Peel also conceded, though, that since the repeal of the Test and Corporation Acts the state had given up trying to control non-established religion. Yet today the argument would be that not even a voluntary association was independent in this sense, and that Parliament could without doubt enforce its will on an unestablished Church if it wanted. Peel's views show us a doctrine of parliamentary sovereignty still in process of reformulation, not yet absolute. Even in this tentative shape, however, it was thoroughly unpalatable to Chalmers and his colleagues. Peel was of course set on a quite different task from theirs, on restoring Conservatism in a polity which after 1832 was reshaped on Liberal lines. From the new dispensation he accepted severe restraint of the political kingdom. He stipulated only that it should be strong in what remained to it. Liberal philosophy, however, allowed no other kingdom to exist. Beyond its bounds lay a state of nature, subject only to the laws of political economy. So on Peel's interpretation, Churches could choose where to place themselves in relation to the bounds, but not beyond them have a second kingdom of their own.

Still, this was just a statement of position, and the attitudes of other English Tory leaders do not imply that they would have spurned a compromise if available. Prominent Scots laymen, in and outside the government, exerted themselves to propose one. Their efforts often owed a good deal to Lord Jeffrey's dissenting judgement on the Auchterarder case, which appealed for a view of statutes taking some to be less absolute in their applicability than others. Conflicts between Church and state, he pointed out, could not all be as exceptional and momentous as the one then before the Bench. There were many more minor examples of ecclesiastical actions with civil consequences, as when a man felt aggrieved at his exclusion from communion. How the courts might discriminate among such cases was by weighing the civil loss against the ecclesiastical loss. At Auchterarder,

Lord Kinnoull's loss was less than the Kirk's loss. The decision ought
therefore to be in the Kirk's favour. This was a pragmatic theory of law, on
a constitutional view containing some element of the federal. 'In the
theory of the constitution,' Jeffrey sensibly observed,

> 'the supreme courts of the country are held to be as nearly incapable
> of doing wrong as the sovereign herself, and, though known to be
> fallible in fact, are presumed to be so equally fallible as not to be trusted
> in the correction of each other's errors.'[17]

The Earl of Aberdeen afterwards busied himself in quest of a corresponding technical solution, but of greater interest were the exertions of Lorne,
about to succeed as Duke of Argyll, who unusually for a nobleman was also
an intellectual. He undertook to coax the English towards an appreciation
of the depth of the issues at stake. In particular, he tried to develop Jeffrey's
view with a definition of the term 'unconstitutional', in relation to statutes
passed by Parliament, which was 'not altogether strange or unintelligible to
the English ear'.[18] What he wanted was to establish a hierarchy of statutes,
in which one like the Act of Security would rank high, 'laws which the united
Parliament of Britain were in future to respect, and which, under the
guardianship of a national treaty, and the Sovereign's oath, were in future
to be preserved inviolate'. By contrast, a more ordinary statute would rank
low, especially in the form it took by dint of the Auchterarder judgement as
just a judicial interpretation. This would make explicit a 'distinction between
a mere civil statute, and constitutional law and principle'. But the task, Lorne
stressed, would have to be consciously undertaken by the government, and
not left to haphazard collisions among the national institutions.[19]

The Kirk was not utterly uncompromising either. Though deadlock
ended the talks in 1838 between Peel's predecessor as prime minister, Lord
Melbourne, and Chalmers, the latter went into them ready to accept that
Parliament might statutorily confirm the General Assembly's own legislation
since 1832, a potential concession on the point of spiritual independence.
Though it became ever harder for him to control the Evangelical hotheads,
even in 1843, we should recall, the Moderate party remained powerful in
the General Assembly. With the Middle Party, formed for the sole purpose
of compromise, it had an actual majority. Right on the brink, with the
different parties polarised, a way back could still be sought. The Kirk was not
entirely friendless in Parliament, where seventy-six votes were cast in support
of a committee on the Claim of Right. On the strength of that the Scottish
philosopher James Ferrier told ministers they had been wrong to give up
their livings unless ejected; they should have hung on till Church and state
felt obliged to deliberate together, as they surely must do in the end.[20]
English pragmatism might thus have been brought to concede that there
was not just one kingdom in Scotland, but two. Nobody at any rate should
have lost from sight the purpose of vindicating Scottish rights without
disrupting the Kirk, or given up all appeal to Caesar to rely on religious
enthusiasm for the upholding of spiritual independence, in what Ferrier's
modern interpreter calls 'a spirit of pietistic laissez-faire'.[21] For in this case

the seceders were by implication agreeing with Peel: that only one kingdom existed, with a state of nature beyond it.

Ferrier wrote with the benefit of hindsight, but it might be granted that till quite a late stage the situation ought to have been more fluid than it appeared. Opinions on each side were not yet cast in the inflexible mould of dogma, and genuine hope of compromise still existed. In fact, the stumbling block that rendered all such hope vain was already there. Strangely, it is to a Scottish, not an English source, to the Court of Session's judgement on Auchterarder, that we have to look for the introduction of a truly uncompromising spirit. It is there we must go – long before anyone at Westminster had intervened or been asked to – for the most comprehensive and contemptuous rejection of the Kirk's claims and for the idea that society must have a sovereign without equal or superior, so that, with the Act of 1712 before it, the Bench simply did not have the option of judging lay patronage to be a matter for the General Assembly.

Here is Lord Gillies, dealing with any reservations that may have arisen on grounds of the Act of Security:

> 'There can be no compact, properly speaking, between the legislature and any other body in the state. Parliament, the King and the three estates of the realm are omnipotent, and incapable of making a compact, because they cannot be bound by it.'

And here is Lord President Hope: 'The Parliament is temporal head of the Church, from whose acts and from whose acts alone, it exists as a national Church, and from which alone it derives all its powers.' There could be no conflict because 'an Establishment never can possess an independent juris-diction which can give rise to a conflict ... It is wholly a creature of statute.' Altogether, 'that our saviour is head of the Kirk of Scotland in any temporal or legislative or judicial sense is a position I can dignify by no other name than absurdity.'[22] It was only when thus prompted by the Bench in Edinburgh that the House of Lords, on the appeal, threw its weight behind this most extreme of the available positions. And it was the two Scots sitting in Westminster Hall, Lords Brougham and Campbell, who then went the furthest of all. Campbell could apparently see no real difference between the Kirk and the Church of England: 'While the appellants remain members of the Establishment, they are, in addition to their sacred character, public functionaries, appointed and paid by the state; and they must perform the duties which the law of the land imposes on them.'[23] So the Lords just confirmed what had been, from Scotland, unqualified assertions of parlia-mentary sovereignty and unqualified denials of the theory of the two kingdoms. How could this have happened? In 1785 the idea that the Court of Session itself might be reformed at Parliament's unfettered discretion had been repudiated. Did it now refuse to the other institutions the same safeguard? The integrity of Scottish society depended on balance and compromise among them. Was it the court's intention to destroy that?

Judges are no better than the times they live in, and perhaps the answer has to be sought from what had changed in Scotland at large to justify the application of, by Scottish standards, novel principles. The judiciary, for example, had indeed been several times reformed by statute meanwhile, so that the reservations of 1785 evidently no longer held. Moreover, the whole of the surviving political constitution had been toppled since 1832. Most Scots assumed that the old Scotland was simply passing away. They regretted it, but thought it unavoidable if they were to have their rightful place in the United Kingdom and the empire. And the process seemed irrevocably bound up with the transfer of powers to the imperial Parliament and government. In the spirit of the age there was something anomalous about the Kirk alone seeking to stand out against the state.

Testimony to this effect came from the Lord President's son, John Hope, who played a yet bigger role in the Disruption. The Tories' last Solicitor General before 1832, then Dean of the Faculty of Advocates, he did much to bring the Auchterarder case to court and was an adviser of notable intransigence to Sir Robert Peel from 1841. Consciousness of a new, British context to events is often evident in his views, as here on the Veto Act: 'The changes contemplated cannot be confined to Scotland. The consideration of these cannot be regarded merely as a Scotch question even if their importance to society in Scotland did not demand the most anxious consideration.' He deplored nationalistic attempts to draw a comparison between Presbyterian tradition and what was now at stake, for in these days such exertions in the name of Scotland could be 'alarming sources of disturbance and confusion to the social system'.[24]

It would be easy to dismiss Hope as extreme and biased, except that key points of his were echoed by others of different convictions. Henry Cockburn stood at the opposite end of the political spectrum, yet he also appreciated what difference a British perspective might make:

> 'There never was such an instance of the habitual ignorance and indifference of Government (all governments) to Scotch affairs as in this of patronage ... Yet because it was as yet merely Scotch, and conducted without turbulent agitation, it was impossible to get any line whatever adopted by ministers.'[25]

When a Scotch affair at length became more than Scotch and a line had to be adopted, ministers were happy to grasp at the ready-packaged solution from the Scotch Court of Session, a doctrine of absolute parliamentary sovereignty. The judges may have thought they had defined the law as it ever was. They were in truth giving expression to a great change that had come over Scotland, an acceptance that it was the British context, not the native tradition, that mattered most.

The judgement certainly ruled out any chance of finding a modern form of semi-independence, of renewing the concepts of 1707, even if obligations towards Scotland were thus disregarded. Everything was declared simply subordinate to Parliament, without further qualification. It was incompetent of the highest courts of the land to declare that Parliament had erred, let alone to correct the error, or consider the strength of another body's case. There could be no superior theory of law, because the law was simply what had been passed by Parliament. To have ruled in any other sense would, of course, have defined parliamentary sovereignty as non-absolute, and have granted that Church and state might exercise some form of co-ordinate jurisdiction.

From this point, the British constitution must have started to elaborate a new theory of itself. Peel's observations even indicate that there might have been scope to do so. But at the decisive moment, it was the Scots judges who took a view allowing no ambiguity. Surely this was an outcome more absolutist than the circumstances called for, or politicians in London could ever have intended or has been altogether good for Scotland and the Union since.

The Kirk could not believe it anyway and reacted in a manner eventually matching the judges' extremism, with a conscious polarisation that made the Disruption unavoidable. In defence of it, one should recall how fantastic the idea must have seemed that the Church of Scotland was a mere creature of Parliament, enjoying rights only at its pleasure – the Church of Scotland of all Churches, whose entire history and tradition spoke of its independence, its capacity to stand alone if need be, whatever the world did to it! Even if by the middle of the nineteenth century it was hard-pressed to maintain its kingdom, still it felt that its wholeness in industrial society could somehow be restored: *nec tamen consumebatur*. Independence, wholeness – it was impossible with these purposes for the Kirk to perceive in society anything other than a federal structure, where sovereignty could not be attributed exclusively to one part.

Over that perception the unitary state did formally prevail, in what can, however, hardly be called a victory. Graham said just before the Disruption: 'These pretensions of the Church of Scotland as they now stand ... appear to me to rest on expectations and views so unreasonable, that the sooner they are extinguished the better.'[26] This was the same man who later admitted that he 'never would cease to regard it with the deepest regret and sorrow, as the saddest event in his life, that he should never have had any hand in that most fatal act'.[27]

The state invited moral defeat by its very insistence that there was no superior theory of law, so that law must then have the primacy over conscience. This, a free people could not be made to accept. Consequently the state had just to look on while great numbers walked out of the national Church, the established position of which it was in principle committed to defend. As a result, there existed no real national Church in Scotland. This was undesirable given the problems of the age, quite apart from the fact that it smashed the compact of 1707.

Yet it did not – as it might have done and as some hoped it would – bring a rapid, let alone ultimate, assimilation of Scotland into England. People saw clearly enough that if Scots had been able in any degree to decide for themselves, the Disruption could never have happened. There might have been a clash between Kirk and courts, but Scottish statesmanship and Scottish public opinion would have ensured a better outcome. For reasons already explained, this realisation generated no strong nationalist reaction.

But still in major respects it did make the Scots more Scottish, more rigid, vehement and intransigent, more concerned with the logic of a position than with its practical effects, though also more respectful of democracy than of hierarchy, above all more resolved to be themselves than to truckle. This was no doubt necessary in a Union which for the sake of its material benefits none wanted broken, but which had changed all the same against the Scots' will. It would in future assert over historical or particular interests new interests of its own, and do so by means of a new doctrine of absolute parliamentary sovereignty. This, like so much else in Victorian Britain, seems ironically to have been in its highest form an invention of Scotsmen, of the judges who pressed home a logical rigour for which Englishmen left to themselves might have had little taste. Whether the resulting Union is better than what a different course could have produced is not for this chapter to answer; enough to observe that the tension within it of Scottish particularism and absolute sovereignty remains unresolved.

The dilemmas of the future were already visible on 18 May 1843. The Revd Thomas Brown tells in the *Annals of the Disruption* how the Revd Walter Wood of Elie had visited Langholm in January of that year, as a member of one among a number of missions sent out by the General Assembly on tours round Scotland to prepare the faithful for an event which all now knew to be inevitable. He addressed a meeting, and complained to it that at Westminster the voice of the Scottish members had been overborne by the English majority:

> I said, on the spur of the moment, that such injustice was enough to justify Scotland in demanding the repeal of the Union. With that, to my surprise, and somewhat to my consternation, the meeting rose as one man, waving hats and handkerchiefs and cheering again and again. No doubt the enthusiastic feelings of the people assisted our object, but I took care not to speak of repeal of the Union at our subsequent meetings.[28]

NOTES

1   From the Revd Thomas Guthrie, quoted in Anon., *Practical Remarks on the Scotch Church Question* (London, 1841), p. 56.
2   M. R. G. Fry, *The Dundas Despotism* (Edinburgh, 1992), chs. ix, x.
3   Lord Cooper of Culross, 'The Central Courts after 1532', in Stair Society, *An Introduction to Scottish Legal History* (Edinburgh, 1958), p. 44; T. B. Smith, *British Justice, the Scottish contribution* (London, 1961), pp. 61, 68.
4   H. J. Laski, *Studies in the Problem of Sovereignty* (New Haven and London, 1917), p. 28.
5   Fry, *The Dundas Despotism*, pp. 7–8, 142–3, 334.
6   Quoted in full in R. Buchanan; *The Ten Years' Conflict*, 2 vols (Glasgow, 1849), vol. ii, pp. 633–47.
7   Hansard, 3rd ser., vol. xxxv, pp. 575–81.
8   Buchanan, *The Ten Years' Conflict*, vol. i, p. 481 and vol. ii, p. 21; R. W. Vaudry, 'The Constitutional Party in the Church of Scotland', *Scottish Historical Review*, lxii (1983), 42–3.
9   T. Chalmers, 'Lectures on the Establishment and Extension of National Churches', *The Collected Works of Thomas Chalmers*, 25 vols. (Glasgow 1835–42), vol. xvii, pp. 264–5.

10 W. E. Gladstone, *The State in its Relations with the Church* (London, 1838).
11 Duke of Argyll, *Autobiography and Memoirs* (London, 1906), p. 174.
12 Buchanan, *The Ten Years' Conflict*, vol. ii, p. 364.
13 C. McIlwain, *The High Court of Parliament and its Supremacy* (New Haven, 1910).
14 C. S. Parker, *Life and Letters of Sir James Graham 1792–1861* (London, 1907), vol. i, pp. 374–5.
15 Ibid., p. 321.
16 Hansard, 3rd ser. vol. lxvii, p. 502.
17 C. Robertson (ed.), *Report of the Auchterarder Case* (Edinburgh, 1838), pp. 361–96; G. W. T. Omond, *The Lord Advocates of Scotland*, 2nd ser. (Edinburgh, 1914), p. 58.
18 Marquis of Lorne, *A Letter to the Reverend Thomas Chalmers* (Edinburgh, 1842), p. 18.
19 Duke of Argyll, *Letter to the Peers* (Edinburgh, 1842), p. 79.
20 J. F. Ferrier, *Observations on Church and State* (Edinburgh and London, 1848), p. 20; J. Bulloch and A. L. Drummond, *The Scottish Church 1688–1843* (Edinburgh, 1973), p. 222.
21 G. E. Davie, *The Democratic Intellect* (Edinburgh, 1961), p. 308.
22 Robertson, *Report*, pp. 1–20, 21–52.
23 Quoted in T. Brown (ed.), *Annals of the Disruption* (Edinburgh, 1893), pp. 27–8.
24 J. Hope, *A Letter to the Lord Chancellor on the Claims of the Church of Scotland* (Edinburgh, 1838), pp. 7, 11.
25 Quoted in I. Maciver, 'Cockburn and the Church', in A. Bell (ed.), *Lord Cockburn: A Bicentenary Commemoration* (Edinburgh, 1979), p. 94.
26 Hansard, 3rd ser. vol. lxvii, p. 502.
27 Parker, *Life and Letters*, p. 395.
28 Brown, *Annals of the Disruption*, p. 69.

CHAPTER THREE

The Sociology of the Disruption

P. L. M. HILLIS

The wee Kirk, the Free Kirk
The Kirk wi'out the steeple
The auld Kirk, the cauld Kirk
The Kirk wi'out the people[1]

THIS CONTEMPORARY RHYME suggested a bleak future for the Church of
Scotland after 1843. Although slightly less pessimistic about the strength of
the 'auld Kirk', Thomas Chalmers confidently predicted that in the Free
Church 'the great bulk and body of the common people, with a goodly
proportion of the middle classes, are upon our side, though it bodes ill for
the country that the higher classes are almost universally against us'.[2] This
chapter tests Chalmers's claim that the Free Church had the support of the
'common people' and a large part of the middle class. It will show that, not
only was the contemporary rhyme too dismissive of the Church of Scotland,
but the situation was also more complicated than Chalmers's statement
would lead one to believe. The sociology of the Disruption varied according
to region and according to the different social groups within each region.
Moreover, social composition was not the sole determinant of religious
adherence since other factors, including the personality of the local ministers and local traditions, played an important role in deciding who stayed in
and who went out of the Established Church in 1843.

In order to test Chalmers's thesis the chapter will look in some detail at
the social composition of Established and Free Church congregations within
the three most obvious regional divisions: Highland, Lowland rural and
Lowland urban. The parishes chosen within each region were those whose
extant records allowed a direct comparison of the Churches' social make-up,
for example Durness Parish Church and Durness Free Church. These
findings are supplemented by an analysis of a range of individual congregations within the relevant region. The most detailed source for studying a
congregation's social composition would have been the communion roll
book but few roll books remain in existence. Therefore, baptismal registers

were used to analyse religious adherence since Church membership was usually a prerequisite for parents wishing the baptism of their child in Church. Although a more lenient attitude was taken towards baptisms in mission stations[3] many Churches insisted on regular church-going before baptism, or at the very least a promise of good attendance.[4] Baptismal registers, if analysed over a period of several years, give an accurate socio-logical insight into a congregation. However, before moving on to the analysis of religious adherence it should be noted that this chapter is largely a preliminary study of a large and complex subject. Its purpose will have been partly served if it encourages others to study the situation in their given locality.

THE HIGHLANDS

One cold winter's Sunday morning the only parishioner who had braved the elements to attend morning service at Carnoch church in Strathconan had to remind his somewhat unenthusiastic minister of the Lord's promise that 'where two or three are gathered together in my name I am in the midst of them … You are one and I am two, and I like a word in the Gaelic.'[5] That the empty pews on this morning were no exception is evidenced by the fact that only twenty baptisms were administered in the church in the thirty-one years after 1883,[6] while on the first Sunday of October 1867 the minister dispensed communion to a congregation of seven people.[7] These figures relate to a parish population in 1861 of 1,612 of whom 177 were children between the ages of 5 to 15 attending school[8]. The biographer of James Cameron Lees, minister of Carnoch from 1856 to 1859, wrote of the 'isolation' and 'mental stagnation'[9] of life and work in Strathconan with few ceremonies to perform, empty pews and hostility from many local people. Smashing the windows of the church was a popular youthful pastime. It was perhaps to the benefit of Lees's mental health that he only spent three years in Strathconan. John MacDougall, minister from 1866, was suspended from his charge in 1897 for inefficiency. Shutting himself up in his manse he lived the life of a hermit. He ceased to attend funerals, celebrated no marriage in twenty-six years and had not administered baptism since 1885. The manse fell into a deplorable condition and the church was filthy with 'seats and floors covered with the droppings of birds'.[10] The loneliness of MacDougall's position had much to do with his suspension.

He might have taken some comfort from his colleagues elsewhere in the Highlands. At Lairg the minister administered thirty-two baptisms between 1855 and 1876[11] in a parish whose population totalled 961 in 1861.[12] Tongue St Andrew's had a roll of twenty in 1891[13] whereas the congregation of Tongue Free Church witnessed 246 baptisms in the six years following 1846.[14] In Durness Free Church on Sunday 8 May 1844 Neil Sutherland watched the baptism of his daughter Aina.[15] Aina's twin brother and her mother had died during childbirth. Neil Sutherland's occupation in the baptismal register was recorded as 'Master of Rover's Bride, Lochinver',[16] with Aina one of 134 baptisms in the Free Church between 1843 and 1848.

By way of a stark contrast, when the Cape Wrath lighthouse keeper, Patrick Ewing Reid, and his wife brought their daughter for baptism[17] at Durness Parish Church, this was one of only thirteen baptisms between 1856 and 1865.[18]

These figures reflect the wider picture of Free Church adherence in the Highlands where the 'ministerial secession varied from 76 per cent in Easter Ross to 35 per cent in the Hebrides and West Highlands ...', figures which held a 'fairly uniform defection to the Free Church by the laity'.[19] Although it has been claimed that in the predominantly Roman Catholic areas of Barra and South Uist the Free Church presence was 'insignificant',[20] South Uist and Barra Free Church had a roll of thirty-seven in 1880, a respectable total by Church of Scotland standards.

Contemporary accounts describe the empty pews left by the Disruption in many Highland parishes. Hugh Miller, editor of the *Witness*, journal of the Free Church, likened the post-Disruption Establishment to a bygone religion: 'The Established Churches have become as useless in the district, as if, like its Druidical circles, they represented some idolatrous belief, long exploded, the people will not enter them ...'[21] Furthermore, in areas where the Free Church was strong Hugh Miller noted a class division between the rival denominations both claiming to be a national Church: '... all who are not creatures of the proprietor, and have not stifled their convictions for a piece of bread, are devotedly attached to the disestablished ministers ...'[22]

Miller's claims are largely supported by Table 3.1 showing the social composition of several Highland Churches. Accepting the situation whereby the exact social make-up of a congregation depended on the sociology of

Table 3.1   Social pattern of the Disruption in the Highlands[23]

Church	Total	Found	Landed and Professional	Skilled	Farm/unskilled
Carnoch Church	20	20	4	0	16
baptisms	percentage		20	0	80
1883–1914					
Lairg Parish Church	32	32	19	4	9
baptisms	percentage		59	13	28
1855–76					
Tain Free Church	175	158	38	51	69
baptisms	percentage		24	32	44
1843–7					
Blair Atholl and Struan	44	31	16	9	6
Free Church	percentage		54	29	19
proposed elders					
and deacons					
1844–84					

the parish, Tain and Blair Atholl show the strength of the Free Church among the small tenant farmers; the largest number of identified elders and deacons at Blair Atholl were from this group. However, the real numerical strength of the Highland Free Church came from farm and unskilled workers, the bulk, as Hugh Miller noted, of the Highland population.[24] Noticeable also is the almost total lack of support for the Establishment from skilled tradesmen. In many parts of the Highlands, therefore, the Church of Scotland was left with very small congregations confined largely to the large landowners, selected professional groups – especially parish school-masters – and employees of the landowner, such as coachmen, grooms, keepers and ploughmen.

This sociological schism between the denominations has led to the Disruption in the Highlands being described as not just an ecclesiastical dispute, but also a class conflict: 'Its battle line was the line of class demar-cation, the line between the small tenantry on the one hand sheep farmers, factors and proprietors on the other.'[25] Thomas Chalmers and Hugh Miller would appear to have been correct in stating that the Free Church was popular especially among certain social groups. This would suggest that the social composition of the Highlands and socio-economic factors up to 1843 explain the pattern of the Disruption in this region. Notable among the socio-economic factors were the Highland Clearances.

It has been argued that the role played by Church of Scotland ministers during the Clearances largely contributed to their unpopularity and the demise of their Church.[26] In some areas the Establishment's association with the Clearances was very close. In the 1820s and 1830s, several Skye ministers were also sheep farmers and acted as factors on the larger estates. Some Hebridean ministers held tacks and like some other tacksmen were prone 'to treat their subtenants with great severity'.[27] Elsewhere, Church of Scot-land ministers, appointed by landowners, often stand accused of either failing to condemn, or actively aiding and abetting in, the Clearances. David MacKenzie, minister of the parish of Farr, read eviction notices to his people in 1818 and 1819.[28] Where people offered resistance to the Clearances, as at Durness in 1841, the parish minister

> made himself useful on the occasion threatening the the people with punishment here and hereafter … According to him all the evils inflicted upon them were ordained of God and for their good, whereas any opposition on their part proceeded from the devil, and subjected them to just punishment here and eternal torment hereafter.[29]

Donald MacLeod summed up the role of the Establishment's ministers during the Clearances:

> The clergy … whose duty it is to denounce the oppressor and aid the oppressed, have … found their account in abetting the wrongdoers, exhorting the people to quiet submission, helping to stifle their cries, telling them that all their sufferings came from the hand of God, and was a just punishment for their sins.[30]

At first sight William Findlater's threats of eternal torment, as described by Donald MacLeod, might seem to explain the well-filled pews in Durness Free Church and empty seats in the Parish Church after 1843. However, the difficulty with this explanation is that William Findlater took most of his congregation with him when he left the Church of Scotland for the Free Church at the Disruption. In a similar manner, David MacKenzie's congregation followed their minister into the Free Church. The Clearances may explain the overall unpopularity of the Establishment but they do not always account for local loyalties and traditions. Other evidence from Durness and Farr indicates that many Church of Scotland ministers have been too readily condemned for their roles during the Clearances, with the Clearances being only one of many factors accounting for the Disruption. These factors explain why many Church of Scotland ministers were followed into the Free Church by large numbers of people.

Despite supporting agricultural changes,[31] some Church of Scotland ministers were concerned about the detrimental effects on their parishioners. Soon after being translated to the Parish Church of Farr, David MacKenzie was asked to give his seal of approval to 'the scheme of clearing Strathnaver, and many other places … but this he absolutely refused to do'.[32] In the *New Statistical Account* William Findlater showed a more ambivalent attitude towards agricultural change than that recorded by Donald MacLeod. William Findlater noted that the 'division of the Parish into such extensive farms has also suppressed almost entirely the middle classes of society …'[33] Furthermore, *Disruption Worthies of the Highlands* gives a different interpretation to the one accepted by many historians,[34] concerning the part played by Findlater during the Durness riots of 1841:

> A party of soldiers was ordered to be in readiness at Fort George … but owing to the representation which Mr Findlater made of the people's cause to the Edinburgh authorities, a special Commissioner was sent to Durness, and the matter amicably settled. So grateful were the people for their pastor's interposition, that they gave a public dinner to himself and other gentlemen who had taken their side.[35]

Findlater's belief that 'any opposition' on the part of the parishioners 'proceeded from the devil' was accepted and put a stop to subsequent resistance. His sermons did 'not denote his abandonment of the people; they were a reflection of what he, and they, thought was correct'.[36]

MacKenzie's reputation as an 'evangelical'[37] alongside a strong family tradition of opposing the intrusion of 'unacceptable' ministers[38] enhanced his popularity. William Findlater's ability to communicate 'correctly and fluently' in Gaelic was also commended.[39] Such factors influenced the pattern of the Disruption beyond the confines of Durness and Farr. In the 1820s and 1830s the effect of patronage, strongly opposed by David MacKenzie's father, altered the position of ministers within Highland society. In the old Highlands many ministers had been drawn from 'among the tacksmen and like them had occupied something of an intermediate position in the social hierarchy'.[40] In the early decades of the nineteenth century, however, the clergy moved in the circles of the farmers, factors and proprietors, away from the bulk of the population. Many ministers could not speak Gaelic while a report to the 1824 General Assembly accused ministers in the north-west of being for the most part 'inattentive to the interests of religion'.[41] In Sutherland ministers were placed in parishes contrary to 'the will of the people'. Previously well-filled churches 'were deserted by their congregations, just because a respectable woman of the world (the Duchess of Sutherland) ... had planted them with men of the world who were only tolerably respectable ...'[42]

The early nineteenth century witnessed a series of revivals in the Hebrides and north-west Highlands which 'eventually carried the greater part of the people into the Free Church'.[43] Associated with this revival were Evangelical ministers like Roderick MacLeod, minister of Bracdale and Snizort,[44] and Robert Finlayson of Lochs and Lewis,[45] the vast majority of whom seceded in 1843. In the context of this revival, a minister's popularity largely depended on the content and style of his preaching and subsequent classification as either a Moderate or an Evangelical. Opprobrium was heaped on the former with terms such as 'dumb dogs' and 'stinking Moderates' not uncommon.[46] While the revivals did not directly effect Durness and Farr, it was important to their minister's future role in the Free Church that MacKenzie and Findlater were seen as Evangelical 'in the exposition of the truth'.[47] But the greatest popular acclaim was reserved for those Evangelical ministers and clergy of the Free Church who unequivocally condemned the Clearances. Eric Findlater, Free Church minister of Lochearnhead, preached a sermon against proprietors, sheep farmers and factors, which proved so popular that he had it published – price sixpence:

> They (landlords) became so blinded with this lust after riches that the strong bond which had for ages knit chieftain and clan became as a wither which were broken in a minute ... a sheep was to rank higher than a man.[48]

The opposition of many landowners to the Free Church, shown in the refusal to grant sites to the new Church, only served to increase its popularity. William Findlater wrote in 1844:

> Here in my old parish I feel pleasure in proclaiming to a poor yet patient people upon the hillside, or under a canvas tent, the glorious principles which have constrained so many of God's dear servants to come out and separate, to deny themselves, take up their cross and follow Christ, and to stand fast in the Liberty wherewith Christ has made them free.[49]

The Free Church congregation in the Parish of Torosay in Mull had to meet in a gravel pit while at Sunart the congregation worshipped in a floating iron church. Landowner opposition often stemmed, not from religious motives, but political considerations. Sir James Riddell, landowner at Ardnamurchan was an Episcopalian like many other landlords, which explains why so few of their names appear in communion rolls and baptismal registers. According to Sir James Riddell the Free Church had shown

> contempt for the existing laws, and led others to disobey them ... Have

they not bid defiance to the powers that be? Have they not broken up society from its very foundation, and sown the seeds of dissension and discord throughout the whole length and breadth of the land ...[50]

It is, however, important to qualify this picture of the Disruption in the Highlands as highlighting the unpopularity of the Establishment both ecclesiastical and lay. In many parts of the region the Church of Scotland continued to attract parishioners, rich and poor. In 1876 Strachur and Strathlachan Parish Church had 80 members of whom 12 were classified as landed and professional, 3 as skilled, 12 as farm and unskilled, and 53 classed as wife, widow, spinster or daughter. Strachur Free Church had a roll of 65 in 1880.[51] Unfortunately occupations were not recorded. Likewise, Tarbert (Lochfyne) Parish Church witnessed 196 baptisms between 1864 and 1875 of which 21 parents were classed as landed and professional, 11 as skilled, 162 as farm and unskilled (mainly fishermen), with 2 giving no occupation.[52] In the nearby parish of Ardrishaig, the Free Church had 49 members in 1875.[53] These parishes do not support the claims made by Hugh Miller and Thomas Chalmers. The Church of Scotland was able to retain a broad appeal in these and other areas where agricultural change was less traumatic and other factors, notably the religious revival, were not apparent.

In the minds of most people in the northern Highlands the Church of Scotland, as an institution, was closely associated with landlord policies, thus the post-1843 Establishment had a restricted social make-up confined to landlords and associated professions and trades. The apparent contradiction between an unpopular Establishment and many of its ministers taking the majority of their congregations into the Free Church is explained by the fact that much of the calumny associated with ministerial roles during the Clearances is unwarranted. In addition, the Clearances were only one of many factors accounting for the Disruption. In many other Highland areas the Free Church was less popular because the issues which led to its popularity further north could not be exploited to the same degree.

THE RURAL LOWLANDS

Here it is more difficult to see discernible patterns which would suggest that the social composition of the Lowlands explains the Disruption. The patterns more closely mirrored the situation outside the northern Highlands. Ardclach Parish Church bordered north-west Aberdeenshire and the Highlands. It witnessed 73 baptisms in the ten years following 1861. Thirteen parents were classed as landed and professional, 1 as skilled, 47 as farm and unskilled, 2 had no occupation recorded and 10 children were illegitimate.[54] Ardclach Free Church had 63 members in 1873 but their occupations were not noted.[55] However, an earlier breakdown of employment in the parish showed 9 landed and professional families, 47 skilled and 219 farm and unskilled families.[56] Table 3.2 examines the extent to which the apparent failure of Ardclach Parish Church to attract skilled workers was repeated throughout the rural Lowlands.

One immediate conclusion which can be drawn from the above analysis

Table 3.2   Social pattern of the rural Lowlands[57]

Church	Total	Found	Landed and Professional	Skilled	Farm/ unskilled
Forgue Free					
Church	134	82	17	22	43
baptisms	percentage		21	26	53
1843–9					
Bowden Free Church	116	85	17	30	38
baptisms	percentage		20	35	45
1843–59					
Kirkintilloch					
Free St David's, New	27	20	3	15	2
communicants	percentage	(7 were	15	75	10
5/11/1845		women with			
		no recorded			
		occupation)			
Cruden Parish Church	307	282	55	15	212
baptisms	percentage		19	5	75
1851– 61					
Glenisla Parish					
Church	156	153	52	20	81
baptisms	percentage		34	13	53
1856 – 60					

is that the Church of Scotland retained a considerable presence, a strength which extended throughout Lowland Scotland. Whereas in Glasgow 63 per cent of ministers left for the Free Church, in the presbytery of Glasgow, which included many rural areas, the percentage fell to 53, falling further to 22 per cent in the neighbouring Dumbarton presbytery. In Edinburgh 62 per cent of the capital's clergy seceded, but in the synod of Lothian and Tweeddale only 43 per cent left. In the Borders and the south-west, walk-outs were even lower, 25 and 20 per cent respectively.[58]

The main sociological difference between the Church of Scotland and the Free Church concentrated upon a higher percentage of skilled trades-men among the congregation and office-bearers of the new Church. In Kirkintilloch Free St David's, eighteen members were proposed as elders or deacons during August 1845. Twenty-two per cent were from landed and professional groups, 5 per cent from farm and related, with 55 per cent classed as skilled tradesmen. There was no recorded occupation for three elders or deacons.[59] This trend mirrored earlier secessions which had drawn support from 'the small tradesmen, farmers, and the craftsmen'.[60] In an anonymous article entitled 'The Large Farm System' a contributor to the *Free Church Magazine* claimed that the 'vast proportion of our country adherents is drawn from the class of small tenants',[61] but in the Lowlands the Established Church could match this claim. The Church of Scotland also could state with justification that the 'common people' and a significant proportion of the middle class were among its members.

The explanation for the Established Church's greater strength in the Lowlands may lie in the absence of the factors which caused its unpopularity in the Highlands. Although patronage was a national issue, placing ministers who could not speak Gaelic in Lowland parishes was not the obstacle to communication thrown up by the English language in the Highlands. Lowland agricultural change was not pursued with the same ruthlessness as in parts of the Highlands. This was particularly true in Ormiston where the Parish Church was able to withstand the secession of its minister and prominent Evangelical, James Bannerman.[62] An additional factor in containing the strength of the Free Church was the existence of Secession Churches in the rural Lowlands, which meant that many of those predisposed to oppose the Established Church had already gone out. The village of Scone was served by its Parish Church and its congregation attached to the United Associate Synod. Both Churches were 'in general very well attended'.[63] Although there were no 'dissenting Chapels' in the parish of Kirkcolm many parishioners went to the 'Dissenting meeting-houses of their several persuasions in Stranraer. There are forty families of Dissenters ...' who belonged chiefly to the United Secession, Reformed Presbyterian and Relief Churches. The parish minister estimated that out of a total population of 426, 191 people did not belong to the Established Church.[64] Nevertheless, in Ormiston there were 'no Dissenting meeting-houses in the parish'.[65] This situation reinforces the argument that the Church of Scotland was able to retain its influence because those factors contributing to its unpopularity in the north of Scotland were largely absent from the Lowlands.

The considerable geographic diversity which existed in Lowland Scotland makes it more difficult to form definite conclusions about the sociology of the Disruption in rural Scotland outside the Highlands. It has been shown, however, that while both Established and Free Churches represented the broad spectrum of rural society, the Free Church held a greater appeal to skilled workers. The absence of rigid class patterns within church-going indicates that social factors were less important than issues such as patronage and local traditions in determining allegiances. Thomas Chalmers's claim has been substantiated but his observation also applied to the 'auld kirk'. The kirk may have been the 'cauld kirk' but it was not the 'kirk wi'out the people'.

THE URBAN LOWLANDS

Given the constraints of a brief chapter it is not possible to study all the Scottish cities in detail. For this reason attention will focus mainly on Glasgow with some reference to A. A. MacLaren's data on Aberdeen.[66] The evidence suggests that although certain trends emerged it is necessary to be cautious about generalisations.

Table 3.3   Social composition of urban congregations[67]

Church	Total	Found	High Status	Low Status	Working Class
Govan Parish Church	826	809	35	32	742
baptisms	percentage		4	4	92
1856–64					
Govan Free Church	60	51	6	11	34
founding members–	percentage		12	21	67
male heads of house					
St Stephen's Church	172	166	59	27	80
of Scotland (Glasgow)	percentage		36	16	48
baptisms 1838					
St Stephen's Free	453	450	50	69	331
Church, baptisms	percentage		11	15	74
1851–65					
St Enoch's Free	241	237	61	44	132
Church (Glasgow),	percentage	26	27	19	55
baptisms 1844–56					
Barony Parish	332	294	68	50	176
Church (Glasgow),	percentage		23	17	60
baptisms					

In looking at the strength of the ministerial secession for Glasgow and Edinburgh, shown above, it is clear that outside the Highlands the urban areas saw the Free Church at its numerically most powerful. Further evidence came from Aberdeen where all fifteen Church of Scotland ministers joined the Free Church. An analysis of Free Church congregations shows widespread support both for those ministers and for many who remained in the Established Church.

A more detailed examination of the patterns of middle-class Church membership indicates that the Church of Scotland had most success among the older commercial and professional families, with the lower middle class adhering in greater numbers to the Free Church (see Table 3.3). Despite having a different social structure to Glasgow the situation in Aberdeen was similar among office-bearers. The identified eldership for 1851 in the eight Free Churches which were former *quoad sacra* churches was composed of high status (16 per cent), low status (82 per cent), and working class (2 per cent).[68]

By way of contrast the status of elders in Barony and St George's Parish Churches, Glasgow, and Govan Parish Church was as shown in Table 3.4.

Two biographies illustrate the difference in middle-class support for the

Table 3.4   Social class of elders[69]

Total	Found	High status	Low status	Working Class
87	76	62	12	2
	percentage	81	16	3

Free Church and the Church of Scotland. David MacBrayne was an elder in
Barony Church, Glasgow. His father, Donald, emigrated from the Highlands
to Glasgow in the early eighteenth century. He joined the firm of Adam
Good & Company, calico and linen printers, High Street, but he later took
over the firm and ran it as a partnership of MacBrayne & Stenhouse. He was
a founder member of Glasgow Chamber of Commerce in 1783, which places
him among the city's most prominent citizens. His one son, David, began
work employed by James Leslie & Company, Albion Street. In 1818 he
founded his own weaving company in Bishop Street, later becoming Barony
Session Clerk and marrying Elizabeth Burns, daughter of Dr Burns, minister
of the Church from 1773 to 1843. David and Elizabeth MacBrayne had two
sons, David and Robert. The former founded the MacBrayne Shipping
Company, now Caledonian-MacBrayne.

Robert Leisk was an elder in Free St Stephen's, Glasgow. In 1850 he was
a merchant at 46 Cambridge Street. Two years later he formed the partnership of Leisk & Eaglesham, manufacturers and warehousemen, 14 Canon
Street. By 1854 the business had moved to 125 Trongate and Leisk was living
at 75 Sauchiehall Street. Four years later the firm changed to Robert Leisk
& Son, merchants and warehousemen, 125 Trongate. Leisk now lived in the
prosperous West End at 24 Oakfield Terrace. The firm remained the same,
although by 1864 it had moved to 75 East Howard Street, until Leisk's death
in the early 1870s. The MacBrayne's, with long roots in the middle class,
were members and office-bearers in the Established Church, but the Leisks,
more upwardly mobile, joined the Free Church.

Church membership, more especially the position of elder or deacon,
was viewed by many as a useful rung on the social ladder. Although from a
different denomination John G. Paton related in his autobiography some of
the motives which encouraged him to accept the post of elder:

> For some years now I had been attached to them as City Missionary for
> their district, and many friends urged me to accept the eldership as
> likely to increase my usefulness, and give me varied experience for my
> future work.[70]

Many aspirant middle-class members of the Church of Scotland may have
felt their route up the social ladder blocked by the upper middle-class
dominance of the Church. One way to circumvent this barrier was to form
a new Church where they would be more powerful. With the greater wealth
brought about by the Industrial Revolution this became a practicable proposition. Moreover, it was from these sections of society that demands for an
extension of the franchise and other reforms were increasingly being made.

The lack of democratic control over the appointment of ministers and office-bearers in the Church of Scotland ran contrary to these wishes. Writing in *McPhail's Journal,* a publication which supported the Church of Scotland, one author caught the mood of the times when he tried to explain why so many lay people had left the Church:

> A variety of motives … affected men's conduct in such emergencies – the love of novelty – the influence of excitement – the force of example – a certain esprit de corps, or the sentiment akin to it, which attaches one to a particular minister or particular congregation … above all, the spirit of the age which is emphatically a spirit of aggressive, restless agitation for an increase of popular power.[71]

The greater appeal of the Free Church to the upwardly mobile middle class should not be seen as a hard and fast rule. It was possible for the personality of the minister to override social determinism and thus allow him to retain his congregation after 1843. Norman Macleod of the Barony Church of Glasgow proved sufficiently popular during the Sabbath controversy of the 1860s to keep all his congregation, even when some threatened secession to form Barony Free Church.[72] Furthermore, Macleod was minister of Loudoun in Ayrshire during the Disruption, but as he recorded:

> The result has been most gratifying. Of ten elders not one has left me! This is singular, as I believe only two in the whole town of Kilmarnock have refused to join the Convocation. The people are nearly unanimous or, at all events, are so attached to me personally that they are about to present to me a gold watch and an address from all parties. I would be very ungrateful to God if I were not both gratified and humbled by this proof of my dear people's good-will to me.[73]

Returning to urban Scotland, one of the most important features of an Established or Free Congregation was the high percentage of working-class members, but the Church of Scotland attracted a higher proportion of unskilled workers than the Free Church which drew larger numbers of skilled tradesmen.

At the Disruption the minister and congregation of St Stephen's, Glasgow, seceded to the Free Church. This move led to a drop in attendance from unskilled workers. When the Established Church reopened in 1855 it was again more successful in attracting the lower working class. The figures for St Enoch's Free Church show a similar pattern of working class adherence to that in St Stephen's Free Church (see Table 3.5).

Many explanations, including not possessing the Sunday best, have been given to explain the failure of the Church to attract higher numbers of the urban poor.[74] However, in the context of the Disruption two possible explanations stand out.

During the Disruption years in Aberdeen, it has been claimed, kirk-session discipline was used by the middle class to impose its values on the working class with sessions reluctant to pursue those of 'socio and economic status'.[75] Consequently the urban poor felt alienated, especially from the Free Church. At first sight the kirk session minutes of St Stephen's Established

Table 3.5   Status of Working class of parents

Church	Total percentage	Working Class group H	group I
St Stephen's Church of Scotland baptisms 1838	80	54 67	26 33
St Stephen's Free Church baptisms, 1851– 65	331	253 76	78 24
St Stephen's Church of Scotland baptisms 1855 – 60	89	53 60	36 40
St Enoch's Free Church baptisms 1844 – 56	132	96 73	36 27

and Free Church would seem to support this theory. Before 1844 the session's discipline had not extended, as was common in most Established Churches, beyond cases of 'antenuptial fornication' and illegitimate births. In July 1850 the Session Clerk of St Stephen's Free Church recorded that

> the attention of the court was called to the conduct of David Thomson … a member of the congregation, who had been seen in May last by several members of the congregation in a state of intoxication, and who being spoken to by them as to the sinfulness of his conduct, had used language unbecoming a member of a Christian Church.[76]

This was just one example of an extension of discipline into other areas including intemperance and dubious business transactions.[77] As has been shown, this tighter discipline corresponded with a fall in attendance from the urban poor, but not skilled workers.

Nevertheless, two important reservations must be made to this theory. Wealthier Church members were not immune from kirk-session discipline. William Ralston, an elder in St Stephen's Free Church, and a coal merchant, was investigated for having faulty weights and measures on his coal-weighing machine.[78] John Smith, an elder of Kirkintilloch Free St David's was asked to explain why he and his wife had separated.[79] Robert Baillie, a deacon at Govan Free Church, was called to answer a charge of drunkenness.[80] An identical accusation was made against John Wilson, a deacon of Ormiston Free Church.[81] Discipline was applied to all social classes in the congregation. There were more cases involving working-class members, but this simply reflected their numerical superiority amongst Church members.

Ormiston and other rural Free Churches were equally vigilant in monitoring the behaviour of their members. At Inveraray Free Church, on 13 December 1845, Catherine MacGregor admitted to the session that

> she is with child and that Donald MacVicar Junior Auchnangoul is the father of her pregnancy. Being interrogated she declares she was guilty of fornication with him about the middle of last spring or shortly

> before seed-sowing time ... Being further interrogated she declares
> that he came into the house about dawn one morning early May last
> and went into her bed where Margaret MacNicol Inveraray was sleep-
> ing with her ...

Donald MacVicar denied this particular piece of seed sowing, but after
taking evidence from witnesses, including Margaret MacNicol, the session
concluded that 'Donald MacVicar is the father of her child'.[82] Of sociological
import to this and many other similar cases is the fact that tight kirk-session
discipline did not deter the rural poor from attending the Free Church.
There must have been a factor unique to the urban Free Church accounting
for the relatively lower attendance from unskilled workers. This factor was
money.

The rural Free Church, especially in the Highlands, was supported by the
Sustentation Fund which in turn was largely made up from contributions
from Churches in the industrial towns. Urban congregations were constantly
urged to contribute. The Deacon's Court of Free St Stephen's heard from
its secretary in September 1843 of the 'indispensable necessity of an effort
being made by the congregation to increase their weekly Sabbath collections ... '[83] One year later 'Mr Burns gave in a statement in reference to the
congregation's contribution to the Central Sustentation Fund along with
lists of Non Subscribers in each district when it was agreed that every exertion
should be made to increase our contribution.'[84] After further discussions 'it
was ultimately agreed that each superintendent should go through his
district, it being very desirable that no member of the Church be left without
an opportunity of contributing to this most important Fund'.[85]

Added to this imperative their own Church had to be built and maintained. Office-bearers were often asked to give their names as security for
loans on the church building and/or donate money.[86] Thereafter members
had to pay for the privilege of sitting in their church. Rent arrears were
vigorously pursued. 'It having been reported that Mrs Fox', of St Stephen's
Free Church, 'occupied a sitting but did not either pay for it or have it
allocated, Mr Clow was appointed to wait upon her and to report. Mr
Dickson was also appointed to wait upon Mr Oswald on the same subject.'[87]
Without the pressing need to build a national Church, from the beginning
the Church of Scotland placed lighter financial demands upon its members.
This largely enabled greater numbers of the urban poor to retain their
membership.

Throughout Highland, Lowland rural and Lowland urban Scotland
skilled workers attended the Free Church in greater numbers instead of
their Parish Church. Artisans had a broader financial back on which to
support the monetary implications of Church membership. Furthermore,
respectability, or the desire to 'get on', was the aim of many tradesmen.
Church adherence may have fitted in with this trend. The aspirant middle
class partly viewed the eldership as a means to further their economic and
social status and many skilled workers saw Church membership, especially
in a new Church where their voice would hold more sway, in a similar light:

Respectability was the ultimate goal, for it represented success in his attempt to guide his life by the standards of his social superiors. In this obsessive quest for respectability is to be found the key to the social outlook of the artisan. To that end he bent the full force of his tenacious character, and sought to display all the signs of an inner respectability. He scrupulously adhered to his self improvement imperatives: civility, especially to superiors, decency in dress, decorum in behaviour, purity of speech ... diligent performance of religious duties ...[88]

From the existing work on urban areas it is possible to suggest certain preliminary findings. The Free Church had special success among two main groups: the upwardly mobile middle class and the skilled artisans. The Established Church held a greater appeal to older commercial and professional groups, the unskilled workers and urban poor. However, the example of Norman Macleod indicates that decisions concerning choice of Church were not always based on straightforward social factors as the personality of the minister could also play an important role.

CONCLUSION

This chapter has suggested that certain broad patterns can be discerned in the sociology of the Disruption. The northern Highlands saw the Free Church at its strongest in terms of numbers, drawing widespread support outside the circle of most landlords and their dependents. Opposition to landlord policies during the Clearances was only one factor accounting for the strength of the Free Church, and in many areas of the Highlands both Free and Established Churches were popular. As a cause of the Disruption in Lowland rural Scotland social factors were less important than the personality of ministers and attitudes towards patronage, with both denominations appealing to a wide range of rural society. The financial demands placed on urban Free Church members dented its appeal to the urban poor, but skilled workers and many of those who aspired to higher 'middle class status' saw their future better served by the new Church. The Church of Scotland continued to find support from large sections of urban society. These broad trends contained considerable local variations with evidence which does not support a strict social determinism as a cause of religious adherence. Thomas Chalmers was correct when he asserted that the 'common people' and 'a goodly proportion of the middle classes' filled the pews in the Free Church. None the less, the Church of Scotland could also claim substantial middle-class support. Chalmers's full claim that the 'great bulk and body of the common people ... are upon our side' only applied to the northern Highlands since outside this area the Established Church could count the working classes among its members. Finally, these local and regional variations show the need for more work on the sociology of the Disruption, especially local studies. Only when these local studies are compared will the wider picture become clearer.

NOTES

The author would like to express his gratitude to the late Revd. Ian Muirhead, who supervised the research into urban congregations, Huisdean Duff, Librarian at Gleniffer High School, Paisley, for his generous help in the analysis of Highland parishes and the editors for their advice.

BR	Baptismal Register
CR	Communion Roll
KSM	Kirk Session Minutes
NSA	*New Statistical Account of Scotland*
SRA	Strathclyde Regional Archives
SRO	Scottish Record Office

1 Quoted in Andrew Tod (ed.), *Memoirs of a Highland Lady, Elizabeth Grant of Rothiemurchus,* 2 vols (Edinburgh, 1988), vol. 1, p. 246.
2 W. Hanna, *Memoirs of the Life and Writings of Thomas Chalmers,* 4 vols (Edinburgh, 1849–1852), vol. 4, p. 333.
3 See e.g. baptisms at Barony Parish Church (Glasgow), Mission Station 1865–73, SRA CH2/173/33.
4 See e.g. Kelvinhaugh Church of Scotland (Glasgow) KSM 19/6/1862, SRA CH2/605/1.
5 Norman MacLean, *The Life of James Cameron Lees* (Glasgow, 1922), p. 73.
6 Carnoch Church, BR 1883–1914, SRO CH2/625/5.
7 Carnoch Church, CR 1867–9, SRO CH2/652/7.
8 1861 Census for Scotland, p. 13.
9 MacLean, *James Cameron Lees.* p. 75.
10 Ibid., p. 92.
11 Lairg Parish Church BR 1855–1908, SRO CH2/738/1.
12 1861 Census for Scotland, p. 10.
13 Tongue St Andrew's CR 1891–5, SRO CH2/509/1.
14 Tongue Free Church BR 1843–2, SRO CH3/449/3.
15 Durness Free Church BR 1843–3, SRO CH3/852/2.
16 No ship called Rover's Bride is listed in Lloyd's register of shipping until 1849, when a boat built in Sutherland in 1845 and based in the port of London sailed to Odessa. Neil Sutherland's Rover's Bride was in all probability either a fishing or coastal trading boat.
17 Patrick Reid, his wife Sarah and their daughter were likely to have travelled to the church along the road from the lighthouse to the Kyle of Durness built by the Lighthouse Commissioners in 1828. *New Statistical Account of Scotland,* 15 vols (Edinburgh, 1845), vol. 15, p. 101.
18 Durness Parish Church BR 1856–1933, SRO CH2/876/1.
19 Callum Brown, *The Social History of Religion in Scotland since 1730* (London, 1987), p. 39.
20 Ibid.
21 Hugh Miller, 'Sutherland as it was and is or how a Country may be Ruined', in John Davidson (ed.), *Leading Articles on Various Subjects* (Edinburgh, 1870), pp. 396–7.
22 Ibid.
23 References for all but Tain Free Church BR 1843–66, SRO CH3/748/4, and Blair Atholl and Struan Free Church, KSM 1844–88, SRO CH3/358/1 are given above.
24 Miller, 'Sutherland as it was', in *Leading Articles,* pp. 396-7.
25 James Hunter, *The Making of the Crofting Community* (Edinburgh, 1976), p. 104.
26 See e.g. Donald C. Smith, *Passive Obedience and Prophetic Protest: Social Criticism in the Scottish Church, 1830–1945* (New York, 1987), pp. 129–41
27 J. L. Buchanan, *Travels in the Western Hebrides from 1782–1790* (London, 1793), pp. 36–7.

28 Smith, *Passive Obedience*, pp. 136–7.
29 Donald MacLeod, *Gloomy Memories* (Glasgow, 1888), p. 58, quoted in Smith, *Passive Obedience*, p. 138.
30 Ibid., p. 137.
31 See Alexander Mearns, 'The Minister and the Bailiff: A Study of Presbyterian Clergy in the northern Highlands during the Clearances', *Records of the Scottish Church History Society*, xxiv (1990), pt 1.
32 Alexander Duff (ed.), *Disruption Worthies of the Highlands* (Edinburgh, 1877), p. 90.
33 NSA, vol. 15, p. 103.
34 Smith, *Passive Obedience*, pp. 137–8.
35 Duff, *Disruption Worthies of the Highlands*, p. 66.
36 Mearns, 'The Minister and the Bailiff'.
37 Duff, *Disruption Worthies of the Highlands*, pp. 94–5.
38 Ibid., p. 91.
39 Ibid., p. 64.
40 Hunter, *The Making of the Crofting Community*, p. 104.
41 Ibid., p. 95.
42 Miller, 'Sutherland as it was', p. 147.
43 Hunter, *The Making of the Crofting Community*, p. 96.
44 Roderick MacLeod, 'The Bishop of Skye, the Life and Work of Rev. Roderick MacLeod (1794–1868), Minister of Bracdale and Snizort', *Transactions of the Gaelic Society of Inverness*, liii (1982–5), 174–209.
45 Roderick MacLeod, 'The John Bunyan of the Highlands, the Life and Work of Robert Finlayson (1793–1861)', *Transactions of the Gaelic Society of Inverness*, liv (1984–6), 240–68.
46 Roderick MacLeod, 'Ministerearan an Arian? A Profile of Nineteenth Century Hebridean Moderates', *Transactions of the Gaelic Society of Inverness*, lii, (1980–2), 243–69.
47 Duff, *Disruption Worthies of the Highlands*, p. 95.
48 Sermon quoted in John Prebble, *The Highland Clearances* (London, 1963), p. 312.
49 Duff, *Disruption Worthies of the Highlands*, p. 68.
50 Report of the Select Committee appointed to inquire into the Refusal to grant Sites for Churches in Scotland, 1847, xiii, 2nd Report, 92–3 quoted in Lionel A. Ritchie, 'The Floating Church of Loch Sunart', *Records of the Scottish Church History Society*, xxii (1985) pt 2.
51 Strachur and Strathlachan Parish Church CR 1876–1929, SRO CH2/340/5, and Strachur and Strathlachan Free Church CR 1880–1902 SRO CH3/946/3.
52 Tarbert Parish Church BR 1864–1976, SRO CH2/904/1. No records are held for Tarbert Free Church in SRO.
53 Ardrishaig Free Church CR 1875–1920, SRO CH3/840/5.
54 Ardclach Parish Church BR 1857–1933, SRO CH2/717/6.
55 Ardclach Free Church CR 1873–1919, SRO CH3/1080/3.
56 NSA, vol. 8, pp. 34–5.
57 Forgue Free Church BR 1843–9, SRO CH3/1044/5, Bowden Free Church BR 1843–59, SRO CH3/834/3, Kirkintilloch Free St David's KSM 1845–80, SRA CH3/362/1, Cruden Parish Church BR 1851–1901, SRO CH2/447/9, Glenisla Parish Church BR 1860–1945, SRO CH2/589/6.
58 Brown, *The Social History of Religion*, p. 39.
59 Kirkintilloch Free St David's KSM 22/8/1845.
60 A. L. Drummond and J. Bulloch, *The Scottish Church, 1660–1843* (Edinburgh, 1973), p. 43.
61 Free Church Magazine, April 1848. The magazines are available at the Free Church offices, 15 North Bank Street, Edinburgh.
62 James A. Wylie (ed.), *Disruption Worthies of 1843* (Edinburgh, n. d.), pp. 18–22.
63 *NSA*, Vol. 10, p. 1073.
64 Ibid., vol. 4, p. 120.

65 Ibid., vol. 2, p. 148.

66 A. A. MacLaren, *Religion and Social Class: The Disruption Years in Aberdeen* (London, 1974).

67 High status groups were well-established middle-class families; low status represented the lower middle class. The working-class category was divided into artisans and unskilled workers. The detailed categories, adapted from MacLaren, *Religion and Social Class*, pp. 218–19, are as follows: A. Professional group: 1. Advocates, partners in legal firms 2. Professors, lecturers, physicians and surgeons 3. Principals, rectors, headmasters; B. Commercial group: 1. Bankers, bank managers and agents 2. Cashiers, principal clerks, accountants, insurance company managers, brokers and agents, company treasurers; C. Large merchant-manufacturing group: 1. Suppliers of capital goods, construction companies, iron-founders, textile manufacturers, wholesalers and importers, distillers, company managers 2. Suppliers of consumer goods and services catering for the middle class, silversmiths, silk mercers 3. Suppliers of food and wines, grocers, vintners, etc. 4. Commission merchants, ship agents; D. Retired-rentier group: 1. Shipowners 2. Landlords, those retired and living on income from rented property, shares or capital 3. Farmers; E. Public servants (I): 1. Druggists 2. Local government officials, building inspectors, architects, surveyors, house factors 3. Shipmasters, marine and civil engineers; F. Public servants (II):1. Teachers, divinity students who were also often city missionaries 2. Clerks, writers; G. Small merchant-tradesmen group: 1. Shopkeepers 2. Self-employed tradesmen, agents living in premises, commercial travellers 3. Foremen, overseers 4. Retired tradesmen and shopkeepers; H. Artisans: 1. Engineers, boiler-makers, joiners, smiths, etc. I. Unskilled workers:1. Labourers, carters, porters, chimney sweeps, etc.

In Table 3.3, high status represents Groups A, B, C, D; low status represents Groups E, F, G; and working class represents Groups H and I.

Govan Parish Church BR 1856–64 (held in the church), Govan Free Church KSM 1844–56, SRA CH3/157/1, St Stephen's Established and Free Church KSM 1838–71, SRA CH3/162/1 and BR 1850–83, SRA CH3/162/17, St Enoch's Free Church BR 1844–91, SRA CH3/525/3, and Barony Parish Church BR 1855–70, SRA CH2/173/31.

68 The churches were Bonaccord, Melville, Union, Holburn, John Knox, Gilcomston, Gaelic (Spring Garden) and Mariners' MacLaren, *Religion and Social Class*, p. 220.

69 See the author's 'Presbyterianism and Social Class in Mid-Nineteenth Century Glasgow: A Study of Nine Churches', unpublished Ph.D. Thesis (Univ. of Glasgow, 1978), p. 287 and also in *Journal of Ecclesiastical History*, 32 (1981), No. 1.

70 John G. Paton, *Missionary to the New Hebrides* (London, 1889), p. 4.

71 *MacPhail's Journal*, 3 (1847), 51–2.

72 Donald MacLeod, *Memoir of Norman MacLeod*, 2 vols (London, 1876), vol. 2, p. 191.

73 Ibid., vol. 1, p. 194.

74 These explanations are discussed in the author's 'Presbyterianism and Social Class', pp. 163–72.

75 MacLaren, *Religion and Social Class*, p. 130.

76 St Stephen's Free Church KSM 15/7/1850.

77 Ibid., 26/11/1847 and 11/8/1847.

78 Ibid., 11/10/1855, 18/10/1855 and 11/12/1855.

79 Kirkintilloch Free St David's KSM 24/4/1845 and 29/4/1845, SRA CH3/262/1.

80 Govan Free Church KSM 18/11/1844.

81 Ormiston Free Church KSM 9/1/1848 and 24/1/1848, SRO CH3/251/1.

82 Inverary Free Church KSM 13/12/1845, 15/12/1845 and 20/4/1846, SRO CH3/584/1.

83 St Stephen's Free Church Deacons' Court Minutes 11/9/1843, SRA CH3/162/6.

84 Ibid., 2/9/1844.
85 Ibid., 10/10/1844.
86 Ibid., 26/6/1849.
87 Ibid., 26/11/1850.
88 T. R. Tholfsen, 'The Artisan and the Culture of Early Victorian Birmingham',
    University of Birmingham Historical Journal, 4 (1954), 146–66.

PLATE 1   *The Famous Stalking Horse Non-Intrusion*

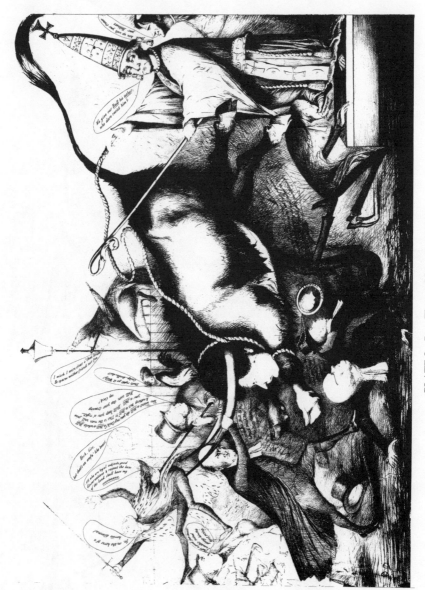

PLATE 2 *Pope Thomas I Issueth his Bull*

PLATE 3 *Clerical Suspension*

PLATE 4 *Modern Martyrs*

PLATE 5   *The Reel of Bogie!! A Clerical Dance*

PLATE 6 Untitled (Thomas Chalmers and friends in the bog)

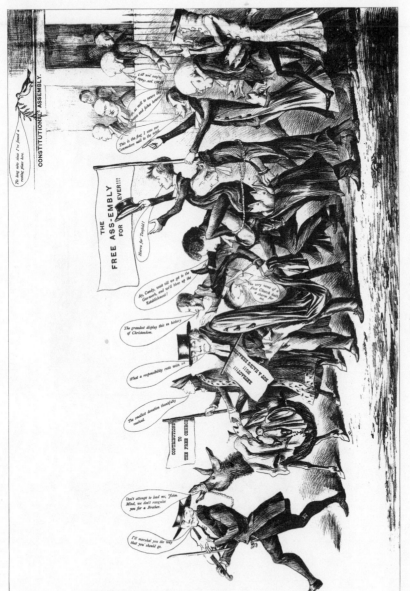

PLATE 7 *The Disruption!*

PLATE 8 'Send Back the Money'

CHAPTER FOUR

Thomas Chalmers and Pauperism

DONALD MACLEOD

THE MOST STRIKING FEATURE of the political theology of Disruption churchmen is the confidence with which they assume the obligation of the state to recognise Christianity and respect Christian values. According to William Cunningham, for example, 'The civil magistrate is bound, in the exercise of his proper authority, in his own province, to aim at the promotion of religion and the welfare of the church.'[1] James Bannerman wrote to similar effect:

> there can be no sound view of political government which restricts it to the care of man's body and bodily wants, and does not assign to it a wider sphere, as charged in a certain sense with the advancement of human well-being, in its moral as well as its material interests.[2]

It was inevitable that churchmen holding such a view of Church–state relations would take a keen interest in public affairs and avail themselves of every opportunity to point out how Christianity bore on matters of public policy. American slavery, Sunday legislation, public education, civil disobedience, Highland Clearances, pauperism: these are only some of the subjects which passed under their scrutiny. Even the briefest treatment of all of these would be impossible in a single essay. We focus, therefore, on one issue: pauperism.

The Free Church attitude to pauperism is linked inextricably with the work of Thomas Chalmers, particularly his opposition to Poor Laws and his social experiments in St John's parish, Glasgow and the West Port, Edinburgh. In his own lifetime that work was widely acclaimed. His biographer, William Hanna, described an English Poor Law Commissioner, E. C. Tufnell, as visiting Glasgow in 1833 and describing the St John's experiment as a 'most triumphant success'.[3] Hanna himself eulogised the work in the West Port: 'At the same cost, among the same class, within the same limits, and during the same time, there never have been accomplished in this or any other land anything like the same educational and spiritual results. It stands the only instance in which the depths of city ignorance and vice have been sounded to the very bottom; nor can the possibility of cleansing the foul basement story of our social edifice be doubted any longer.'[4]

The adulation was not confined to Chalmers's contemporaries. Dr Hugh Watt described the work in Glasgow as

> a success beyond anything that Chalmers himself had predicted or anticipated. He had demonstrated that, by the thorough application of the normal parochial care of the Church, with adequate organisation, the problem of poverty could be coped with, even in a populous city parish of the poorest classes.[5]

Watt was equally enthusiastic about the West Port: 'The evangelization of Edinburgh's western slum was a glorious sunset to his labours.'[6]

Yet even in his own lifetime Chalmers's work had its critics. Dr W. P. Alison, Professor of Medicine at Edinburgh University, campaigned strenuously for a Scottish Poor Law modelled on the English pattern, arguing that Scotland did less for the relief of poverty than any other country in Europe. Despite Chalmers's plea that the parochial system without a poor-rate was perfectly adequate, Alison won the battle and a Scottish Poor Law was passed in 1844. Even among the Evangelical clergy there were those such as Patrick Brewster of Paisley who strongly opposed Chalmers's policy: so strongly, in fact, that, although he detested patronage, Brewster could not bring himself to follow Chalmers into the Free Church in 1843.

Recent scholarship has tended to side with the critics. Stewart Brown, for example, while describing the St John's experiment as an impressive demonstration of Chalmers's social ideal in action, went on to say, 'In truth, the programmes never succeeded in achieving his main object – the formation of a closely-knit working-class community, united by Evangelical ideals, and centred upon the parish church.'[7] Brown is equally critical of the work in the West Port, describing it as 'less than successful'[8] and arguing that it led to no significant improvement in social conditions. 'The great mass of West Port inhabitants', he maintains, 'remained rootless, impoverished and often homeless.'[9]

Donald C. Smith is more scathing. He speaks of Chalmers's 'harsh and inhuman, not to say unchristian, Malthusian presuppositions'[10] and dismisses the St John's experiment as 'falsely praised'.[11] Smith sets these criticisms in the context of a blanket condemnation of all the Scottish Churches in the nineteenth century:

> So closely aligned was the Church in sympathy and outlook with the privileged classes that it was incapable of seeing, much less denouncing – as did the Scottish reformers in their day – the cruelties and injustices which were being inflicted upon the weak and underprivileged members of society. Indeed, it is not too much to say that the Church itself, in no small way, unknowingly contributed to and perpetuated the oppression of the poor.[12]

There is considerable truth in these criticisms, even in the charge of heartlessness. Watt describes the aim of the St John's experiment as dealing with *poverty*. But *poverty* is probably the wrong word. Chalmers repeatedly conveys the impression that what he was really concerned with was *pauperism*, and he distinguished sharply between the two. A poor man was a man who was unable to provide a proper subsistence for himself and his family.[13] A pauper was a man who was supported by relief legally awarded to him out of a compulsory Poor Fund. Chalmers entertained little hope of eliminating poverty and even used the words of Christ to buttress his opinion: 'We are able to affirm on the highest of all authorities that the poor shall be with us always, or, in other words, that it is vain to look for the extinction of poverty from the world.'[14] From this point of view, poverty was something against which the wisdom of man could make no headway. The only hope was charity. Compassion could soften 'the wretchedness of a state against the existence of which no artifice of human policy seems to be at all available'.[15] Chalmers even carried this to the extraordinary length of surmising that in the millennial age itself 'the state of poverty shall be at times exemplified'. The difference would be that 'the sufferings of poverty' would be unknown, because of 'the vigilance and promptitude of such sympathies as are quickened and kept alive by the influence of the gospel'.[16] Loving relations and friends would ensure that the poor would be provided for.

But society could, Chalmers thought, make some headway against pauperism, which he described as 'a moral nuisance' which led to seething discontent, to parishes intoxicated with litigation, to the destruction of family virtues, to the extinction of diligence and to the chilling of 'the wider charities of life'.[17]

Such an analysis posed the grave danger that Chalmers would divert his energies from fighting poverty to fighting pauperism and deluding himself that the reduction of the one was the reduction of the other. He often seems to have gloried, not in increases in the number of people helped, but in decreases. The boast was not how much had been disbursed but how little, and sometimes the consuming passion seemed to be to reduce the number of applications:

> for, in proportion to the pains bestowed on each new application, was it hoped, that the number of them would be greatly diminished, by the very knowledge, on the part of the population, of the now more searching ordeal through which they had to pass.[18]

And an *ordeal* it certainly was.[19] Every applicant was deemed guilty until proved innocent and one cannot but wonder whether any but the desperate or the unscrupulous would ever have submitted to such humiliation. The obvious presumption that every applicant was a malingerer must have deterred many of the poor from presenting themselves.

Another suspicion, too, gradually dawns: that Chalmers never touched, and maybe never even thought of, those at the bottom of the social heap. His whole territorial system with its proportions, its deacons, its schools and its visitors was for *residents*; and that meant those who at least had some kind of roof over their heads – the kind of people who today could give an address to a DSS office. The plight of such people was often appalling. Yet beneath them was a group even more wretched: the homeless, address-less, demoralised, ravished poor. There appears to have been little place for them in Chalmers's plans.

This becomes painfully clear if one turns from *Christian and Civic Polity of a Nation* to General Booth's classic, *Darkest England and the Way Out* (London, 1890). Booth's concern was with 'the submerged class' and he applied a graphic criterion: the London cab-horse. Such a horse had three privileges: 'a shelter for the night, food for its stomach and work allotted to it by which it can earn its corn'.[20] Booth reckoned that three million Englishmen (a tenth of the population) fell below this standard. These were the people he targeted: 'there is a depth below that of the dweller in the slums,' he wrote, 'It is that of the dweller in the street, who has not even a lair in the slums which he can call his own.'[21] Booth was sceptical of 'the Utopians, the economists and most of the philanthropists' who propounded remedies. Their schemes were relevant only to those whose condition least needed amelioration. Even if adopted immediately they would affect only 'the aristocracy of the miserable'. It is difficult to believe that Booth did not have Chalmers in mind when he went on to say:

> No one will ever make even a visible dint on the Morass of Squalor who does not deal with the improvident, the lazy, the vicious and the criminal. The scheme of social salvation is not worth discussion which is not as wide as the Scheme of Eternal Salvation set forth in the Gospel... . If the Scheme which I set forth in these and the following pages is not applicable to the Thief, the Harlot, the Drunkard, and the Sluggard, it may as well be dismissed without ceremony.[22]

This did not mean that Booth was indifferent to morality and salvation. As much as Chalmers's, his first concern was the salvation of souls: 'I must assert in the most unqualified way that it is primarily and mainly for the sake of saving the soul that I seek the salvation of the body.'[23] The difference was that he, unlike Chalmers, was willing to give *immediate* relief. 'What', he asked,

> is the use of preaching the Gospel to men whose whole attention is concentrated upon a mad, desperate struggle to keep themselves alive? ... (they) cannot hear you any more than a man whose head is under water can listen to a sermon.[24]

Part of the reason for Booth's attitude probably was that he was less judgemental than Chalmers, acknowledging the influence of social environment on human behaviour. Again, he expressed himself graphically:

> The bastard of a harlot, born in a brothel, suckled in gin, and familiar from earliest infancy with all the beastialities of debauch, violated before she is twelve and driven out into the streets by her mother a year or two later, what chance is there for such a girl in this world – I say nothing about the next?[25]

But behind this there lay a different concept of social responsibility. The Church, according to Booth, had to give first aid, regardless of merit or future reformation. If a London cab-horse fell, it was picked up. There was no question of debating how he came to stumble before getting him on his feet again: 'If not for his own sake, then merely in order to prevent an obstruction of the traffic, all attention is concentrated upon the question of how we are to get him on his legs again.'[26] Chalmers's measures would not have reached these depths. Assiduous deacons, schools, prayer-meetings and savings banks could provide no lifeboat for those who, in the words of South (quoted by Booth) were 'not so much born into the world as damned into it'.[27] Chalmers was in the business of 'building up character', not of providing clean death-beds for prostitutes.

There is a curious inconsistency here in Chalmers's application of the Establishment principle. With all his Disruption colleagues, as we have seen, he believed that it was the duty of the state to promote Christianity. This meant that the civil power had the same general responsibilities towards the kingdom of God as a private individual.[28] Does it not follow, then, that the civil power has the same responsibilities as a private individual towards the poor? Chalmers did not believe that the building of churches should be left to *laissez-faire*. He sought government help. Yet he objected to legally enforced provision for the poor. The inconsistency is inexplicable. In terms of the parable of the Good Samaritan the state has no more right than the priest or the Levite to pass by on the other side.

Sometimes, too, there is a peculiar Pelagianism in Chalmers's policy on pauperism. Care for the poor could be left to the charity of kindness to the exclusion of the charity of law because of the nobility of human nature (not least that of the poor themselves). He wrote:

> on the simple abolition of a compulsory assessment for the relief of new applicants, there would instantly break forth from innumerable fountains, now frozen or locked up by the hand of legislation, so many refreshing rills, on all the places that had been left dry and destitute by the withdrawment from them of public charity, as would spread a far more equal and smiling abundance than before over the face of society.[29]

Indeed, some of his statements in this vein are quite extraordinary, especially for a man who, in other connections, laid such stress on the depravity of man. 'Nature,' he wrote, 'when simply left to the development of her own spontaneous and inborn principles, will render a better service to humanity than can be done by the legal charity of England.'[30] Similarly, he allowed himself to say,

> such is the recoil of one human being from the contemplation of extreme hunger in another, that the report of a perishing household, in some deepest recess of a city lane, would inflict a discomfort on the whole neighbourhood, and call out succour, in frequent and timely forthgoings, from the contiguous families.[31]

Apart from all else the morality of this is extremely dubious. It leaves the care of the destitute to those just as destitute. The use of the word *'contiguous'*, too, is interesting. Relief will come from those who *see* and are moved to compassion. What of those who are not contiguous and do not see and yet have far greater resources? Besides, here again there is a radical inconsistency. Evangelism was not to be left to the contiguous population. It was to be aggressive, Chalmers insisted. Why should the provision of relief – the attack on poverty – not also be aggressive? Society's inertia in relation to poverty is even greater than its inertia in relation to Evangelism. The affluent will redistribute their wealth only under compulsion.

But what is astonishing is the theology itself. Chalmers's view of 'the deepest recesses of a city lane' is idyllic. This is not to say that there is no nobility there. But there is also, surely, a good deal of depravity: Rachmanite landlords, loan-sharks, extortioners and, above all, considerable numbers of men and women who would take whatever steps are necessary for survival (or to secure alcohol).

Chalmers had an equally romantic view of the aristocracy. In a pamphlet, *Churches and Schools for the Working Classes,*[32] he declared:

> nothing delights me more than to assure the people of the humbler classes, of the great disposition which exists among the upper classes to do them good, if only they knew how. I confess I do not give them much credit for skill or intelligence in setting about it. They are, I think, great blunderers; but, so far as the disposition is concerned, they have a great disposition to do all they can for the working classes. I never fail to mention this. There is often great odium and contempt in the vocation of a go-between, but I glory in being a go-between from the higher to the lower classes, carrying messages of substantial kindness from the one, and bringing back expressions of gratitude from the other.

No other passage in Chalmers's extensive writings is more difficult to thole than this! Would anyone today seriously suggest that, left to themselves, the landed gentry and the boardrooms they dominate would contribute to charity sums equal to those they are forced to surrender by Income Tax, Capital Gains Tax, Corporation Tax and Death Duties? A fallen world needs the charity of law as surely as it needs the law of charity.

This theological lapse on Chalmers's part is closely related to another problem in his approach to pauperism: the almost total lack of biblical reference. *Christian and Economic Polity of a Nation* contains virtually no exegesis. This would be understandable if the subject were one on which Scripture had little to say. But this is hardly the case. The *poor* are a major biblical category. For example, the article on *ptochos* in Kittel's *Theological Dictionary of the New Testament* occupies thirty pages.[33] More important, our obligations to them form a major topic in Christian ethics. What other conclusion can we draw from such a passage as Galatians 2: 10 ('Only they would that we should remember the poor; the same which I also was forward to do')? Yet Chalmers hardly ever interacts with this material. This is why he is vulnerable to the charge that he owed more to Malthus and Adam Smith than to the Gospel and the Epistles.[34] In fact, Chalmers appears to have accepted Malthus's theory unreservedly:

> However obnoxious the modern doctrine of population as expounded by Mr Malthus may have been, and still is, to weak and limited sentimentalists, it is the truth which of all other sheds the greatest brightness over the earthly prospects of humanity – and this in spite of the hideous, the yet sustained outcry which has risen against it.[35]

This Malthusianism led Chalmers to a profound pessimism. The produce of the soil could not be made to increase at the same rate as the population; the industrial nations would always have a surfeit of labour; and the future of the lower classes was grim. They faced either increased drudgery or increased destitution.

The problem, of course, was a real one and it is important to notice that the solution Chalmers proposed was far from Draconian. He advocated a postponement in the average age of matrimony; and even here he did not contemplate any legislative action. All that was necessary was 'the formation of a higher taste for comfort and decency among the peasantry themselves'.[36] In other words, if people set decent standards for themselves they would not rush into precipitate matrimony and excessive child-bearing. 'The tendency to excessive child-bearing', he wrote elsewhere, 'can only find its thorough and decisive counteraction among the amended habits, and the moralised characters, and the exalted principles of the people themselves.'[37]

In essence, Chalmers was saying that an illiterate and uncultured population would be guilty of heedless breeding. The basic difficulty with this is that, whether true or false, it is not a political *theology*. It may be promulgated by a theologian and advanced as an element in a Christian polity, but it remains simply a politico-economic theory for which no theological proof was (or could be) offered. In fact, if we were to test it by the Scriptures we would find it seriously wanting. Biblically, it is good to be fruitful and multiply; biblically, it is an honour for a man to have many sons; biblically, we must not fear to reproduce; biblically, we should expect the sweat of our brows to be sufficient to earn our bread.

All this should have alerted Chalmers to the inadequacies of the Malthusian solution. It ignored the fact that over-breeding was often the result of poverty, not its cause. Indeed, over-breeding was almost inevitable when huge numbers of people were crammed into tiny living areas, sleeping promiscuously in states of almost total nudity. According to one report, in some of the hovels

> ten, twelve, and sometimes twenty persons of both sexes and all ages sleep promiscuously on the floor in different degrees of nakedness. These places are, generally as regards dirt, damp and decay, such as no person of common humanity would stable his horse in.[38]

On the other hand, Chalmers and Malthus were also blind to the possibility that the problem of starvation arose, not from the limited productivity of the soil, but from the inequities of distribution. What would they have thought of our modern situation where European farmers are paid *not* to cultivate their land and European fishermen are paid to *decommission* their boats, while in India and East Africa, for example, millions are starving? (Paradoxically, in these countries a high birth-rate is generated, not by dissipation, but by the fears arising from a high rate of child mortality.)

It is difficult to ascertain the precise extent of Chalmers's personal familiarity with the writings of Adam Smith. It was probably fairly limited. There is no doubt, however, that he was an ardent advocate of *laissez-faire*, at least in the sphere of commerce. Government might safely withdraw from it altogether 'and abandon it to the love of gain, and the spirit of enterprise, and the sharp-sighted sagacity, that guides almost all the pursuits of interest'.[39]

It should be noted, however, that Chalmers's application of the principle of *laissez-faire* was certainly not a complete social policy. But even in commerce, its influence, if unfettered, would be extensive. Companies would be left to the full force of the market. There would be no limited liability for bankrupts. There would be few, if any, statutory provisions for the health and safety of workers. Above all, there would be no regulation of the labour-market. The price of labour would be a question simply of market forces and there would be no relief for the able-bodied unemployed. Their only recourse would be to seek work elsewhere.

Yet Chalmers would not have shared the idea that there was sufficient work for all, provided they 'got on their bikes'. He knew that there were far more labourers than jobs. His solution was that the (Christianised) labouring classes should marry later and have smaller families. But this was a long-term solution at best, and far removed from, for example, Booth's conception of the urgency of the situation. Booth saw that he needed not merely a long-term solution but lifeboats for immediate deployment. He was utterly contemptuous of *laissez-faire*.

'Let things alone', the inexorable laws of supply and demand, and all the rest of the excuses by which those who stand on firm ground salve their consciences when they leave their brother to sink, how do they look when we apply them to the actual loss of life at sea? Does 'Let things alone' man the lifeboat? Will the inexorable laws of political economy save the shipwrecked sailor from the boiling surf?[40]

Laissez-faire produced coffin-ships, not lifeboats: 'no law of supply and demand actuates the volunteers who risk their lives to bring the shipwrecked to shore.'

There are two problems here. One is that, as we have seen already, Chalmers is not really engaging in political theology. He is merely lending the weight of his authority as a churchman to a purely secular economic theory. The second is that he is not thinking rigorously enough. *Laissez-faire* is essentially a plea that the current injustices and imbalances of society be canonised. Scottish society in Chalmers's day was not the result of *laissez-faire*. It was the result of greed, rapacity and violence. It was not by *laissez-faire*, for example, that the Duke of Sutherland had come to 'own' the county of Sutherland. But once he had it, 'Leave things alone!' was certainly in his interest. Nor was it by *laissez-faire* that the East India Company had come to enjoy a monopoly in the riches of the sub-continent. At any given moment, society is a complex of injustices. Financial power, political power and media power are all in the hands of a tiny group of people. That being so, *laissez-faire* is a plea that we leave these people in possession of their privileges – a plea often reinforced by the totally spurious argument that if we do not 'leave things alone' the political order will collapse and we shall find ourselves overtaken by anarchy and confusion.

Clearly, then, in assessing Chalmers there is much to be said on the debit side. But that is by no means the whole story. For one thing, as Owen Chadwick points out, there is no doubt that Chalmers cared: 'His entire theory of an established Church rested on this compassion for the poor.'[41] Had he been driven by naked ambition he might have found easier roads to preferment. Besides, on the road he chose he had few predecessors and even fewer successors. Certainly, those of us who engage in sedate academic evaluation of his work are in a very vulnerable position. If Chalmers, who at least tried, is to be condemned, what is to be said for the rest of us? He was as far removed as could be from the type of clergyman lampooned by Booth: 'He is paid to preach, and there he considers his responsibility ends, the rich excepted.'[42] Of no one was that less true than of Chalmers. He visited his parish assiduously, canvassed politicians, solicited funds, played with children, corresponded, entertained and pamphleteered – all to advance his objective of not only saving the elect but humanising and moralising the entire population.

Secondly, there can be no denying Chalmers's very real achievements. On several occasions he did, to use Booth's metaphor, literally launch a social lifeboat. Whatever the St John's experiment was, it was not an experiment in *laissez-faire*. Nor was its success limited to reducing the number of paupers and the cost of supporting them. Unfortunately this is the aspect highlighted by contemporary reports, not least Chalmers's own. Hanna's use of Tufnell is typical. Enthusiastic as the English Poor Law Commissioner's endorsement was, it emphasised the administrative rather than the humanitarian advantages of the St John's experiment. 'Its chief virtue', he wrote,

> seems to consist in the closer investigation which each new case of pauperism receives, by which means the parish is prevented from being imposed on; and as it is well known by the poor that this severe scrutiny is never omitted, attempts at imposition are less frequently practised.[43]

Chalmers's friends argued in similar vein: an expenditure which had amounted to £1,400 per annum was reduced to £280; an income of £300 was proving sufficient to finance the pauperism of a parish of over 10,000.[44] But these arguments, surely, were often *ad hominem*. Critics protested that Chalmers's scheme was impracticable. Church door collections could never support the poor. Chalmers proved that they could: in other words, the experiment *was* economically practicable.

There is no evidence that the poor themselves thought they suffered as a result. They certainly showed no inclination to move from St John's to other parishes. In fact, according to Hanna[45] more paupers moved in than moved out. Besides, the deacons did have power to give immediate short-term relief and, for all their caution, were still liable to be conned (as by the lady who persuaded one to finance the funeral of her very-much-alive husband and was caught out only when she applied for similar help in respect of her even more lively daughter). Jobs were found; friends and relations persuaded to help; and families kept from breaking up.

Nor were the deacons merely poor-managers. Certainly, their primary and stated role was to relieve distress: the first time the Church in Scotland had taken its ministry of compassion seriously. But pauperism took up only a fraction of their time. Chalmers's own assessment, based on reports submitted to him, was that 'the time spent by each of his deacons on the pauperism of the parish did not on an average exceed three hours a month'.[46] For the rest of the time, far from being cold, officious bureaucrats, they were friends and familiars to the people, on hand to give support, counsel and advice. It was known that they had money to give. It was also known that this was not all they had to give. Years later, Chalmers's successor, Dr Patrick MacFarlan, testified that the system 'worked well in all respects'.[47]

After the Disruption, Chalmers engaged in similar work in the West Port of Edinburgh. The long-term effects of this were probably minimal because the population was highly mobile. Yet again there were real achievements. Every home was assiduously visited. Education was placed within the reach of all who wanted it (not a single child was known not to be at school). Children were provided with shoes and clothing. Teachers and a missionary were employed and Sunday Schools and Sunday services were organised. Basic practical skills (sewing, knitting and washing) were taught and a savings bank was established. Chalmers was realistic about the results, especially on the spiritual plane. He knew of only ten conversions, but he was not discouraged:

> People may say that ten is a very small number. Now, I would meet this by the enlightened remark of Mr Wilberforce, who said that such was the power of Christianity, that for every one that it spiritualised and Christianised, it moralised fifty.[48]

In fact when Chalmers presided at the first-Communion service in March 1847, there were 132 communicants, 100 of them from the West Port, 'a locality which, two years ago, had not one in ten churchgoers from the whole population'.[49]

Chalmers also initiated decisive remedial action in 1846, when the Highland potato crop was devastated by blight.[50] There had been similar disasters before, but never of this magnitude: 'A human tragedy on a scale unparalleled in modern Scottish history, it was unprecedented in severity and duration.'[51] By the end of 1846 it was estimated that at least three-quarters of the crofting community were entirely without food. Nor was starvation the only threat. The winter was exceptionally cold and stormy, and disease (cholera, typhus, dysentry and scurvy) was rampant. Chalmers was one of the first to realise the gravity of the situation. Indeed, he was alarmed by the fact that the nation was underestimating the tragedy. Convinced 'that the public have a most inadequate view of the efforts necessary to keep our suffering population alive'[52] he gathered as much information as he could. The Free Church, conscious of a special responsibility since many of the victims were its own members, set up a Committee of Relief and appointed a Special Collection for Sunday, 6 December. The total contribution (£15,000) was the largest ever taken up by any Church in Scotland for such an object.

But even when supplemented by the liberality of other Churches and charities the sum was far from adequate; and if Chalmers had ever been a blind devotee of Adam Smith, he abandoned him now. Private philanthropy could provide no remedy for tragedy on such a scale. Massive government help was required. On 6 March, 1847, Chalmers wrote to the *Witness*, expressing the fear that the government would 'so economise as to put human life in jeopardy'. 'Is it right in the government', he asked,

> to abstain from their grants in the hope that we, the public, will do all? ... we have a very strong impression that without their gratuities, there is the utmost danger that many in a state of helpless infirmity or of hopeless and forlorn widowhood, will be left to perish.[53]

Confronted by catastrophe, Chalmers no longer saw it as a priority to distinguish between deserving and undeserving poor or to calculate the demoralising effects of state help. He saw only that people desperately needed relief. The government, unfortunately, did not share his view. Their attitude was summed up in the words of Sir Charles Trevelyan, Assistant Secretary to the Treasury:

> Next to allowing the people to starve of hunger, the greatest evil that could happen would be their being habituated to depend upon public charity. The object to be aimed at, therefore, is to prevent the assistance given from being productive of idleness and, if possible, to make it conducive to increased exertion.'[54]

With such assumptions it was hardly surprising that the priority became not to do as much as possible for the suffering community but to make relief unpalatable. In this they certainly succeeded. For six days of back-breaking labour an unmarried crofter received nine pence worth of meal, at a time when the lowest wages on the open market were about six shillings a week.[55]

Clearly, then, Chalmers had no aversion in principle to launching a social lifeboat. On the other hand, his aversion to a statutory Poor Law did have some justification. Apart from the obvious problems (that poor-relief *did* discourage neighbourly assistance and that it *was* open to unscrupulous exploitation) there were two serious drawbacks.

First, receipt of it carried a social stigma, and for this reason many of the 'sturdy poor' shrank from it. Hugh Miller referred to a class of poor

> who bore up in their honest and independent poverty, relying for support on the provision of their heavenly Father, but who asked not the help of man, and who, in so many instances, would not receive it even when it was extended to them.[56]

Smith[57] is dismissive of Miller's attitude, which reflected, he thought, a longing on the Church's part for the return of the ' "good old days" of the 18th century when the poor were content to suffer want and privation in silence because of their pride and independence and religious character.' But the feelings Miller indicates were real enough. Some would rather have died than 'go on the parish' or, what was worse, enter the poorhouse. Besides, the pride involved was often a complicated one. For example, it involved a reluctance to let the world know that one's family were not providing support. If a mother had boasted of 'her boy' all her life it would be very difficult at the end to admit that he didn't care.

There is a fascinating glimpse into this now lost world in J. M. Barrie's novel, *The Little Minister*.[58] An old woman waits to be taken to the poorhouse and the doctor tries to comfort her:

'Why, after you have been there a week, you won't be the same woman.'
'That's it!' cried Nanny with sudden passion. 'Na, na: I'll be a woman on the poor's rates. Oh, mither, mither, you little thocht when you bore me that I would come to this!'

'You will often get out to see your friends', was all Gavin could say.

'Na, na, na,' she cried, 'dinna say that; I'll gang, but you maurna bid me ever come out, except in a hearse. Dinna let onybody in Thrums look on my face again.'

She then give her final instructions: 'If it could just be said to poor Saunders when he comes back that I died hurriedly, syne he would be able to haud up his head … Oh, mither! … I wish terribly they had come and ta'en me at nicht … It's a dog-cart, and I was praying it micht be a cart, so that they could cover me wi' straw.'

Chalmers knew the Scottish poor better than his critics. There had to be poorhouses. But far better was, wherever possible, that relations and friends be persuaded to provide the necessary support. For Barrie's nanny, the poorhouse was a fate worse than death. For others, being on the parish made their poverty official. From that moment on, they were trapped in one simple, desperate identity: pauper.

Secondly, the Poor Laws did not work: at least not in the form in which they were envisaged in the nineteenth century. Scotland obtained its Poor Law in 1845. Admittedly, it fell far short of what those who fought for it had hoped for. In particular, it offered no relief for the able-bodied unemployed: applicants had to prove physical or mental disability before they qualified for help. However, this did not apply to the corresponding English law, and yet there is no evidence that the position south of the Border was any better than it was in Scotland. In fact, the description given by Booth suggests the opposite. A tenth of the population of England belonged to the 'submerged classes': if they were left to what they could earn, they would be dead of starvation in a month. A Poor Law, even an ideal one, could offer a partial solution. But it did not deal with the causes of poverty; and its very existence tended to create the illusion that the problem was being dealt with. This is why in 1849 a well-informed observer could still write: 'pauperism, in all its phases, is thriving'.[59]

The final point to be made in Chalmer's defence is that he was never given the resources he asked for. His central idea was that the Church, not the state, should assume responsibility for the poor. But he never imagined that the parochial organisation he inherited was adequate for the task.

NOTES

1   W. Cunningham, *Discussions on Church Principles* (Edinburgh, 1863), p. 209.
2   J. Bannerman, *The Church of Christ* (Edinburgh, 1869), p. 363.

3 W. Hanna, *Memoirs of Dr. Chalmers, D.D. LL.D.*, 2 vols (Edinburgh, 1854), vol i, p. 588.
4 Ibid., vol ii, p. 697.
5 H. Watt, *Thomas Chalmers and the Disruption* (Edinburgh, 1943), p. 63.
6 Ibid., p. 341.
7 S. J. Brown, *Thomas Chalmers and the Godly Commonwealth in Scotland* (Oxford, 1982), p. 143.
8 Ibid., p. 361.
9 Ibid., p. 363.
10 D. C. Smith, *Passive Obedience and Prophetic Protest: Social Criticism in the Scottish Church 1830–1945* (New York, 1987), p. 113.
11 Ibid., p. 118.
12 Ibid., p. 120.
13 T. Chalmers, *Christian and Civic Polity of a Nation* (Edinburgh, 1856), p. 246.
14 Ibid., p. 244.
15 Ibid., p. 247.
16 Ibid., p. 246.
17 Ibid., p. 264.
18 Ibid., p. 284.
19 Ibid., p. 294.
20 W. Booth, *In Darkest England and the Way Out* (London, 1890), p. 20.
21 Ibid., p. 24.
22 Ibid., p. 36.
23 Ibid., p. 45.
24 Ibid., p. 45.
25 Ibid., p. 47.
26 Ibid., p. 19.
27 Ibid., p. 47.
28 See Cunningham, *Discussions on Church Principles*, p. 225.
29 Chalmers, *Christian and Civic Polity of a Nation*, p. 248.
30 Ibid., p. 255.
31 Ibid., p. 253.
32 T. Chalmers, *Churches and Schools for the Working Classes* (Edinburgh, 1846), p. 21.
33 E. Bannmel, 'Ptochos', in G. Kittel (ed.), *Theological Dictionary of the New Testament*, 10 vols (Grand Rapids, 1964–76), vol. vi, pp. 885–915.
34 Mary T. Furgol in A. C. Cheyne (ed.), *The Practical and the Pious* (Edinburgh, 1983), p. 119.
35 T. Chalmers, *On the Power, Wisdom and Goodness of God as Manifested in the Adaptation of External Nature to the Moral and Intellectual Constitution of Man*, 2 vols (London, 1833), vol. ii, p. 49.
36 Quoted in Henry Hunter, *Problems of Poverty: Selections from the Economic and Social Writings of Thomas Chalmers D. D.* (London, 1912), p. 47.
37 Chalmers, *Christian and Civic Polity of a Nation*, p. 16.
38 Quoted in Smith, *Passive Obedience and Prophetic Proest*, p. 35
39 Chalmers, *Christian and Civic Polity of a Nation*, pp. 15, 16.
40 Booth, *In Darkest England* p. 42.
41 Cheyne, *The Practical and the Pious*, p. 70.
42 Booth, *In Darkest England*, p. 42.
43 Hanna, *Memoirs of Dr. Chalmers*, vol. i, p. 588.
44 Ibid., p. 584.
45 Ibid., p. 585.
46 Ibid., p. 587.
47 Ibid., p. 587.
48 Chalmers, *Churches and Schools*, p. 16.
49 Watt, *Thomas Chalmers*, p. 341.
50 See J. Hunter, *The Making of the Crofting Community* (Edinburgh, 1976), pp. 50–72.
51 Ibid., p. 50

52 Hanna, *Memoirs of Dr. Chalmers*, vol. ii, p. 713.
53 *Witness*, 6 Mar. 1847, p. 2.
54 Hunter, *Making of the Crofting Community*, p. 66.
55 Ibid., p. 66.
56 *Witness*, 28 Mar. 1840, p. 2.
57 Smith, *Passive Obedience and Prophetic Protest*, p. 116.
58 J. M. Barrie, *The Little Minister* (*The Uniform Edition of the Works of J. M. Barrie*, Cassel & Company Ltd, London, n. d.), pp. 52 ff.
59 George Bell, *Day and Night in the Wynds of Edinburgh* (Edinburgh, 1849), p. 12.

PART TWO

The Disruption and Scottish Culture

CHAPTER FIVE

Adrift among the Reefs of Conflicting Ideals?

Education and the Free Church, 1843–55

DONALD J. WITHRINGTON

TO DETERMINE JUST WHAT the Free Church contribution was to Scottish schooling, or to Scottish education in general, is not the simple matter it may seem at first. By 1847, we are told, there were in operation in Scotland over 500 schools which were supported in some form by the Free Church Education Committee[1]; in 1850–1, by varying accounts, that number had risen to at least 640 or to just over 700.[2] With about 950 legal parishes in the country, this seems to represent a remarkable addition to educational provision. But the returns to the religious and educational census of 1851 show that at least 124 of the Free Church schools had been in existence before – some well before – the Disruption, and had been taken over, ready-made as it were, in or since 1843.[3] Also, since nearly 200 teachers on the Free Church payroll in 1847 had previously been employed on their own private adventure or in private subscription schools, the number of transferred schools may well have been even larger.[4] Perhaps over a third of Free Church schools in 1847 and a fifth or even a quarter in 1851 – when their numbers were at an all-time high – had been taken over into the Educational Scheme and were not, therefore, additional to the national provision. The contribution in schooling was still remarkable, but not so substantial as has so often been made out.

The 1851 census returns gave details of school numbers, and enrolled pupils, according to their religious and other affiliations. Comparatively, how did the Free Church stand in these? The census noted 719 schools which claimed Free Church connection, accounting for 13.7 per cent of the Scottish total, teaching 17.1 per cent of all Scottish pupils. The same lists show 1,094 parochial and side schools in the legal system, representing 20.1 per cent of schools and 24.5 per cent of scholars. More surprising, and revealing, are the 914 schools which declared a direct connection with the Church of Scotland as a sect – Assembly schools, schools of the Society in Scotland for Propagating Christian Knowledge (SSPCK), Gaelic and other society schools, sessional and other schools supported by congregations, etc. – in all, 17.4 per cent of the total, enrolling 16.9 per cent of all pupils in the

country: in effect, a virtual match of the Free Church effort. Meanwhile, all
the other Scottish sects together provided only 237 schools (4.5 per cent),
which accommodated only 7.6 per cent of all scholars.[5]

Yet the returns for each of the denominations, and for the national
system, were dwarfed in number by the 2,321 schools in 1851 which were
recorded as having no formal religious attachment – 428 of them maintained by groups or societies, 1,893 by private individuals on their own
adventure, together accounting for 44.3 per cent of Scottish schools and
teaching 33.9 per cent of Scottish pupils. In a country which, it was widely
believed, demanded that all education, to be really worthy of the name,
should be consistently infused with religious truth (however that might be
defined) and also carefully supervised by Church authorities, the census data
were deeply worrying – and not least to Free Churchmen. Early expectations
that their educational enterprises would come to dominate in the nation at
large, and would reinvigorate a weakened religious attachment in the whole
country, had not been fulfilled, and this at a time when rising crime rates,
drunkenness and immorality of all kinds seemed only to underline the
continuing threat of political upset and social breakdown.

If it had not achieved the hoped-for ascendancy in numbers, then what
about the quality of Free Church schooling? In the early months and years
of the Disruption there was much criticism of the lethargy and incompe-
tence of parochial schoolmasters, particularly of those who had remained
in post in 1843 or who filled vacancies created then, just as there was much
trumpeting that the Free Church schools contained the liveliest, best-
educated and professionally-ablest teachers. Again, we need to exercise
some caution here. First, there is good evidence in many areas across the
whole of Scotland, that the standards of teaching, the extent of the curriculum offered, and the quality of supervision of the public schools had
steadily improved in the 1830s and early 1840s – some of this owing to the
activities of Evangelical clergy who had seceded.[6] Yet Free Churchmen, in
their public pronouncements in the aftermath of 1843, were quick to deny
that anything of value could be found in connection with a wholly detestable
Erastian Establishment: thus a 'residual' schoolmaster was bound to be as
tarnished as a 'residual' minister. Secondly, there was some serious questioning within the Free Church itself about the quality and efficiency of teachers
who had been admitted to the Educational Scheme in the early days of the
new Church – in 1847 Dr Robert Candlish, in a telling comment to the
Assembly, remarked that there were many teachers in their schools in the
Highlands 'whose heart is perhaps more thoroughly qualified than the head
is'. Even apparently impeccable sources can mislead us about the nature as
well as the extent of the Free Church contribution. In 1865, Dr John
Cumming, one of Her Majesty's Inspectors of Schools, was keen to
demonstrate to a royal commission chaired by the Duke of Argyll the
impetus which the Disruption had given to Scottish schooling.[7] He took the
example of the parish of Forgue, on the borders of Aberdeenshire and
upper Banffshire, which before 1843 had had only one parish school

teaching 70 pupils, but in 1865 supported two parochial schools, two Free Church schools and another, with 400 scholars in all. Cumming had clearly gone to the *New Statistical Account*[8] for the minister's report, written in 1836, but he failed to add, as the minister had, that there were then also 'five or six elementary schools taught by females on their own adventure' and that 'scarcely anyone between 6 and 15 years of age cannot read'. In 1843, the same minister told a government commission on the poor laws that, as before, one or two more schools would be requisite, but also that 'most of the people can read and write'.[9] We are left to wonder whether the five schools of 1865 reached a larger proportion of the population than those of 1836 or 1843 and were teaching the elements any more extensively or effectively, and whether the Disruption had had anything like the towering influence Cumming claimed for it.

But where did the Free Church get all its teachers from? It is frequently said that it was forced into setting up an alternative school system to the parish-school one because very large numbers of teachers, and parochial masters in particular, were summarily ejected from their teaching posts by heritors, kirk sessions or local Established presbyteries as soon as they made their allegiance to the new Church evident. Yet as late as 1847 it was reported to the Free Church Education Committee that only 80 ex-parochials – the number is sometimes given as 77 – had joined the Educational Scheme.[10] To be sure, there will have been others who left teaching and went more or less directly into the Free Church ministry; but even allowing for them (and their numbers would not have been significantly large), there were obviously not the wholesale dismissals or resignations among the thousand-or-so parochial masters which have often been assumed. As it happens, we know that in Fife, only in 4 parishes out of 60 were the public schoolteachers certainly ejected[11] and in the borderlands of West- and Midlothian no parochial master in the presbytery of Linlithgow was 'removed or had retired in consequence of his secession'.[12] Indeed, in Fife by the late 1840s, only in 28 or perhaps 30 parishes were there any schools connected with the Free Church, while of 28 parishes in Stirlingshire in 1850, only 8 had Free Church schools. If large numbers of parochial schoolteachers did not come over into the new Church, what about the teachers in other schools which were closely tied to the Establishment? In April 1844, the *Free Church Magazine* was noting that as few as 39 out of 146 Assembly schoolteachers had joined the Educational Scheme since the Disruption[13] – a number later estimated at 60, but still fewer than might have been anticipated. Certainly, more were to be recruited from the SSPCK: by 1847, it appears, some 75 – following a legal judgement that confirmed the Establishment's right to control and manage these schools.[14] In fact, by far the largest number of Free Church teachers who, in 1847, were being supported by Education Committee funding were not those dismissed from public appointments, but private adventurers and subscription schoolteachers: what we do not know is how many of them may have been persuaded into throwing in their lot with the new Church because it promised the security of a stated stipend, rather than from a strong commitment to Free Church principles. What seems clear enough, however, is that, while the stories of harsh and unjust dismissals of schoolmasters by a deeply wounded Establishment had great propaganda value at the Disruption, there were other and more positive reasons for the wideranging education policy that was developed by the Free Church leadership.

'The functions of any Church, and especially of any Church that aspires to the character of national', declared the Free Church Education Committee in May 1843, 'cannot be considered as completely fulfilled till provision is made for the training of the children and the young persons connected with it, from the lowest elementary school to the first institutions of science and learning'.[15] The Assembly agreed, and so laid down the basic outline of its policy: 'having given a shock to the existing religious and educational establishment, by withdrawing ourselves from them, then we are bound to furnish Scotland an equivalent'.[16] Yet even in the most euphoric days of the 'release from bondage', there were those in the Church who resisted this view – 'some disposition was manifested at the time of the disruption to postpone all efforts for school erection', it was admitted in February 1844[17] – and offered opposition to it on three main counts. First, it was said that the new Church should not cut itself off from the national educational heritage, but should put its principal effort into loosening the legal grip of the Establishment on its management and supervision. Secondly, since the parochial schools were known to teach the Bible and Shorter Catechism, there did not need to be an embargo on Free Church parents' continuing to use these schools – so long as there was no highly objectionable proselytising in them against the Free Church and attempts were meantime made to open up the masterships to Free Church candidates. Thirdly, it was contended that the new Church would have problems enough in financing the building of churches and paying the stipends of an unendowed ministry, without launching into less needful (yet substantial) expenditure on its own system of schools – apart, that is, from providing work for those teachers who were directly dismissed for having joined the Free Church.

The first argument was met by the response that an antagonistic government would be bound to defend all the privileges of the Establishment, and also by the contention that the Free Church should distance itself from ministries and governments (Tory or Whig/Liberal) which had been so obstructive to it and which had increasingly demonstrated a lack of commitment to promoting religious truth in the land.[18]

The third argument was quickly weakened by events: plans were laid, and then swiftly backed by promised subscriptions, to raise £50,000 (and then £60,000) for the building of 500 or more new Free Church schools; also, in 1843 and 1844, the sums gathered through congregational collections for teachers' stipends actually left a balance in hand – and there seemed to be no limit to the readiness with which the Church at large would pay for this or its other schemes.

But the second argument – that there was no essential theological barrier to Free Church parents electing to keep their children in the national schools – was much more difficult to overcome, and the response to it was to attack anything that was connected with 'the unmitigated, Erastian anti-Christ of the Scottish Establishment'. In October 1843, the Glasgow Assembly was prompted to state that 'we as a Free Church are for ever separated from the endowed schools of the land'. While the new Church insisted that it was the 'historic Church of Scotland', the progeny of a new Reformation which would reinvigorate a great ecclesiastical tradition, it condemned the Establishment for having become 'the great persecutor of true Presbyterianism': thus the blessings of a pure scriptural education could only be found in the schools of the Free Church, in schools intended 'not for the support of a sect, but for the regeneration of Scotland'. In sharp criticisms of landowners who refused sites for Free churches and schools, it was interestingly claimed that they were in truth acting not so much in favour of the Established Church, as against 'the stricter and more serious religion' which the Free Church was bringing to the country.[19] Hence, opposition to the Free Church policy was unpatriotic and, moreover, displayed a near-treacherous lack of faith in the God-driven destiny which awaited the new Church. The *Free Church Magazine* in February 1844 still felt obliged, however, to reassure Free Church parents that it was not 'extreme' to withdraw their children from the parochial schools,[20] on the grounds that the Disruption had 'dissolved the moral police' in the parishes, where only the Free Church schools now provided that vital godliness in teaching which was demanded by 'the whole Scottish Christian peasantry'.[21]

But that was not the whole story either. From the day of the Disruption itself, there had been concern about the likely counter-attacks which might be made by the political and religious Establishment – such as the one which came in August 1843 with the passing of Lord Aberdeen's Benefices Act and its 'democratising' of the appointment of parish ministers. What was especially worrying was the possibility that there would be moves to strengthen and extend the parochial schools in order to contain or weaken Free Church attachment in the localities. Even before 1843 there had been a campaign for a substantial improvement in the stipends and in the accommodation of the parochial schoolteachers, and this was revived in 1843–4. If the state acted quickly, then the existing discrepancy between the stipends of parochial and Free Church teachers would be even more marked; and if it became possible for the national schools to charge no fees or to reduce them to a mere pittance, then Free Church children and Free Church masters alike might return to the more comfortable haven of the old endowed system. There was a recognisable edginess in the way in which rumours were reported in the journals – for example, that the Duke of Sutherland intended to 'stud' his properties with new schools, 'thick as stars in the milky way', to draw back his tenantry into the Established Church,[22] even before Peel and Graham could bring in legislation (another rumour) to provide unprecedentedly generous levels of funding for an extended parochial school structure. The Free Church's answer was to act immediately, and so 'pre-occupy' the land with its own schools that any such government scheme would be thwarted and made insupportable in Parliament[23] and also to convince its own membership that the future security of their Church would depend on their success in carrying through the enterprise. Still there was opposition within the ranks – 'some entertain a different view', it was reported in April 1846[24] – and the *Free Church Magazine* warned, with a touch of desperation, against any decision to delay in the hope that the government might reform the parish schools and open them up to Free Church teachers: 'it is by the means of the school system alone that the Establishment possesses any real power to inflict permanent injury upon the kingdom' and thus it had to be challenged. The Free Church had to cover the land with their own schools, 'were it only on the principle of self-preservation'.[25] From such a standpoint, even the continued existence and certainly the growth of the Free Church itself was at stake, and it explains Robert Candlish's approach in 1845 to his old voluntaryist enemies, in the hope that 'all Evangelical Dissenters should unite and set up an efficient system of schools over the whole kingdom, withdrawing all their children from the parochial schools'[26] – but among them suspicion had died hard and the approach was unanswered.

This offensive against the Establishment, very noticeable in and after 1845, did not arise only from anxieties that government might act to support and strengthen the old parochial schools. What had not been anticipated in the exhilarating days of 1843 and 1844 – i.e. financial problems – beset the Free Church in the two following years,[27] and would never retreat thereafter, not only in respect of education but also of nearly all the church schemes, including that for the sustentation of the ministry. Promised subscriptions to the school-building fund were slow in coming or were not paid at all; and the annual collections for schoolteachers' salaries were no longer keeping pace with the rising numbers of new teachers applying for admission to the Educational Scheme. It was even the case that some Free Church landlords were holding back from supporting the erection of new schools where there was already an adequate supply of school places.[28] The old arguments against the policy of virtually unlimited expansion of the Educational Scheme began to revive.

A somewhat subdued Assembly in 1846 concluded that its Education Committee lacked the energetic leadership and thrusting organisation which the situation demanded, and its convener, Dr William Cunningham of New College, was brusquely replaced by Robert Candlish.[29] In the debate on education, in a typically fiery speech, Candlish all but ignored any hesitancies about or questioning of the expansionist policy and pushed aside the current financial difficulties (apart from suggesting that deacons courts might substitute monthly house-collections for church-door givings to improve congregational returns), as he whipped up renewed enthusiasm for the Church's educational enterprises. They were, he told the Assembly, to plan for 1,000 schools and to set about at once to gather such a vast endowment that they could avoid their present hand-to-mouth existence. Above all he stressed to his audience the essential role that their schools played in maintaining and increasing awareness of their distinctive Free Church principles, on which alone their Church could stand and by which it must grow. At a time when Romanism and Puseyism were threatening true religion, and when it seemed that governments had lost their way in religious matters (e.g., the recent huge endowment of Maynooth College for the training of Irish Catholic priests), there could be no relaxation. And in his capacity as editor of *Lowe's Edinburgh Magazine*, Candlish offered yet further reasons for restoring what he called the 'old Scottish association of religion and learning':

> The masses of our population are leavened in a fearful degree with the principle – not merely of practical ungodliness and speculative Infidelity – but a sort of desperate Atheism, prepared to defy all power, whether of earth or heaven ... Again, in the other classes of the community, ignorance and superstition so prevail as to make them the ready prey of priestly usurpation ... If there be a wholesome element still working in the community at all, it is almost wholly in that middle order to which the religious electors belong ...

And that middle order was where the Free Church had its greatest political, social and religious strength. Candlish felt that he had to convince the middle order that 'the really great questions yet outstanding are all mixed up with religious considerations' and that when politicians proffered 'not a whisper now of the exclusive right of the Church to educate', it was even more vital for the nation that the Free Church should march ahead with its army of energetic and thoroughly religious schoolteachers in an ever-expanding Educational Scheme. The future of their Church, and the future of the nation as a God-fearing community imbued with the 'right' attitudes and amenable to the 'right' policies, depended on it.[30]

The 1846 Assembly instructed Candlish and the Education Committee to present a revised and reinvigorated educational plan at its meeting a year later. In that 1847 report, Candlish put an extraordinary emphasis on the character and quality of the teachers who were to be employed under the scheme:[31] they had to be much better remunerated in order to ensure their high intellectual and professional capabilities (there were to be three different grades of teachers with parallel grades of stipend); and he proposed a very elaborate structure of regulations for their appointment, admission, 'ordination', supervision and inspection, and for their disciplining and dismissal – all emphasising the importance of their religious character and also their subordination to the ministers and to the Church courts. According to Hugh Miller, Candlish seemed bent on subjecting the teachers to clerical domination; indeed, the scheme had an awkward sacerdotal, even Jesuitical, flavour which, he believed, would repel rather than attract teachers and would not draw in the funding which it required.[32]

In fact, the particulars of Candlish's proposals were largely lost to view in the furore that accompanied the Education Committee debate on another but related matter. A new arrangement for government-funded grants in aid of school-building (and, later, of teachers' stipends) had been announced by the Privy Council Committee on Education in December 1846, and there seemed to be an easy way out of the Free Church's problems of financing its schools, since these grants were now to be made to Churches other than the Establishment.[33] One group in the Assembly insisted that the Free Church must reject all dealings with an unregenerate government, unless it accepted the Disruption demands of 1842–3. A larger grouping opposed acceptance because, by the Privy Council regulations, the grants were to be made to the Churches as *sects*. Having come out in 1843 as 'the national church unestablished', this grouping would not allow the Church to be categorised as a sect, nor regarded as different from Episcopalians or Roman Catholics. A still weightier grouping also emerged in opposition, and argued that the Privy Council was wrongly applying to Scotland a divisive form of educational support which had also been forced on England because of the unbridgeable theological differences among the English denominations – whereas in Scotland the vast bulk of the people shared the same Presbyterian theological standards. It was their view that government should be persuaded to legislate for the reform and considerable extension of the existing national, state-endowed system, for they believed that the state alone had the resources to overtake the 'educational destitution' of the largely unchurched districts of the great towns; and they emphatically opposed the Free Church's acceptance of any Privy Council grants because, by doing so, the Church would actually obstruct the possibility of Scotland gaining the educational legislation which it needed. Led by James Begg and Thomas Guthrie in the Church courts and by Hugh Miller outside, they attacked what they saw as sectarianism working against the national interest, partly because it would stir up obstructive inter-denominational troubles in the schools where they saw no need for them, partly because they believed it would weaken the Free Church among the people if it were seen as having party rather than national advantage as its leading concern.

Candlish recommended that the Assembly accept the grants, while adding a preliminary statement that the Church disputed and could not agree with the principles on which Privy Council made them. Successive, fierce debates ended in the Assembly of 1850 with his winning a very substantial victory against a final effort led by James Begg to persuade his fellow Churchmen to act positively in favour of national education, even to the point of offering government the schools attached to their scheme as part of a new national system which would incorporate all the old parochial schools and such new ones as were needed, the whole taken out of the hands of individual Churches and put in the care of elected representatives in each parish or locality.[34] For Candlish there was no security in such an arrangement for the 'religious character' of the schooling he wanted, and he was very dismissive of Begg's arguments. Thereafter, Candlish was frequently accused of parading such a blinding sectarianism that he was 'the divine in the Free Church most conspicuous against National Education',[35] yet he would have claimed that it was for the future of the nation that he opposed Begg's proposals and then the succession of attempts in parliament in 1849–56 to legislate for an expanded national schooling based in the old parochial system. He rejected these proposals, not because they were national, but because they lacked a thorough-going security for the proper religious character of the education they would offer. He would support a national structure which gave such a security (unlikely as it was that that would ever be offered), but until then, as he remarked to the 1851 Assembly, they should 'proceed as if there were nothing whatever on the *tapis* but only the great Educational Scheme to which this Church stood pledged'.

The debates in the Free Church on its educational policies and practice certainly did not end, as is sometimes implied, with Candlish's resounding victory in May 1850. The embittered exchanges about schooling did not die away, but were to become intertwined with yet more educational controversies – this time arising from sharply contrasting views about the Free Church's role in higher education in Scotland.

In the early months of the new Church, swift agreement had been reached on two matters concerning post-school education: the need to provide model schools, or teacher-training institutions, in Glasgow and Edinburgh to replace those from which Free Church teachers and students had withdrawn or would soon be ejected by the Establishment; and the requirement which was undoubtedly laid on the Church to provide its own theological training for its new ministry, starting with the small core of professors – with Thomas Chalmers at their head – who had resigned from the Divinity Halls in Edinburgh and Aberdeen. But, right from the beginning, the Education Committee had more adventurous plans in mind. It wished to see an 'entire' educational system under the aegis of the Free Church[36] – elementary schooling everywhere, but also intermediate schooling (grammar schools, German-style gymnasia, mercantile schools, academies) with bursaries to ensure their accessibility, and the whole structure topped off not only with 'four Divinity Halls but four complete Colleges'.[37] By May 1844, it was reported that many in the Church were becoming anxious that a year had slipped by 'without maturing the scheme for a Free Church University', at least one, to be based on the emergent 'new college' for divinity students in Edinburgh. W. H. Hetherington, editor of the recently founded *Free Church Magazine*, demanded swift action by the ensuing Assembly:

> From the week of the disruption … we felt strongly that the safety and success of the Free Church depended much on the adoption of such a measure … Why leave the youth to be warped and biassed, and to the danger of having their principles at least diluted with those who reject our claims and would trample our course? Rather let the full curriculum be forthwith instituted… . The Free Church University would thus stand forth as a monument of our indomitable resolution not to be put down, our determined purpose to carry out the full benefit of our system, in every direction and in every sphere.[38]

Not only would the university help to safeguard the future of the church; it would also be so constructed as to be 'the centre and focus of all the educational improvements of the age' and add still more to the reputation and standing of the Free Church in the country.[39]

Plans were afoot in Edinburgh to reform and extend the theological training once a full compliment of professors was appointed, as well as to begin teaching some arts subjects. Endowment, however, was slow in coming, so in the mean time a modest curriculum along the old lines was offered there and something of a holding operation was put in place in Aberdeen (where its one professor received the support of local ministers). There were no regular divinity classes in Glasgow or St Andrews – the Free Church theology students in these regions were expected to go to Edinburgh – but there and in Aberdeen arrangements were made for the supervision of Free Church students attending non-theological classes.

The Education Committee's plans here, as in schooling, provoked some opposition. There was, it was argued, no invincible reason for Free Churchmen to withdraw from the ancient national universities: no religious tests were applied to the students, and the professors were formally required to sign the Confession of Faith. Further, it would be foolish to cut themselves off from the large bursary funds which were intended to be of service to the whole people of Scotland. Once again, the voices of caution were swept aside in the exhilaration of 1843–4. While progress was slow, even in Edinburgh, until £12,000 was gathered in donations for the building of New College,[40] once a tutor in classics and a professor of moral philosophy were appointed, followed by professors of natural science and logic the first steps towards constructing a complete university were readily visible.

But the question of the extent and character of the Free Church's commitment in higher education was still under discussion when, in 1845, Parliament highlighted two issues which served to sharpen the disagreements in the Free Church Assembly. The first occurred when MPs friendly to the Free Church and the Dissenting Churches moved to abolish all religious tests for university professors of non-theological subjects.[41] As might be expected, this proposition was violently opposed by the old Moderates in the Establishment. But more surprisingly, it was also attacked by Candlish and his coterie of younger Evangelicals in the Free Church. The Moderates wanted no change in any law which gave the Church of Scotland a privileged position in national education and upheld the traditional connection of the national Church with the national universities. Its Free Church opponents attacked the bill because it would weaken or entirely remove the direct religious connection: what they wanted was not an abolition of the test but a substitute test which would be so framed as to be acceptable to the Free Church. Both parties were made very anxious by the fact that Peel and Graham, impressed by the wide support which the bill seemed to have when it was introduced in the House of Commons (including the support of the ancient universities themselves), allowed it to go forward to a second reading. By now, however, James Graham had changed his mind and opposed its progress, and the bill was defeated, though only by a very narrow margin. Graham, it seems, was driven to change his opinion in the matter because of the threat he perceived to the existing universities from a full-blown Free Church university. Dr James Bryce in the Established Assembly in May 1845 had warned his fellow commissioners of what might lie ahead if the university tests were abolished: then 'infidel professors will shut your classrooms against the pious youth of the country ... who will be sent to the sectarian institution where security is afforded that their minds shall not be poisoned by infidel and anti-Christian doctrines'.[42] No doubt Graham had taken such warnings to heart; what he also wanted to avoid was the possibility that, if abolition was carried, the Church of Scotland might try to set up its own sectarian college or colleges and so plague Scotland with 'sectarian teaching and the prevalence of religious discord', previously avoided in its higher education. The failure of the bill was a relief to the high-flyers in the Free Church, who had before them the prospect of their own alternative higher education with close ties to evangelical religion: for them education at all levels should be the servant of the true faith – 'education without religion', stated the *Free Church Magazine* in April 1846, 'is destructive of all true religion'.[43]

In the same session of Parliament which debated the abolition of university tests in Scotland, the government introduced a bill to establish a new university in Ireland. In an attempt to avoid confrontations among the Irish Catholics, Episcopalians and Presbyterians, Peel proposed the erection of the Queen's University on the pattern of London – an administrative unit, having the power to grant degrees, with control over the curriculum and examinations, and having (under the Crown) the patronage of appointments, etc. – while its three constituent teaching colleges in Cork, Galway and Belfast, on the Scottish pattern, would be non-residential, without any religious tests for students, and with teaching by the lecture system. In Ireland, the colleges were forbidden to allow any teaching of a distinctive religious or sectarian nature within their buildings. Candlish and his Free Church group, having been outraged by the government's grant to Maynooth, now recoiled at the vast endowment envisaged for this 'godless' Irish university – and reacted by claiming that, if it were ever to be put into the hands of this government or any other, then higher education in Scotland would be opened to the doctrines of infidels and deists rather than to 'the principles and influence of the gospels'. With governments the enemy of true Protestantism, it was as well if the Free Church had no truck with them. Little wonder that in 1847, when Candlish proposed – however reluctantly – that the Church should accept the Privy Council grants for school-building,[44] he felt obliged to explain to the Assembly that in doing so he might seem 'to set aside some arguments that he had been thought to hold'; and no wonder at all that Guthrie and Miller were astounded by the volte-face, and concluded that a new and even more virulent sectarianism had taken grip of him.

The events of 1845 gave a head of steam to the efforts to push forward with the Edinburgh college – but the unexpected financial constraints were to limit the expansion into arts teaching and held back the making of additional appointments in theology and the reformed and extended divinity curriculum which had been suggested. At the same time, in May 1845, it was decided to begin more seriously the process of establishing a fully equipped Divinity Hall in Aberdeen,[45] a decision which was not welcomed by the College Committee with its strong representation of Edinburgh professorial members. They argued that it was in the best interests of the church to 'complete' the college in Edinburgh, 'at headquarters', in preference to expending money and manpower on any extension of theological training elsewhere. To the dismay of William Cunningham, Principal of New College after David Welsh's death in April 1845, and the convenor of the College Committee, there was a second Assembly in October of that year in Inverness which, despite Cunningham's protestations, directed the committee to act positively – if also at a suitably measured pace – to erect an 'equivalent' college in Aberdeen, and not the wholly subordinate institution with severely limited functions which Cunningham had wanted. The makings of another confrontation, and of yet more division in the Church, were there for all to see.

The Free presbytery of Aberdeen distrusted Cunningham and the Edinburgh and College-dominated Committee, and acted to overcome the inevitable delaying tactics which would be employed against the Aberdeen Hall.[46] To Cunningham's fury, it sent out a circular to all presbyteries, inviting their observations on 'college extension', and received remarkable support in favour of the Aberdeen plan as agreed by the Inverness Assembly. Yet the College Committee did manage to prevaricate and to delay any effective decisions in the next two years, but in doing so provoked increasingly unrestrained criticisms of their manoeuvrings – not all from the north, it should be noted, but many from the west of Scotland – and complaints that Cunningham was bent on 'starving out' the Aberdeen project. In the run-up to the Assembly of May 1848, it was well known that there would be a very public clash over college policy, about which the *Free Church Magazine* was full of foreboding.[47] In the Assembly itself, some extraordinarily intemperate remarks by Cunningham only served to weaken and undermine his cause – while he also managed to upset Candlish very badly. Candlish had now embraced the position that a strong Free Church college in Aberdeen was crucial for maintaining the supply of ministers and teachers from a region which contained 'a full half' of the Free Church membership, and had decided that it should take precedence over any university extension in the capital.[48] However, Candlish was for once on the receiving end of a very astute piece of political management during the course of the debate, in which a moderating motion he had introduced was pushed aside and disregarded. The Assembly gave Cunningham a temporary respite – when in trouble, send the question down again to the presbyteries of the Church! – but this did nothing to quieten the controversy. In 1848–9, newspapers up and down the country reported the verbal scufflings in the Church courts, and a stream of pamphlets was produced on the 'college question', in one of which Candlish described it as 'a fertile and never-ending source of mutual suspicion and alarm, an interminable bone of contention'.[49] One development that greatly concerned Candlish was that both sides were busy in the presbyteries attempting to commission as ministers and elders in the next Assembly only those who committed themselves to vote in a particular way before hearing any debates – it all seemed to him like a return to the politicking of pre-Disruption times, and destructive of the peace of the Church.

The later years of this controversy need only be sketched in. The battle lines were well set, and a number of wealthy Free Church laymen in Aberdeen stole a very effective march on what they regarded as an Edinburgh cabal, by providing a substantial amount of money for the building of the Aberdeen hall and beginning its construction without reference to Edinburgh.[50] Cunningham was enraged but virtually helpless, and turned a torrent of abuse on the men of the north, all the time trying to block or circumvent or ignore recommendations from the Assembly or the Commission. Finally, in 1852, came the unequivocal order that the Aberdeen hall should be funded and manned for the task of giving a complete training to the theological students of the Church.[51] In 1853, Parliament passed an act which, in effect, abolished the religious tests for non-theological professors in the Scottish universities. Thus another blow had been delivered on Cunningham, since with appointments open to Free Churchmen, and with one immediate transfer from New College to Edinburgh University, all hope of persuading the Church to expand that college into a Free Church university had effectively gone. Then, despite some skirmishing in the intervening Assemblies, by 1856 Glasgow also had the go-ahead for its full and equivalent theological hall.

William Cunningham, that doughty old campaigner of Disruption times, withdrew almost entirely from all public activities in the Church, and into an estrangement from Candlish which would not be healed for a decade.[52] The college controversy, just as the controversy over national schooling had done, disrupted personal relationships, produced new and violent antagonisms, and was used to call into question the probity and credibility of individuals and causes – all within a Free Church which had prided itself only a few years earlier on its harmony and unity of purpose.

In the early 1850s, the controversy over national schooling – and over what kinds of relationship with the state were acceptable – still remained alive and very troublesome. Guthrie's and Begg's support for an extended state-endowed system of schools based on the old parochial structure of school provision, managed by elected representatives on local committees with no religious tests applied to them, and attempting to overcome the problems of denominational differences in local communities by allocating particular times of the school day for religious observance and religious teaching (by sect separately, and with parental rights to withdraw their children at these times) were anathema to Candlish and his supporters.[53] Guthrie was incensed by accusations that he and Begg held 'the principles

of Atheists, Deists, and Infidels', and in a letter to Fox Maule wrote of the
'jealousies and bigotry and narrow-mindedness' of the Education Committee from which he resigned in 1851 – 'these men are never without a pair of
Free Church spectacles'.[54] Meanwhile, once again showing that curious
identity in the attitudes of the old Moderates in the Established Church and
the high-flyers in the Free Church, a very Tory, Establishment journal
remarked huffily in 1851 that 'Dr Begg, Dr Guthrie and a few others ... have
already passed over to the secular camp'.[55] The war of words went on
unabated.

What Candlish called 'the *quaestio vexata*, the difficult question of a right
national system of education'[56] was kept to the fore throughout the earlier
1850s, as a stream of bills were presented to Parliament, latterly government
bills introduced by Lord Advocate Moncrieff, a very prominent Free Kirk
elder. They were uniformly opposed by the old Moderates in the Church of
Scotland who would contemplate no weakening of the connection, however
tenuous in practice, between the national Church and national schooling,
and they were supported by the bulk of the landowners and the Anglican
Establishment south of the border: having lost ground with the abolition of
university tests in 1853, they were especially aggressive in their opposition
thereafter. The same bills, even when in the name of Moncrieff, were as
consistently opposed by Candlish and his group – but often more obliquely
and less publicly and prominently – on the grounds that there must be no
division between secular and religious schooling, that absolute security must
be given for a religious teaching steeped in Evangelical Protestantism and
that, in the management of schools, ministers (and perhaps Church courts)
should have a leading if not a predominating role. Candlish seems to have
shown an extraordinary aptitude at this time, in appearing to be ready to
support this or that bill in his more public pronouncements, yet always
managing to reserve his own final position. The failure of the bills of the
1850s, generally so heartily supported by Begg and Guthrie among many
others in the Free Church, may not after all have been wholly due to the old
Church Moderates and their allies:[57] it may owe more than has been
imagined to the calculated machinations of Candlish and his band of
hardliners.

On the face of it, it seems thoroughly unlikely, within a decade or so of
the glorious episode of the Disruption, that the Free Church should be
openly spoken and written about as a house deeply, even irrevocably, divided
against itself. Yet this is what happened, and much of that disharmony
stemmed from intensely held, divergent views about education. One pamph-
leteer in 1855 posed the question:

> Is it asked now, why is the Free Church of Scotland torn by dissensions,
> shattered by factions, and threatened with premature dissolution ...
> The Free Church has reached a *crisis* in her history ... or, whether the
> crisis being passed, they were now in a catastrophe ...[58]

The title of his pamphlet, *Clerical Misrule*, gives the author's own answer;
after condemning the intrusive 'interference of ministers with what does not

truly concern them, the secular affairs of the Church', he makes it plain that education should be judged a mainly secular concern:

> Should we not anticipate a remodelling of our Educational Institutions, by the introduction of a national scheme, by men – laymen, whose education and habits and social intercourse with denominational memberships, have fitted them for mutual cooperation for the salvation of our common country? ...[59]

The question of national schooling, therefore, would have been better left to the more open-minded and more worldly-wise laymen. The fact that it had been appropriated and then badly mishandled by ministers had been, in the Free Church, a prime cause of faction and dissension. It was the ministers, and not the 'Churches', who were blocking sensible and generally desired reforms such as the reconstruction of Scottish schooling. Ministers were, in effect, disabled from their appointed wider work in the world by their 'education, habits and social intercourse', which tended to imprison them in their cliquish reservations. Such comments were not particularly novel in 1855 – the writer of the pamphlet draws quite heavily on earlier publications by Thomas Guthrie – but they clearly reflect a growing exasperation in the mid-1850s with current Church organisation and Church management, and show also the impact on some Church members of the recent battles over educational policy and other issues in the Free Church. It is a curious but important by-product of those controversies.

This was not the only criticism of ministers which was also closely allied to educational matters. The author berates 'our more conspicuous ecclesiastics (we do not, although some say Bishops)' who habitually gathered themselves together in something 'like a metropolitan cliqueship', and aims his barbs at the 'headquarters mentality' which had also drawn the fire of the supporters of college expansion. Indeed, it seems likely that it was the college controversy which first brought these criticisms of the 'metropolitan hierarchy' firmly into the public domain, in journals, newspapers and pamphlets. In the earliest years of the Disruption there had been much need of a continuing and decisive leadership concentrated in relatively few, strong and reliable hands. It was, apparently, too easy for those who had grasped or been given power to retain it. But from 1848 onwards there are more and more complaints about the packing of Assembly committees and about the private conferences of a 'few leading members of Assembly' to patch up quietly this or that dispute in order to contain any potentially dangerous debating on the floor of the house.[60] In the aftermath of the school and college controversies, with the ministers and elders and presbyteries in the north-east and in the west of Scotland especially alive to the ever-present dangers of 'centralisation', there is little doubt that the Free Church in Assembly became rather more difficult to handle.[61]

Yet there was still another, and more important, by-product of the educational battles in the Free Church in the later 1840s and early 1850s. In their contests with Candlish, both James Begg and Thomas Guthrie remarked on the deeply traditionalist and often very unbending concept he had of ministry and service in the community, and in particular on his view of the relationship between religion and education. Both were provoked into retaliation against what they considered was an outmoded vision, no longer acceptable in the mightily changed society of mid-nineteenth-century Scotland. It was Guthrie who led the most brutal assault, and it is sufficient to quote from only one publication. Guthrie found himself unable to attend a public meeting in Edinburgh on national education, at which he had been asked to speak, on 9 April 1850; but he sent a letter to be read out to the meeting, and this was published very soon afterwards:

> For the godly upbringing of the young, I think we must look not so much to the teachers of man's appointment, as of God's – to parents and pastors; to the care of Christian ministers, elders, deacons and Sabbath schoolteachers. I should be very sorry to see the people of Scotland trusting the godly upbringing of their children to the education of the common school ... I do not think an ordinary school is the fittest place for winning the young mind to Christ or training it for heaven.
>
> I think, and have come on mature reflection to believe, that churches as such have nothing to do with secular education, beyond giving to it – as to various schemes of patriotism and philanthropy – all due encouragement ... To me it does not appear to be the duty of a church of Christ to spend the monies and energies that should be sacred to redemption, and reserved for the gospel, on mere secular knowledge – on the multiplication table, the problems of Euclid, the metaphysics of Aristotle, the metamorphoses of Ovid, book-keeping and vulgar fractions.... I am opposed to the attempt now making to bring all education, secular as well as religious, within the hands of the clergy and of the church courts ... Ability to read the Word of God is necessary for a full and free understanding of Scripture ... and, if no other party were there to furnish the people with this key, to instruct in the simple elements of reading would be clearly the duty of the Church ... but I think that the Church of Christ was not set up to teach the ordinary branches of secular knowledge.
>
> ... the denominational system of education ... is in its very nature calculated, if not to propagate, certainly to perpetuate, and to stereotype divisions which, as brethren and Christians, we ought to use all lawful means of removing ... If our children may learn cricket and football together – I may be blind as a mole – but I cannot see why they cannot learn the ABC together and the multiplication table together ... or read the common Bible and the common Catechism ... It is bad enough to have such barriers in the churches; it is making matters worse to extend them to the school ...[62]

It is hard to conceive that anything could be more distinctive and irreconcilable than the principles on which Candlish and Guthrie took their separate stands in forming their educational policies. It should be no surprise to us, therefore, to find the Free Church being blown about, as it surely was, amid the reefs (submerged and too often uncharted) of such conflicting ideals.

NOTES

1 *Proceedings of the General Assembly of the Free Church of Scotland, May 1847* (Edinburgh, 1847), p. 124.
2 *Proceedings of the General Assembly of the Free Church of Scotland, May 1850* (Edinburgh, 1850), p. 195.
3 *Registrar General's Report and Tables with Reference as to Religious Worship and Education, 1851* (London, 1854), Tables H and I.
4 Ibid., Table A (Suppls I and II).
5 Ibid. See also Thomas Gordon, *Education in Scotland: its actual Amount* (Edinburgh, 1854), pp. iv–viii. Gordon rightly points out that the tables for day schools give an account only of those which sent in returns, and are unlikely to be complete. But that should not be significant for the analysis here: the Free Church was anxious that the census should show it in the best light, and the number of schools claiming Free Church attachment in the tables is larger than any registered elsewhere by the Church itself. The grouping most likely to be affected by non-returns are the private adventurers. On the basis of enrolled pupils according to the census, 1 in 7.84 of the population was at school in 1851; if we make the calculation from the total number of 'scholars' entered in the occupation tables in the main census, the figure is 1 in 6.75. Both indicate that the country was well provided with schooling.
6 The most easily accessible source here is the *New Statistical Account of Scotland,* 15 vols (Edinburgh, 1845): individual entries may be dated from c.1833 to c.1843.
7 I. J. Simpson, *Education in Aberdeenshire before 1872* (Edinburgh, 1947), p. 177: 'Dr Cumming ... informed the Education Commission that all, or nearly all, the Free Church schools were needed to supply the deficiences in Scottish education.'
8 *New Statistical Account,* vol. xii, pp. 609–10.
9 *Parliamentary Papers,* Reports from Commissioners, Poor Laws in Scotland, Appendix, part II (1844), vol. xxi, p. 723.
10 *Proceedings of the General Assembly of the Free Church of Scotland, May 1847* (Edinburgh, 1847), p. 124: it was stated that only 50 ejected masters were actually receiving salaries; Hugh Miller, *Thoughts on the Educational Question, or the 'Battle of Scotland'* (London, 1850), p. 21.
11 James M. Beale, *A History of the Burgh and Parochial Schools of Fife* (Edinburgh, 1983), p. 182.
12 Andrew Bain, *Education in Stirlingshire* (Edinburgh, 1965), p. 147: in Falkirk 'the desire to plant and support a Free Church school came less from the need to employ a seceding master than from a determination to be independent of the Established Church in all things'.
13 *Free Church Magazine* (Apr. 1844), 97.
14 *Proceedings of the General Assembly of the Free Church of Scotland, May 1847* (Edinburgh, 1847), p. 124.
15 *Proceedings of the General Assembly of the Free Church of Scotland, May 1843* (Edinburgh, 1843), p. 146.
16 Ibid.
17 *Free Church Magazine* (Feb. 1844), 36.
18 For the background to this, see D. J. Withrington, 'The Free Church Educational Scheme, 1843–50', in *Records of the Scottish Church History Society,* xv (1964), 107; there is a very good account of the political factors at work in I. G. C. Hutchison, *A Political History of Scotland, 1832–1924* (Edinburgh, 1986), ch. 3.
19 *Free Church Magazine* (June 1844), 178; (June 1846), 26.
20 *Free Church Magazine* (Feb. 1844), 38.
21 Ibid., 39.

22 Ibid., 38.

23 Ibid., 38–9.

24 *Free Church Magazine* (Apr. 1846), 100.

25 Ibid.

26 *Free Church Magazine* (Feb. 1845), 49.

27 Withrington, 'Free Church Educational Scheme', pp. 107–8.

28 *Fifeshire Journal*, 8 and 20 June 1848.

29 *Proceedings of the General Assembly of the Free Church of Scotland, May 1846* (Edinburgh, 1846), pp. 186–7; and see *Free Church Magazine* (June 1846), 97–101.

30 *Lowe's Edinburgh Magazine*, NS, i (Nov. 1846), 5, 66.

31 See the very full report in *Free Church Magazine* (June 1847).

32 Miller, *Thoughts*, p. 21.

33 Withrington, 'Free Church Educational Scheme', pp. 108–10.

34 Ibid., pp. 112–13.

35 *An Appeal for Scotland to the Parliament of 1851, or What should Lord John Russell do?* (London, 1850), pp. 10–11; W. G. Blaikie warned the new editor of the *North British Review* in 1850 that 'a decidedly narrower spirit was now guiding the councils of the church than in the days of Chalmers and Welsh' (J. Shattock, M. Wolff (eds), *The Victorian Periodical Press: Samplings and Soundings* (Leicester, 1982), p. 155).

36 *Free Church Magazine* (Apr. 1846), 100–1; and *Free Church Magazine* (Sept. 1845), 309–11, for proposals initiated by James Begg for the erection of a grammar school-cum-liberal arts college in Oban, to serve the Gaelic-speaking youth of the western Highlands and Islands.

37 R. S. Candlish, *College Extension* (Edinburgh, 1849), p. 19.

38 *Free Church Magazine* (May 1844), 129.

39 Ibid., 130.

40 *Free Church Magazine* (June 1845), 154–9: report of building committee to Assembly.

41 *Hansard's Parliamentary Debates*, lxxx (1845) cols 11–23 (esp. 20) and lxxxii (1845) cols 227–79 (esp. 249–50).

42 *Macphail's Edinburgh Ecclesiastical Journal and Literary Review*, xi (1851), 326.

43 *Free Church Magazine* (Apr. 1846), 97–101 (leading article on 'Education in Scotland').

44 *Proceedings of the General Assembly of the Free Church of Scotland, May 1847* (Edinburgh, 1847), pp. 158–60.

45 *Proceedings of the General Assembly of the Free Church of Scotland, June 1845* (Edinburgh, 1845), p. 218.

46 *Proceedings in the Presbytery of Aberdeen relative to the Erection of Buildings for Divinity Classes, Library and Presbytery Hall* (Aberdeen, 1850), pp. 3–7.

47 *Free Church Magazine* (Feb. 1848), 41; *Free Church Magazine* (May 1848), 145–6.

48 Candlish, *College Extension*, p. 19.

49 Ibid., p. 13.

50 *Proceedings in the Presbytery of Aberdeen*, pp. 7–9.

51 *Proceedings of the General Assembly of the Free Church of Scotland, May 1852* (Edinburgh, 1852), pp. 113–21.

52 The *Life of William Cunningham* by Robert Rainy and James Mackenzie (London, 1871) is a very revealing source for the period covered in this chapter, partly because of the wide range of sources which are called upon and quoted, mostly because of the commentary by Rainy on Cunningham's intentions and actions and on his relationships with other major figures in the Free Church – all reflecting Rainy's own youthful recollections of his early days in Edinburgh and his lifelong interest in the Church as a political and administrative machine.

53 Withrington, 'Free Church Educational Scheme', pp. 112–13.

54 Thomas Guthrie, *Letter on National Education* (Edinburgh, 1850), p. 5; D. K. and C. J. Guthrie (eds), *Autobiography of Thomas Guthrie, and Memoir*, 2 vols (Edinburgh, 1875), vol. ii, pp. 288–90.

55 *Macphail's Edinburgh Review*, xi (1851), 223.
56 *Proceedings of the General Assembly of the Free Church of Scotland, May–June 1851* (Edinburgh, 1851), pp. 342–3.
57 J. D. Myers, 'Scottish Nationalism and the Antecedents of the 1872 Education Act', *Scottish Educational Studies*, iv (1972), 73–92.
58 Anon., *Clerical Misrule: or the Voice of Chalmers on Church Offices and Finance, specially addressed to the Deaconship by Some of the People* (Edinburgh, 1855), p. 5.
59 Ibid.
60 Privately expressed complaints were no doubt made earlier; from 1848 they are made very public – see *Free Church Magazine* (June 1846), 166–7; *Free Church Magazine* (June 1848), 161.
61 The editor of the *Free Church Magazine*, W. H. Hetherington, a close ally of Candlish's, felt called upon to defend centralisation and tight control of the Church's business in March 1848: ibid., 83.
62 Guthrie, *Letter on National Education*, pp. 5–7. Guthrie returned to the same topic again and again. On 18 June 1855 the *Witness* printed a letter from him, of which this extract is quite typical – 'He believed if all the ministers ceased to interfere with the secular business of the Church and, like the Apostles, gave themselves wholly to the ministry and to prayer, leaving the management with confidence to the piety, wisdom and energy of the lay members, they would prosper more than hitherto … The ministers were not the lords of God's heritage; they were the servants of Christ … '.

CHAPTER SIX

Deism and Development
Disruptive Forces in Scottish Natural Theology
PAUL BAXTER

THE DISRUPTION OF 1843 split the Church of Scotland and, combined with the effects of earlier secessions from the national Church, helped to make Scottish society more secular, notably by its effect on the educational system. Contemporary scientific culture was far from being wholly secular: indeed some of its leading practitioners were devout Christians who were not embarrassed by frequent references to the Creator in a treatise about zoology or geology. It has been suggested that natural theology, the enterprise of displaying God's attributes in His works, helped to cement over sectarian differences about doctrine and form of worship.[1] Yet the very openness and accessibility of natural theology could turn it into a kind of Trojan horse from which deists and anti-clerical forces could mount surprise attacks on orthodox belief.

This chapter suggests that around the time of the Disruption, a disruption of a different kind was taking place in Scottish natural theology. The main focus is on the work of four men: David Brewster,[2] Thomas Chalmers,[3] Hugh Miller[4] and John Fleming.[5] All belonged to the Evangelical wing of the Church of Scotland before joining the Free Church at the Disruption. All were deeply interested in science, perceiving close links between the study of the natural world and the higher theology of God's revealed word. Their names appear together in the writings of some contemporary Free Church propagandists, eager to prove that the Church was not backward-looking or anti-scientific.[6] Other connections can also be traced. Brewster attended Edinburgh University between 1793 and 1800, whilst Chalmers, a year older than him, spent two sessions at the University between 1799 and 1801. Chalmers and Brewster both attended the lectures of John Robison in natural philosophy, Dugald Stewart in moral philosophy and John Playfair in mathematics. Fleming also attended Edinburgh University, although not until 1802, but afterwards he and Chalmers were ministers of neighbouring parishes in Fife.[7]

As a young man, Brewster shared Chalmers's and Fleming's intention of entering the ministry, although he soon abandoned the aim, apparently because of his extreme nervousness of public speaking, after being licensed to preach in 1802. Afterwards he supported his work in science by journalism and editing. He was a prodigious experimenter, the author of hundreds of papers on optics, and a consistent critic of the undulatory theory of light.[8] Championed by a Cambridge-based school of physicists, including William Whewell and George Airy, the theory in the 1830s was gaining ground against the older particle view of light. Brewster's increasing isolation in the scientific community, combined with a somewhat irascible personality, help to explain his failure to secure a university appointment until 1838, when he was made principal of the United Colleges of St Leonard and St Salvator at St Andrews. He became principal of Edinburgh University in 1859. Besides his specialised research, he contributed a vast amount of material on almost every branch of science to the general periodical press, notably the *Edinburgh Review* and the *North British Review*. Many of these articles blended popular accounts of new discoveries with observations on the moral and religious bearings of scientific inquiry.

The combination of scientific erudition with strong Evangelical beliefs and an unswerving commitment to the political and economic well-being of the Church is best exemplified in the personality of Thomas Chalmers. His interest in scientific subjects was manifested in his early years as a minister in Fife, when he had actually been a supporter of the Moderate party in the Church and had spent much of his time lecturing at St Andrews. Converted to an Evangelical view of the Gospel in 1810, his fascination with chemistry, mathematics and geology survived his new-found seriousness about his clerical duties. In 1816, now minister of the Tron Church in Glasgow, he chose astronomy as the subject of a dazzling series of discourses aimed at illustrating the extent of the divine concern for man's moral destiny.[9] In 1833, Chalmers contributed one of the Bridgewater Treatises, a series of eight commissioned works which rank amongst the classics of nineteenth-century natural theology.[10]

Chalmers made no significant discoveries as a scientist. He is perhaps remembered most as an ecclesiastical politician who navigated the Evangelical party through the difficult waters of the Disruption to a secure future outside the Established Church. Earlier, his organisational skills had been exercised in home missionary work in the St John's parish of Glasgow, where he made determined efforts to extend religious influence amongst the poorest classes. Yet his scientific interests were sometimes revealed even in apparently unrelated concerns. He regarded his attempts to reinstate the old parish system of voluntary donations for the poor as 'experiments' which would conclusively prove that compulsory provision was unnecessary and undesirable.[11] As a theologian he also maintained that true theology was 'simply the result of Bacon's inductive method applied to the book of Revelation, as true science was the result of the same method applied to the book of nature'.[12] Chalmers infused Evangelical thought with a new-found openness to secular learning, building on rather than ignoring or rejecting the achievements of the eighteenth-century Enlightenment.

Fleming spent twenty-six years as a minister before his reputation as a mineralogist and zoologist led him into academic life. After a series of papers submitted to the Edinburgh-based Wernerian Natural History Society, he had his first major work, the *Philosophy of Zoology* published in 1822.[13] He was involved in a number of geological controversies and earned a certain amount of notoriety for the ferocity of his attacks on theories he regarded as inadequate. In 1834 he became professor of natural philosophy at King's College, Aberdeen. After the Disruption, he was made professor of natural science at the Free Church's New College in Edinburgh.

The odd man out of the four appears to be Hugh Miller, in that he was younger (born 1802), received little formal education and never held a university appointment. Perhaps one of Scotland's greatest exemplars of the self-taught man, Miller was both an important figure in Evangelical science and an effective campaigner for his party in the Church. As editor of the *Witness* newspaper he contributed fiery polemics on ecclesiastical politics alongside articles about geology; his discoveries – of evidence for life-forms no longer present in creation – in the fossils of the Old Red Sandstone formation followed earlier work by Fleming, with whom he became friendly during the 1830s.[14]

The Church of Scotland (and, after 1843, the Free Church) could not make any claims of uniqueness for a clergyman who wrote works on zoology (Fleming) or a theologically inclined geologist (Miller). Nor was there anything particularly unusual about a natural philosopher concerned with the religious implications of physical theories (Brewster) or even a theology professor (previously a minister) who had drawn big congregations for a series of astronomical sermons (Chalmers). The religious flavour, sometimes fervour, which penetrated early nineteenth-century science was not confined to Scottish Evangelicals. Anglican Broad Churchmen like William Whewell and Adam Sedgwick were also enthusiastic in tracing marks of the Creator's wisdom and goodness in the natural world.[15] Nor was there anything particularly new about the theological enterprise in which they were engaged. The intellectual foundations of natural theology were laid in the early Christian era in the assertion that, from the evidence of design in the world, it was possible to infer the existence and some of the attributes of a designer.[16]

In the eighteenth century the triumphs of the Newtonian world view appeared to confirm the orderliness and regularity of nature.[17] Everywhere was balance and fine adjustment of part to part. Some natural theologians found in this a guarantee that the social and political order was also divinely ordained. William Paley, the foremost natural theologian of the late eighteenth century, invoked the living world to establish the essential benevolence of the Creator. Evidence of pain and suffering was minimised. 'It is', wrote Paley,

> a happy world after all. The air, the earth, the water, teem with delighted existence. In a spring noon, or a summer evening, on whichever side I turn my eyes, myriads of happy beings crowd upon my view.[18]

Well into the nineteenth century, natural theology continued to provide a common culture, linking clergymen and men of science. Scottish Evangelical intellectuals like Chalmers belonged to this culture, although they were keenly aware of the limitations of natural theology in bringing fallen men to a recognition of their path to salvation. Although Chalmers often expressed these reservations, they were not intended to undermine the whole enterprise. The balance between advocacy and criticism was a subtle one to maintain, and an Evangelical emphasis on the unique status and destiny of man could easily appear muted amidst enthusiasm for a natural world characterised by its predictability and orderliness.

Indeed, a major element in Chalmers's thinking was the intelligibility and reliability of the external world, and the absence from observable nature of miraculous phenomena.

> Once, in a season of miracle, did the word take the precedency of Nature, but ever since hath Nature resumed her courses, and is now proving, by her steadfastness, the authority of that, which she then proved authentic by her deviations. When the word was first ushered in, Nature gave way for a period, after which she moves in her wonted order, till the present system of things shall pass away and that faith which is now upholden by Nature's constancy, shall then receive its accomplishment at Nature's dissolution.[19]

God could and did intervene in nature, for instance in answer to prayer, but such acts were hidden from view, higher up the chain of causes and effects. The constancy of nature was evidence of adaptation between the mind of man and external nature, since the expectation of constancy was a pre-existing belief, not one arising from experience.

The notion of an ordered, law-like universe lent weight to Chalmers's social philosophy, in which society was held to be part of external nature, a divine product beyond the reach of human tampering. The political economy of this God-given regime combined elements from Adam Smith with the law of population set forth by Thomas Malthus. Smith's concept of an invisible hand which derived beneficial results from the interplay of competing individuals contrasted with the gloomier Malthusian principle which held that population growth was for ever tending to outstrip food supply.[20] Yet Chalmers's interpretation of Malthus made the law essentially benign, as moral restraint (allowed only a very limited role by Malthus) became the key to man's social elevation.[21] Later marriage and smaller families meant greater prosperity for the poorer classes. Given the benefits of Christian education, they were transformed by Chalmers from Malthusian victims into agents of their own destiny.

Such was the intellectual rationale for Chalmers's opposition to compulsory poor-relief and for his hostility to any 'artificial' attempts at rebuilding society. It did not matter whether the scheme was inspired by Christian teaching or by overtly atheistic ideas such as those of the socialist and co-operative pioneer, Robert Owen. No Utopian, Chalmers was nevertheless optimistic about the future destiny of man. To the labouring classes in particular, he held out the prospect of 'gaining, every generation, on the distance which now separates them from the upper classes of society'.[22] Indeed, universal Christian education provided 'a guarantee for the progressive conquests, and at length the ultimate triumph, of good over evil in society'.[23]

Chalmers's dominant position in the Free Church makes him an obvious starting-point for a study of Evangelical natural theology. John Fleming, by contrast, wrote little about theological and devotional topics and almost nothing on social and political issues. Yet it is possible to find echoes of Chalmers in Fleming's discussions of the natural world. In his *Philosophy of Zoology*, he set forth a view of the animal kingdom in which there waged 'a wasteful war', where '[t]ribe is divided against tribe, and species against species'.[24] This was not, however, a complete overturning of the comfortable, harmonious world of Paley, rather a plea for seeing nature in a more balanced, less one-sided way. For instance, the Scottish zoologist was concerned that those seeking evidence of design and adaptation often looked only at the ways certain animals protected themselves against predators whilst ignoring the interests of the predators themselves. What benefited the victim deprived the hunter and if, for instance, the white covering of the alpine hare and the ptarmigan effectively hid them from their enemies, 'the eagle, the cat, and the fox ... would be in danger of starvation and death'.[25] Naturalists who took such a limited view missed the real purpose of the white covering, which, according to Fleming, was to keep the animal warm in winter.

Fleming fought hard against all attempts to force nature into imperfect, man-made categories. Just as Chalmers sought to dispel what he saw as man-made, visionary theories about society, which ignored the workings of the true, divinely ordained legislation, so Fleming put to flight all the imperfect attempts at system building of philosophical naturalists, who failed to do justice to nature in all its complexity. At various times, Huttonian geologists,[26] diluvialists (who looked for geological evidence of the Mosaic flood)[27] and disciples of the anatomist Georges Cuvier[28] felt the stings of his methodological lash. Fleming's whole career as a naturalist was characterised by an unwillingness to enlist in any particular theoretical camp. The geologist Sir Charles Lyell was even moved to warn his friend that he was being labelled 'the Zoological Ishmael'.[29]

David Brewster's lifelong opposition to the undulatory theory of light has also been explained by Morse[30] and Cantor[31] in terms of an unwillingness to bequeath to future natural theologians the unwelcome baggage of a discarded theory. The undulatory theory could not explain all the observable phenomena, including selective absorption and refractive dispersion, as well as certain photochemical effects such as the blackening of silver salts. In addition, it postulated the existence of a transmission medium, the luminiferous ether, for which there was no independent evidence. To allow such a hypothetical entity into the sanctum of established science would be to profane the temple. Although Brewster was happy to use the undulatory hypothesis in order to make predictions and suggest experiments, it could not possibly be a true theory.

To the Evangelical natural theologians, it was not knowledge of the natural order which presented a threat to orthodox belief, but human attempts to go beyond what was actually known about this order. During the Disruption years, they perceived such threats to be increasing. It was an age of mechanics' institutes, popular lectures and cheap literature; an age when orthodox Christianity had to contend with cults and philosophies which promised much to the initiate. It was also an era of industrialisation, of rapid growth in the size of the urban working classes, of Chartism, of periodic industrial unrest and of disease epidemics, including a major outbreak of cholera in 1832. Both the working classes and their social superiors in the middle ranks of society were in search of solutions, sometimes based on social reform, science or Evangelism, often on some combination of the three. Such changes provide the background not only for Chalmers's social experiments in Glasgow but also for the growth of heretical and anti-clerical movements, many of which looked to science and even to a version of natural theology for their intellectual rationale. In Scotland during the 1830s and 1840s, the most important secularist group centred on the teachings of the lawyer-turned-phrenologist George Combe, author of the best-selling work, *The Constitution of Man*.

Phrenology, now surviving only on the remote fringes of pseudo-science, enjoyed an enormous following in the early to mid-nineteenth century.[32] It originated in Austria in the work of the physician Franz Josef Gall[33] and was brought to Britain by his pupil Johann Gaspar Spurzheim.[34] Its basic propositions were very simple: the brain, as the organ of the mind, manifested a different physical development in different individuals. Much as people varied in muscular physique, in the size of their bones and lungs, so too could they vary in their cerebral endowment. This endowment showed on the surface, not only of the brain, but also of the skull which enclosed it. The brain was not a single homogeneous organ; rather, it consisted of many faculties, each one located in a different area, each one corresponding to a different mental characteristic. From the size of the associated parts of the skull, the individual's strengths and weaknesses could be 'read'. Conclusions could be drawn about his career prospects, suitable choice of marriage partner and general moral character.

The phrenologists were especially interested in the extremes of human achievement and depravity: phrenological texts were often illustrated with drawings of the skulls of great artists and composers, as well as those of notorious murderers. Phrenology was both an entertaining do-it-yourself science and the basis of a social philosophy, with implications for education, and the treatment of prisoners, paupers and the mentally ill. It also became a stick with which to beat orthodox religion.

In 1820, George Combe helped to found a Phrenological Society in Edinburgh, which initially embraced a wide range of religious opinion. Among other founder members was the Church of Scotland minister David

Welsh, a prominent Evangelical who went on to become professor of Church history at Edinburgh University. In 1826, there were five other clergymen members, including the Revd Robert Buchanan, another leading Evangelical.[35] By this time, clashes were breaking out in the Society between theologically orthodox phrenologists and the heterodox school under Combe's leadership. Combe's lectures in the winter of 1826–27 and a privately circulated *Essay on the Constitution of Man* ventured into the sensitive territory of man's moral condition and prospects.[36] Combe held out the hope that, by a prolonged process of education, the majority of the race could be brought into a state where the superior faculties, the moral sentiments and intellect, regained their natural position of command. Enlightened man would come to discover and obey the 'natural laws', which amounted to divine commands and regulated all aspects of our existence.

These ideas were set out in greater detail in Combe's full-length treatise on *The Constitution of Man*, first published in 1828.[37] Soon to become a bestseller and a target for clerical anathemas, its appearance caused a split in the Phrenological Society and the resignation of Welsh and other clergymen. It also triggered a pamphlet warfare which reached its height in 1836, when Combe was an unsuccessful candidate for the chair of logic and metaphysics at Edinburgh University.[38] Hostilities continued into the 1840s.

Combe and his supporters – who included the educationalist James Simpson, the astronomer John Pringle Nichol, the publisher Robert Chambers, and Charles Maclaren, editor of the *Scotsman* newspaper – had by this time given up any hope of reaching an accommodation with Evangelical opinion. Indeed, they were openly opposed to attempts by the Established Church to maintain its dominant influence on the national education system and privately scornful of all the main tenets of orthodox belief. Sympathetic reviewers nevertheless regarded *The Constitution of Man* as a work of natural theology: for instance, the *Scotsman* thought it had 'considerable analogy to the Bridgewater treatises'.[39] Evangelical critics, on the other hand, linked Combe's philosophy of the natural laws with deistic ideas which had gained wide currency in revolutionary France.

To answer Combe, the Evangelical party recruited William Scott, a lawyer and a former member of the Phrenological Society, who had vehemently attacked the *Essay on the Constitution of Man*. Scott's replies are interesting for their social pessimism and for their dark and hostile image of the natural world. His strategy was to admit the truth of phrenology and then to demonstrate that it did not lead logically to Combe's doctrine of the natural laws. He tried to collapse the hierarchical view of the faculties, arguing that the moral sentiments could just as well be directed towards selfish ends as could the lower faculties. Conversely, the lower propensities, such as philoprogenitiveness (the love of one's offspring) could incline an individual to acts of utter disinterestedness. In any case, the predominance of the lower faculties was evidence of adaptation, not of mismatch, between man's mental constitution and the external world. Man was a fallen creature whose survival depended on the exercise of these more brutish elements in his nature. Nor could the world of non-human nature offer any glimpses of a kinder, less painful regime:

> Mr Combe can never get rid of the unquestionable fact that the animal creation are constantly suffering evils of the most appalling description, which they are altogether incapable of avoiding. In most cases, the highest enjoyment of the one is attended by the laceration, destruction and death of another.[40]

In administering an antidote to Combe, Scott travelled far from the 'happy world' of Paley, or even from the 'wasteful war' which Fleming had described, where at least '[l]imits' were assigned to its ravages and 'the excess only of the population is cut off'. In his social views, Scott also manifested a conservatism deeper and darker than Chalmers's, despite apparently winning the Church leader's approval for his work.[41] Reiterating the law of Malthus in its bleakest form, Scott suggested that periodic hunger would provide the lower classes with the only effective incentive to work, and keep in check the activity of their lower faculties.

Scott's strategy was not the only one by which to attack Combe, and Brewster and Fleming preferred to cut the knot rather than to untie it: like other members of academic and professional élites, they poured scorn on the whole enterprise of phrenology, not just on *The Constitution of Man*.[42] However, the Evangelical periodical press generally followed Scott and tried to prise the natural laws away from the faculty psychology.

Even with a large popular following, phrenology could be pushed to the margins of science: indeed, its appeal to the ill-educated and to women was eagerly seized on by its enemies as proof of its absurdity. It was much harder to dismiss as marginal whole tracts of material from geology, morphology and a wealth of other sciences ranging from astronomy to social statistics. This extraordinary range of sources characterised the anonymous work *Vestiges of the Natural History of Creation*, published in 1844.[43] It was in fact written by a member of Combe's circle, the Edinburgh publisher and bookseller Robert Chambers, and it followed the example of *The Constitution of Man* in becoming a bestseller.

With the benefit of hindsight, *Vestiges* has been labelled a forerunner of Darwin's *Origin of Species*.[44] Certainly it anticipated Darwin in suggesting that species were not fixed and that existing plant and animal life had arisen out of a succession of now extinct species, which could be traced, albeit in a fragmentary way, in the fossil record. There were, however, enormous differences between *Vestiges* and *Origin*; and indeed between their respective authors.

Vestiges was based on wide reading rather than on painstaking fieldwork. Its explanation of species change – an inherent progressive tendency in living matter – was closer to that of the French naturalist Lamarck than that of Darwin, though Chambers mistakenly attributed to Lamarck the view that pressure from the environment was the main cause of change. The bold aim of *Vestiges* was to argue for a grand principle of development, as comprehensive and important as the law of gravitation. As with *The Constitution of Man*, natural theology provided the framework: *Vestiges* abounded with references to the 'Almighty Deviser', the 'Divine Author', the 'Great Ruler of Nature'.[45]

Words like 'charlatan' and 'sciolist' recurred in the torrent of abuse which was heaped upon the book's anonymous author.[46] They could not disguise the deep anxiety he had aroused amongst men of science holding orthodox religious beliefs – from Adam Sedgwick at Cambridge University to Hugh Miller in Scotland. Yet close study of reactions to *Vestiges* reveals differences of opinion over what should be preserved from the rather loosely constructed edifice of natural theology which they had collectively fashioned.

For the Scottish Evangelicals, suspicion immediately fell upon the nebular hypothesis. This theory originally related uniformities in the solar system to its origins in a gaseous cloud, from which planets had condensed and separated. The theory, put forward by the French natural philosopher Pierre Simon Laplace,[47] had been generalised to other solar systems by the astronomer William Herschel to explain the existence of nebulous clouds, which even telescopes of increasing power had failed to resolve into stars.[48] Perhaps, reasoned Herschel, these clouds were not star clusters but true nebulae, the parents of star systems like our own.

Despite the parentage of the nebular hypothesis in the work of an 'infidel' French philosopher, British natural theologians cheerfully integrated it into a theistic view of Creation. At one level, the notion of a gradually cooling earth made sense of geological changes requiring significant amounts of heat.[49] At a more sublime level, the nebular hypothesis brought a new teleological element into natural theology. The earth's history could be seen as part of a still grander and longer process by which physical nature was shaped and eventually made ready for living matter, and finally for man.

In Scotland, the popularisation of the theory by Professor J. P. Nichol, a friend and supporter of Combe, did not lessen its acceptability to religious opinion.[50] Indeed, before *Vestiges*, the hypothesis had no more fervent supporter than David Brewster. Elsewhere I have documented in detail the speed and completeness with which he abandoned the theory when he saw how it had been used by Chambers to argue that the whole of nature, both organic and inorganic, was ruled by a principle of development. In 1838, Brewster had defended the nebular theory against accusations of fostering atheism.[51] As late as 1844 he had referred to it as 'a law of progressive creation, in which revolving matter is distributed into suns and planets'.[52] After reading *Vestiges*, he was describing the nebular cosmogony as a hypothesis 'improbable in its very nature and … gratuitous in all its assumptions'.[53] Through the 1850s he continued to attack the theory with all the zeal of a convert recoiling in horror from past mistakes. To such an extent did he conflate the nebular and development theories that he hailed Darwin's theory of evolution as 'the more offensive offspring' of the nebular theory, 'the great parent heresy'.[54] *Vestiges* had a similar effect on Miller's attitude to the nebular cosmogony[55] although he and Brewster soon found additional ammunition in Nichol's own loss of confidence in the theory, following the apparent resolution into stars of the nebula in the Orion constellation.[56]

Not all critics of *Vestiges* agreed with Brewster's strategy. Adam Sedgwick, author of one of the earliest and longest critiques, pointed out some of the problems which attended the nebular theory, such as its failure to account for the motion of comets and the retrograde motion of the satellites of Uranus. Nevertheless, he continued to regard it as a 'splendid vision' and hoped that it would triumph over these difficulties.[57] Even when the theory's fortunes were definitely waning, some of its erstwhile supporters were at pains to rescue it from the taint of the undesirable company it had been keeping. One reviewer (in a journal which supported the rump of the Established Church after the Disruption) asked whether Brewster would similarly abandon the theory of gravitation because Laplace had used it in support of 'godless materialism'.[58]

The Evangelical attack on the nebular hypothesis was a symptom of their disaffection from any theology of nature which ceded too much to the reign of natural law. Deprived of the nebular hypothesis and its associated vision of the earth's history, Brewster suggested that direct divine intervention might have occurred even in physical events, as well as in the creation of life.[59] Miller, in writings just before his death in 1856, wondered whether during earlier geological periods, 'breaches [of the order of nature] ... were scarce more exceptional than the observance'.[60] Another Evangelical, the Revd John Duns, who succeeded Fleming in the chair of natural science at New College, was driven to express regret at the 'distrust of the simple acknowledgement of the probable presence of miracle in the different stages of the building up of the world'.[61]

There was a growing tendency to see nature, not as a balance of forces held in check by the will of the Creator, but as a balance frequently upset. The Evangelicals were losing confidence in the voluntaristic notion that laws, as mere expressions of the divine will, meant no exclusion of the Creator from his realm. Their view of nature became more 'catastrophist', more highly charged with the threat of sudden, violent disaster. This doom-laden position had to some extent been prefigured in the debates following the publication of *The Constitution of Man*. *Vestiges* was recognisably a product of the same secularist school: indeed, Combe and Nichol, as well as Chambers himself, were high on the list of suspected authors.[62]

It would be left to another generation of Evangelical intellectuals to come to terms with the development theory, although in a Darwinian rather than a Vestigian form. Livingstone has provided a valuable survey of this process, giving the lie to the notion that creationism was the normal Evangelical position in the late nineteenth century.[63] Of particular importance in the Scottish context is the theologian James McCosh, who studied under Chalmers and eventually became president of Princeton College, New Jersey.[64]

There was an enormous conceptual shift involved in accepting that species could be formed out of other species rather than individually created. Brewster, Miller and other Scottish Evangelicals resembled other scientific contemporaries who failed to make this change. In the 1840s, the Evangelicals were actually moving in the opposite direction, towards a universe subject to decay and dissolution, sustained and repaired by acts of divine intervention. The need to combat a rising tide of secularism, stirred up by the false science of *The Constitution of Man*, and of *Vestiges*, helped to impel them along this path. This need was particularly acute in an era of religious upheaval and fragmentation: the timing of *Vestiges*, one year after the Disruption, could hardly have been worse in this respect.

It would be an exaggeration to suggest that either the publication of *Vestiges* or the Disruption itself led to the emergence of a distinctively Evangelical or 'Free Church' style of science, since a wariness of 'natural laws' and all-embracing theories had been evident, at least in embryonic form, well before the 1840s. The appearance of *Vestiges* did, however, encourage the establishment of the chair of natural science at New College in 1845, to which Fleming was appointed.[65] From the beginning, some in the Free Church had wanted New College to be more than a mere theological college and offer the entire range of university subjects. Even those who took a narrower view of New College recognised that science was becoming something of an ideological battleground and that the Free Church clergy would need to be intellectually armed for the fray. Fleming specifically referred to the challenge posed by the *Vestiges* in the debate at the Free Church General Assembly in Inverness in 1845, when the decision to establish the chair was taken.[66]

Although these ecclesiastical and scientific issues undoubtedly played a part in the process, in the case of Brewster and Miller it is tempting to look for secondary reasons in their personal and social experiences. Brewster, as an opponent of the undulatory theory of light, was an increasingly isolated and embittered figure in the scientific community. At St Andrews, he became embroiled in further controversies with the ruling Moderate establishment. After the Disruption, his adversaries tried unsuccessfully to eject him from his post of principal for having quit the Established Church.[67]

Miller also reaped a bitter harvest during his later years. By the late 1840s, he was increasingly prone to ill health, brought on partly by the rigours of his early life as a stonemason and partly by the pressures of editing the *Witness*. By the 1850s, his mind, as well as his body, showed signs of illness and he began to suffer from terrifying visions. In December 1856, after a particularly horrifying experience of this kind, he wrote a farewell note to his wife and shot himself. It is perhaps not too fanciful to suggest that men suffering these kinds of dislocations in their personal lives should increasingly view the natural world as a place that was disordered and out of joint.

NOTES

1   John H. Brooke, 'The Natural Theology of the Geologists: Some Theological Strata', in L. J. Jordanova and R. S. Porter (eds), *Images of the Earth: Essays in the History of the Environmental Sciences* (Chalfont St Giles, 1979), pp. 39–64.
2   David Brewster (1781–1868). The only full-length biography of Brewster is by his daughter, Margaret Maria Gordon [née Brewster], *The Home Life of Sir David Brewster* (Edinburgh, 1869). Many aspects of Brewster's career are covered in A. Morrison-Low and J. R. R. Christie (eds), *'Martyr of Science': Sir David Brewster 1781–1868* (Edinburgh, 1984). This contains the fullest

bibliography of Brewster's work (pp. 107–36) and a bibliography of works about him (pp. 137–8).

3 Thomas Chalmers (1780–1847). For biographies of Chalmers, see William Hanna, *Memoirs of the Life and Writings of Thomas Chalmers*, 4 vols (Edinburgh, 1849–52); Hugh Watt, *Thomas Chalmers and the Disruption* (Edinburgh, 1943). Several biographies appeared in the nineteenth century but Hanna's is by far the most detailed. For more recent studies, see Stewart J. Brown, *Thomas Chalmers and the Godly Commonwealth* (Oxford, 1982); A. C. Cheyne (ed.), *The Practical and the Pious Essays on Thomas Chalmers (1780–1847)* (Edinburgh, 1985).

4 Hugh Miller (1802–56). For the principal biographies of Miller, see P. Bayne, *The Life and Letters of Hugh Miller*, 2 vols (London, 1871); W. M. MacKenzie, *Hugh Miller: A Critical Study* (London, 1905); W. Keith Leask, *Hugh Miller* (Edinburgh and London, 1896). MacKenzie is perhaps the most perceptive in discussing Miller's scientific work. A brief recent biography appears in George Rosie, *Hugh Miller Outrage and Order: A Biography and Selected Writings* (Edinburgh, 1981). See also *Dictionary of Scientific Biography*, s.v. 'Miller, Hugh' by M. J. S. Rudwick.

5 John Fleming (1785–1857). For biographies of Fleming, see John Duns, 'Memoir' in John Fleming, *The Lithology of Edinburgh: edited, with a memoir by the Rev. John Duns, Torphichen* (Edinburgh, 1859); Alexander Bryson, 'Memoir of the Rev. John Fleming, D.D., F.R.S.E.', *Transactions of the Royal Society of Edinburgh*, 22 (1861), pp. 655–80. The latter contains a fairly full list of his publications. See also *Dictionary of Scientific Biography*, s.v. 'Fleming, John', by L. E. Page.

6 See e.g. the claim by Fleming's biographer, the Revd. John Duns, that 'Scotland might be lawfully proud of such a group of men, whose scientific labours are associated with her Christianity, as that which contains the names – Thomas Chalmers, Hugh Miller, John Fleming and David Brewster' ([Duns], 'Scottish Natural Science', *North British Review*, 28 (1858), p. 79).) For more on the biographical links amongst these four men, see Paul Baxter, 'Science and Belief in Scotland, 1805–1868: the Scottish Evangelicals', unpublished Ph.D. Dissertation (Univ. of Edinburgh, 1985).

7 For details of Fleming's meetings with Chalmers, see Hanna, *Memoirs*, vol. 1, p. 178.

8 For an introduction to Brewster's optical studies see *Dictionary of Scientific Biography*, s.v. 'Brewster, David', by E. W. Morse.

9 Thomas Chalmers, *A Series of Discourses on the Christian Revelation Viewed in Connection with the Modern Astronomy* (Glasgow, 1817). For a discussion of the *Discourses* see David Cairns, 'Thomas Chalmers' Astronomical Discourses: A Study in Natural Theology', *Scottish Journal of Theology*, 9 (1956), pp. 410–21.

10 Thomas Chalmers, *On the Power, Wisdom and Goodness of God as Manifested in the Adaptation of External Nature to the Moral and Intellectual Constitution of Man*, 2 vols (London, 1833).

11 For an assessment of Chalmers's efforts to deal with pauperism in St John's, see Andrew L. Drummond and James Bulloch, *The Scottish Church 1688–1843: The Age of the Moderates* (Edinburgh, 1973), pp. 172–7.

12 Quoted in *Dictionary of National Biography*, s.v. 'Chalmers, Thomas'.

13 John Fleming, *The Philosophy of Zoology: or a General View of the Structure. Functions and Classification of Animals*, 2 vols (Edinburgh, 1822).

14 Miller's first major geological work was *The Old Red Sandstone: or, New Walks in an Old Field* (Edinburgh, 1841). Later works included *Footprints of the Creator: or, The Asterolepis of Stromness* (London, 1849) and the posthumously published *The Testimony of the Rocks: or, Geology in its Bearings on the Two Theologies, Natural and Revealed* (Edinburgh, 1857).

15 For accounts of the Anglican Broad Church scientists, see Walter F. Cannon, 'Scientists and Broad Churchmen: An Early Victorian Network', *Journal of British Studies*, 4 (1964), pp. 65–88; Susan Faye (formerly Walter F.) Cannon, *Science in Culture: The early Victorian Period* (Folkestone, 1978).

16 For a general account of the history and use of the design argument see *Dictionary of the History of Ideas*, s.v. 'Design Argument', by Frederick Ferre.

17 A good introduction to natural theology and its relevance to British science in the eighteenth and nineteenth centuries is John H. Brooke, 'Natural Theology in Britain from Boyle to Paley', in J. H. Brooke, R. Hooykaas and C. Lawless (eds), *New Interactions between Theology and Natural Science* (Milton Keynes, 1974), pp. 5–54.

18 William Paley, *Natural Theology: or Evidence of the Existence and Attributes of the Deity Collected from the Appearances of Nature* (London, 1802), p. 490.

19 Thomas Chalmers, 'The Constancy of God in His Works an Argument for the Faithfulness of God in His Word', in id., ... *The Collected Works of Thomas Chalmers*, 25 vols (Glasgow, 1835–42), vol. 7, pp. 239–40. The world would of course eventually come to an end, so even the constancy of nature was a temporary regime, but one in which we could nevertheless repose full confidence. For a discussion of this topic, see Crosbie Smith, 'From Design to Dissolution: Thomas Chalmers' Debt to John Robison', *British Journal for the History of Science*, 12 (1979), pp. 59–70.

20 Adam Smith, *An Inquiry into the Nature and Causes of the Wealth of Nations*, 2 vols (London, 1776); Thomas Robert Malthus, *An Essay on the Principle of Population, as it Affects the Future Improvement of Society with Remarks on the Speculations of Mr Godwin, M Condorcet and Other Writers* (London, 1798).

21 This reinterpretation of Malthus's ideas is discussed in Robert M. Young, 'Malthus and the Evolutionists: The Common Context of Biological and Social Theory', *Past and Present*, 43 (1969), pp. 109–45.

22 Chalmers, *On the Power, Wisdom and Goodness of God*, vol. 2, p. 51.

23 Ibid., vol. 1, p. 184.

24 Fleming, *Philosophy of Zoology*, vol. 2, p. 6.

25 Ibid., p. 21.

26 Two major geognostic schools confronted one another in early nineteenth-century Scotland. The neptunists, inspired by the teachings of the German geognost Abraham Gottlob Werner, argued for the primacy of water as a geological agent. The vulcanists followed the eighteenth-century Scottish natural philosopher James Hutton in stressing the importance of heat, particularly in forming granite, porphyry and basalt, and in producing solid rock out of sediments (a process in which intense pressure also played a part). Fleming's papers to the Wernerian Natural History Society frequently criticised the Huttonians for failing to pay sufficient attention to observable phenomena.

27 For an account of Fleming's attacks on the diluvial theory, see L. E. Page, 'Diluvialism and its Critics', in C. J. Schneer (ed.), *Towards a History of Geology* (Cambridge, Mass., 1969), rep. in C. A. Russell (ed.) *Science and Religious Belief: A Selection of Recent Historical Studies* (London, 1973), pp. 210–23.

28 See e.g. Fleming, *Philosophy of Zoology*, vol. 2, p. 138, where he criticises Cuvier for placing limits on the Creator's resourcefulness by maintaining that there were certain invariable co-occurrences of different organs in animals. This principle, useful in reasoning about the form and habits of extinct animals from fragmentary fossil remains, enabled Cuvier to infer, for instance, that a hoofed animal would be a herbivore.

29 Charles Lyell to John Fleming, 3 Feb. 1830, in Katherine M. Lyell, *Life, Letters and Journals of Sir Charles Lyell, Bart*, 2 vols (London, 1881), vol. 1, p. 259.

30 E. W. Morse, 'Natural Philosophy, Hypotheses and Impiety: Sir David Brewster Confronts the Undulatory Theory of Light', Ph.D. Dissertation, (Univ. of California, Berkeley, 1972).

31 G. N. Cantor, 'Brewster on the Nature of Light', in Morrison-Low and Christie, *Martyr of Science*, pp. 67–76.

32 For general accounts of phrenology in Britain, see David de Giustino, *Conquest of Mind, Phrenology and Victorian Social Thought* (London, 1975); Roger Cooter, *The Cultural Meaning of Popular Science: Phrenology and the Organisation of Consent in Nineteenth Century Britain* (Cambridge, 1984).

33 F. J. Gall's works included *On the Functions of the Brain and of Each of its Parts* (transl. of *Sur les Fonctions du Cerveau* (Paris, 1822–5)), 6 vols (Boston, 1835).

34 J. G. Spurzheim's works included: *The Physiognomical System of Drs Gall and Spurzheim* (London, 1815); *A View of the Elementary Principles of Education* (Edinburgh, 1821).

35 'List of Members of the Phrenological Society', *Phrenological Journal*, 3 (1825–6), pp. 478–80.

36 George Combe, *Essay on the Constitution of Man, and its Relations to External Objects* (Edinburgh, 1827).

37 George Combe, *The Constitution of Man Considered in Relation to External Objects* (Edinburgh, 1828).

38 See e.g., Anon., 'Scott's Harmony of Phrenology with Scripture', *Edinburgh Christian Instructor*, 5 (1836), pp. 587–94; Anon., 'Combe's Constitution of Man', *Presbyterian Review*, 9 (1836–7), pp. 92–118; Anon.,'The Harmony of Phrenology with Scripture', *Church of Scotland Magazine*, 3 (1836), pp. 366–76, pp. 445–54.

39 'Literature', *Scotsman*, 28 Oct. 1835 (review of Combe). *The Constitution of Man*, 4th edn. (1835).

40 William Scott, *A Few Last Words to Mr Combe on the Subject of the Natural Laws* (Edinburgh, 1828), p. 13. See also id., *The Harmony of Phrenology with Scripture, shewn in a refutation of the Philosophical Errors contained in Mr Combe's 'Constitution of Man'* (Edinburgh, 1836).

41 George Combe to J. P. Nichol, 22 Nov. 1836, National Library of Scotland MS7387 f. 193 notes that Chalmers had 'pronounced a high eulogium on Mr Scott's book' in his class.

42 For a sociological analysis of reactions to phrenology, see Steven Shapin, 'Phrenological Knowledge and the Social Structure of Early Nineteenth Century Edinburgh', *Annals of Science*, 32 (1975), pp. 219–43. For Brewster's views on phrenology, see e.g. [David Brewster], 'Dr Roget's Bridgewater Treatise – Animal and Vegetable Physiology', *Edinburgh Review*, 60 (1834), p. 178. For Fleming's comments see John Fleming to Patrick Neill, 28 Oct. 1835, in Fleming, *Lithology of Edinburgh*, pp. lxxii–lxxiii.

43 [Robert Chambers], *Vestiges of the Natural History of Creation* (London, 1844). For a general account of *Vestiges*, see Milton Millhauser, *Just before Darwin Robert Chambers and Vestiges* (Middletown, Conn., 1959).

44 For opposite views on Chambers as a forerunner of Darwin, see A. O. Lovejoy, 'The Argument for Organic Evolution before the *Origin of Species*, 1830–1858' in Hiram B. Glass, Oswei Temkin and William L. Straus (eds), *Forerunners of Darwin, 1747–1859* (Baltimore, 1968); M. J. S. Hodge, 'The Universal Gestation of Nature: Chambers' *Vestiges* and *Explanations*', *Journal of the History of Biology*, 5 (1972), pp. 127–51.

45 [Chambers], *Vestiges*, p. 168 ('Almighty Deviser'), p. 198 ('Divine Author'), p. 376 ('Great Ruler of Nature').

46 For a bibliography of contemporary reactions to *Vestiges*, see Millhauser, *Just before Darwin*, pp. 229–32.

47 Pierre Simon Laplace, *Exposition du Système du Monde*, 2 vols (Paris, 1796), vol. 2, pp. 301–3.

48 William Herschel, 'Astronomical Observations Relating to the Construction of the Heavens, Arranged for the Purpose of a Critical Examination, the Result of which Appears to Throw some New Light upon the Organization of the Celestial Bodies', *Philosophical Transactions of the Royal Society of London*, 101 (1811), pp. 269–345.

49 For a discussion of the influence of the nebular hypothesis on a 'directionalist' view of the earth's physical history and on debates about geological causation, see Philip Lawrence, 'Heaven and Earth – the Relation of the Nebular Hypothesis to Geology', in W. Yourgrau and A. D. Breck (eds), *Cosmology, History and Theology* (New York, 1977), pp. 253–81.

50 The main work by Nichol in which the theory was described was *Views of the Architecture of the Heavens: In a Series of Letters to a Lady* (Edinburgh, 1837).

51   [David Brewster], 'M. Comte's *Course of Positive Philosophy*', *Edinburgh Review*, 67 (1838), pp. 276–7.
52   Id., 'The Earl of Rosse's Reflecting Telescopes', *North British Review*, 2 (1845), p. 212.
53   Id., '*Vestiges of the Natural History of Creation*', *North British Review*, 3 (1845), p. 480.
54   David Brewster, 'The Facts and Fancies of Mr Darwin', *Good Words*, 3 (1862), pp. 8–9. For discussions of the relationship, supportive and otherwise, between the 'nebular' and evolutionary theories, see Ronald L. Numbers, *Creation by Natural Law Laplace's Nebular Hypothesis in American Thought* (Seattle, 1977); Stephen G. Brush, 'The Nebular Hypothesis and the Evolutionary Worldview', *History of Science*, 25 (1987), pp. 245–78.
55   Miller wrote, or at least, as editor, approved an item ('The Nebular Theory', *Witness*, 26 July 1845) in which Nichol was commended for not abandoning the nebular hypothesis, despite the resolution of some nebulous clouds, previously thought to be true nebulae. In an undated but presumably later letter, he asked:

> How, I marvel, are the Astronomical Geologists to get on without their nebula matter. It will be a tremendous downfall if, like mere vulgar Christians, – people like you & I, – they have to believe in Creation after all. It was of course High Science to hold that worlds were formed out of fire-mist; but it will be mere Theology to hold that they have been created out of nothing. (Hugh Miller to Alexander Rose, n.d., in Mary Tweedie Stodart Rose, *Alexander Rose, Geologist and his Grandson Robert Traill Rose, Artist* (Edinburgh, 1956), p. 14)

56   For the recantation of his support for the nebular theory, see J. P. Nichol, *Thoughts on Some Important Points Relating to the System of the World* (Edinburgh, 1846), especially pp. 65–6.
57   [Adam Sedgwick], 'Natural History of Creation', *Edinburgh Review*, 82 (1845), p. 19.
58   Anon.,'Notes on Theology and Science', *Macphail's Edinburgh Ecclesiastical Journal*, 7 (1849), p. 135.
59   [David Brewster], 'Murchison's *Siluria*', *North British Review*, 21 (1854), p. 544.
60   Hugh Miller, *Sketch-book of Popular Geology: Being a Series of Lectures Delivered before the Philosophical Institution of Edinburgh* (Edinburgh, 1859), p. 207.
61   [John Duns], 'Genesis and Science', *North British Review*, 27 (1857), p. 333.
62   In 1848, suspicion of Chambers was great enough for him to withdraw as candidate for Lord Provost of Edinburgh (see Millhauser, *Just before Darwin*, p. 3). From 1860, and possibly earlier, until at least 1877, the British Museum Library Catalogue listed Combe as author. (Information supplied by staff of the inquiry desk, British Library Humanities and Social Sciences Main Reading Room.)
63   David N. Livingstone, *Darwin's Forgotten Defenders: The Encounter between Evangelical Theology and Evolutionary Thought* (Edinburgh, 1987).
64   For a recent study of McCosh, see J. David Hoeveler, *James McCosh and the Scottish Intellectual Tradition: From Glasgow to Princeton* (Princeton, NJ, 1981).
65   For details of Fleming's lectures at New College, see John Fleming, *The Institutes of Natural Science, Exhibiting the Arrangement Followed in the Lectures delivered by Dr Fleming, in the New College, Edinburgh* (Edinburgh, 1846).
66   Reported in *Witness*, 30 Aug. 1845.
67   See Robert Anderson, 'Brewster and the Reform of the Scottish Universities', in Morrison-Low and Christie, *Martyr of Science*, pp. 31–4.

CHAPTER SEVEN

The Disruption in Fiction

ANGUS CALDER

WHY DOES THE GENERAL or common reader in Scotland possess no myth, however remote from documented fact, of the Disruption of 1843? Why has an event which engaged the minds and passions of men regarded as great in their generation almost no resonance for our contemporaries, even in Edinburgh – which saw the climactic drama – a city not backward in emphasising historic traditions, nor, of course, in selling them to tourists? Michael Fry has argued that the Disruption was one of those episodes of a 'Scottish Revolution' in the 1830s and 1840s 'qualified by the destruction they wrought in an ancient polity to stand with almost any other of the national revolutions in Europe during the previous fifty years'.[1] This is not an exaggeration. Many historians now see this as the period in which Scottish independence was at last, and decisively, lost. Yet our children don't know who Miller was, let alone Chalmers.

Several causes can be suggested for this national amnesia. The most obvious is the rapid secularisation of the Scottish intelligentsia after the First World War. Traditions of religious revolt, which had obsessed even the aesthete Stevenson, became increasingly unmentionable. By the last quarter of the twentieth century, a notion that ministers, of every denomination, were and always had been enemies of radical thought and rebellious behaviour was taken for granted. Knox could not be ignored and was ritually lampooned (as in *Mary Queen of Scots got her Head Chopped off*, that popular play from the eighties by Liz Lochhead) even by those who had no sympathy at all for Tory, Catholic or Episcopalian counter-traditions. But the Covenanting rebels of the seventeenth century were deprecated when not wholly occluded: the spate of publication and republication of works about and from their crises dried up in the third decade of our century. By the eighth, well-illustrated and printed memoirs of once-famous missionaries turned up for a few pence in jumble sales. The otherwise admirable movement to create a secular, pluralist, independent nation shuddered away from the Presbyterian themes of the past as if all Calvinists had been Orangemen, all elders Holy Willies.

The Churches themselves, for the most part, now doctrinally evasive and resolutely ecumenical, had no interest in countering such absurdities. Your best chance of getting a sight of relevant books was in a Free Presbyterian shop in Stornoway. So a second cause of amnesia was the reticence of those who knew most. Even the amazing Hugh Miller, whose works of autobiography and natural history had retained for decades 'classic' status, had eventually to be rescued from the waters of Lethe by a journalist, George Rosie, who prefaced his biography and anthology of 1981 with the point that none of its subjects' books were now in print.[2]

But these factors would have counted for much less had just one potent work of fiction fixed, mythologically, an image, however much at variance with documents, of the drama of 1843. Though Scott, from the 1930s on, fell steeply from fashion himself (a turgid Tory tartaniser, as the nationalistic radicals misconceived him), *Old Mortality* continued to present a vivid projection of the Covenanters, and those who now perversely chose to elevate Hogg and even Galt critically above the Wizard of the North rediscovered notable counter-fictions by these men (*The Brownie of Bodsbeck*, *Ringan Gilhaize*), dealing with the same matter. So, playing off all three, a young writer, Harry Tait, could produce a memorable rewriting of myth in his *Ballad of Sawney Bain* (1990). The Covenanters retain mythic presence; the clerics and laity of the Disruption have lost it.

Fictions about the latter's doings have been few. It would be facile to suggest that this is because those most inward with Disruption values had wholesale contempt for literary and other arts, or that the most talented writers of the Free Church heyday were completely alienated from it. Margaret Oliphant, one of the most accomplished and prolific Victorian novelists, came from a Free Church family. Stevenson, self-exiled from puritan Scotland, was nevertheless touched by tales of the Covenanters. The problem – as I think we shall conclude – is not that the men of the Disruption and their heirs were unbendingly puritanical in their rejection of fiction, it is, rather, that they proved to be too reasonable, too worldly, even too Laodicean, to be ranged with Bruce's soldiery, die-hard Cameronians and doomed Jacobites in the 'pageant' of Scottish history. They contended in debate, they chose 'sacrifice': but they landed comfortably poised on their feet. They challenged the premises of the British state – up to a point – but they did not shake the class structure emerging with industrialisation. None of their missions had the glamour attached to the wanderings of that independent Scottish Protestant, Livingstone. Their intellectual, architectural and social achievements merged into the mass of Scottish 'Victorianisms'; their diverse polemical positions into the complexities of sectarian and political debate. Their nemesis was that the fundamentalist seceders of 1900 eventually came to replace them in the Scottish mind – men who, however rebarbative, clearly stood for something distinctive.

This chapter deals with the three most notable novels that present the events of 1843 directly. The first, Lydia Miller's *Passages in the Life of an English Heiress*, was published in 1847,[3] just after the death of the great Chalmers, who features not unvividly in its strange pages. Lydia Miller was Hugh's wife, and her book illuminates positions which he did not disavow, even if he did not fully share them. Since it vanished without trace after one edition (the one copy in the National Library of Scotland (NLS) is falling apart) it cannot be seen as an ideological *agent* of any importance. Its interest, on the contrary, lies in its air of having been ideologically *acted upon*: it reveals cultural cross-currents moving hither and thither the thinking of bourgeois Free Churchers in Miller's Edinburgh.

William Alexander's *Johnny Gibb of Gushetneuk*[4] was, in contrast, highly successful, in newspaper serial form and in popular and deluxe bound editions. In the introduction to its seventeenth edition (Edinburgh, 1912), Alexander Mackie hailed it as a 'local classic ... a work of undoubted genius'. He foresaw, however, that its rich use of Aberdeenshire Doric would present a problem for new readers. 'The dialect will not die yet awhile, but there is little doubt that under a compulsory English education its purity and breadth of vocabulary are already on the wane.'[5] Unsurprisingly, this very factor has educed lavish praise from nationalistic critics in the last couple of decades, and the work is now re-established as a 'Victorian classic' (albeit, out of print.) Alexander was a left-liberal journalist, editor of the *Aberdeen Free Press*, and his view of the Disruption as it affected the rural parish of his own youth was undoubtedly influential. It provides us, *inter alia*, with an opportunity to assess Hume Brown's judgement in his still more influential *History of Scotland* that the Evangelicals of the 1830s and 1840s characteristically asserted 'the rights of the people in opposition to the privileged classes'.[6] If we accept Alexander's fiction as documentary (and it was certainly intended to be so), the verdict will be yes, up to a point. Alexander, in fact, makes the Disruption seem incidental in changing relationships in the countryside involving the Anglicisation of lords, the growth under them of big farmers and the invasion of commerce.

Alexander begins the twenty-sixth of his forty-nine chapters (each originally seen as a self-contained episode in the bi-weekly *Free Press*): 'In the parish of Pyketillim the great event of the Disruption was not seen in any of its grand or striking features.'[7] Quite so. One of the book's many merits is that it conveys how the Disruption, occurring along existing fault-lines in class-divided Scottish society, nevertheless did not 'disrupt' communities traumatically. Wholly sympathetic to the Free Church as Alexander was, he was far too shrewd and humane to idealise its beginnings as millennial, or even, at grass roots, wildly exciting.

His plotting involves quiet use of an Anglicised pro-Establishment laird as *deus ex machina* distributing just deserts, so that the story's very shape resists the egalitarian animus of its eponymous, unheroic, hero.

Robin Jenkins's *The Awakening of George Darroch*, published in 1985, is the work of a distinguished but unlucky writer, whose works have often, in recent years, slunk belatedly into print just as predecessors have fallen out of it. Soon after its appearance, the jury of a national literary prize, wishing to consider *Darroch*, found that its publisher had gone bust and all remaining

copies were warehoused in South-West England. Luckily, a Penguin paper-
back was already on the way, but the book never made the splash which its
vast merits deserved.

As Glenda Norquay has observed, it was 'not surprising' that Jenkins
should take on the Disruption as the subject of his first and only historical
novel. He is interested in what might be called the 'problem of Good' and
the damage which seekers of extreme 'good' can do in a 'relative and
conditional universe'.[8] He presents the Disruption in a starkly dramatic way,
at times in scenes recalling those of late-medieval morality plays, except that
he deploys the psychological insights of a post-Freudian novelist. In 1982,
before *Darroch*'s publication, he went on record about his view of its subject.
Working on the Disruption, he 'very soon became aware that it had not really
been a passionate spiritual crusade but merely a gentlemanly disagreement
over theological matters'. Except in one respect, the Evangelicals

> all wholeheartedly supported the Establishment, and when they spoke
> of their religious beliefs they did so in stilted, stereotyped, lifeless
> language ... You may imagine I found this a drawback, for my hero was
> an Evangelical and to make him representative I had to have him too
> speaking in that dreary conventional way.[9]

Hoping to find an epic crusade, Jenkins found only 'genteel' argument. If
he had read Lydia Miller's novel, this would have confirmed him in his
judgement that the Evangelicals were disastrously timid and respectable.

It is worth recalling the juncture in the history of prose fiction at which
Lydia Miller's book appeared. As Ina Ferris has shown in her brilliant study,
The Achievement of Literary Authority (1991) – subtitled *Gender, History, and the
Waverley Novels* – the vast critical success of Walter Scott had depended in
part on the conviction that he had rescued the novel form from female
practitioners who had confined it to the presentation of domesticised society
under conventional restraints. According to the orthodoxies of critics, who
were almost invariably male, female novelists were indecent when, like Lady
Morgan, they ventured on to high historical ground and dealt with sexual
passion; boring, if worthy, when, like Maria Edgeworth, they moralised
didactically. Francis Jeffrey had damned Edgeworth with faint praise: 'she
scarcely makes use of a single tint that is warmer than real life'. As Ferris puts
it, 'the writerly fitness of women was perceived as a function of their
enclosure'.[10]

Lydia Miller was unfortunate in that she launched herself as a writer of
fiction in the very same year (1847) that saw the publication of *Jane Eyre* and
Wuthering Heights by Charlotte and Emily Brontë, novels which showed how
the discourses of Romanticism could be stirred-in with domestic matter to
profoundly exciting effect, and a year before Mrs Gaskell's *Mary Barton*.
Lydia Miller's available models were Scott and Galt – for 'manners painting'
of Scottish life, Austen and Ferrier for drawing-room scenes, and nobody of
great merit for the serious treatment of Church affairs in a contemporary
context. Her *Passages* have the awkward character of a 'historical' fiction
grafted together with a novel of contemporary domesticity and a 'novel of

ideas' of the kind familiarised by the age of Enlightenment. Their 'historical' import is signalled by the full title: *Passages in the Life of an English Heiress or Recollections of Disruption Times in Scotland*. Only four years after the event, Miller is claiming to 'recollect' the Disruption as Scott and Galt had memorialised the transition to industrialism. She is laying claim to the high ground of 'history'. Occupying this, Scott had satisfied critics that the novel, associated with the typically male discourse of history, could provide more than mere amusement in an idle hour. Her need to maintain an elevated, quasi-male stance in judgement is one reason why her heroine, a fount of 'historical' judgement, cannot be allowed any girlish passion or domestic interests, despite her youth. Had Miller held back for a decade or two, the examples of the Brontës, digested, might have shown her how to use a first-person female narrator judgementally (*Jane Eyre*) or how to intercut points of view to achieve 'historical' depth (*Wuthering Heights*). She displays at various points in her novel qualities of a successful 'realist' writer of fiction: descriptive passages are conventional but sturdy, she has some ear for dialogue and she can present 'character' vividly. But it may be doubted whether she could ever have engaged without reservation in the dangerous trade of novel-writing. She, like her husband, might be called a 'liberal intellectual', at ease in 'polite society' with civilised adversaries. But as we shall see, *Passages* rises at one point to a frenzy of hysterical sectarianism, and its author must always have been aware of the deep prejudice against fiction which was instinctive in Evangelical circles. As William Donaldson puts it:

> To the extreme evangelical fiction was simply a lie and as such intrinsically immoral. Indeed, the form was regarded with varying degrees of distrust by religious activists of every kind. Fiction corrupted the reader. It inflamed the passions and made vice interesting.[11]

The liberal wing of the movement nevertheless would move cautiously into the arena of didactic opportunity created by the newspaper press from the mid-fifties. A serialised novel could inculcate good evangelical principles. Donaldson, however, cites the instance of the greatly popular, now forgotten David Pae, author of some 50 full-length serial novels:

> Despite his sincere desire to make evil serve the ends of good Pae was caught in an insoluble dilemma: the more deeply he entered the imaginative domain the more important fictional elements became. In engaging with fiction at all he tacitly endorsed the very things he wished to destroy.[12]

Lydia Miller was less daring than Pae. Her novel betrays overweening consciousness on her part of what she should *not* do, with moral and political imperatives interfused. She should not risk titillating erotic passion. She should not, in the age of Chartism, abet stirrers of class discord. Over and beyond this, she should not, by offering any elaborate, suspenseful plot, draw readers too far into the shadow-world of novelistic fiction. She must provide the literary equivalent of the vegetarian haggis.

What we know about Lydia Miller herself indicates that she could draw on personal experience of the Highland rural society in which her novel opens, of the fashionable Edinburgh society to which it moves, and of the Southern England in which it ends; but also, that she was not fully at home in any of these spheres.

Lydia Mackenzie Fraser was the daughter of an Inverness businessman who lost his fortune. While he was in trouble, she was brought up by relatives in Surrey. She also sojourned in Edinburgh, staying with Burns's publisher George Thomson and mingling with the second rank of *literati* – the Ballantynes, Mrs Grant of Laggan, Tennant who wrote 'Anster Fair' and the painter Thomson of Duddingston – if not with the aristocrats whom she presents in her novel. After her father's death, her mother, who had her own income, went to live in the bustling little town of Cromarty. Lydia was excited to learn that a stonemason of the town, one Hugh Miller, was publishing poetry. The Burns cult was well developed. She sought to attract Miller's attention, and he was soon smitten with her '*petite* figure, waxen clearness of complexion, and childlike appearance'. Despite her mother's disapproval, romance blossomed. By Hugh Miller's own admission she 'taught him to understand the love poetry of Burns'.[13]

Miller determined to marry her only when his station in life was more respectable. In late 1834, after three years of courtship, he was offered and accepted the post of accountant in a bank. They finally married in January 1837. Despite a hostile account of her 'evil' personality, left by Miller's nephew Hugh Williamson and discovered by George Rosie in the NLS, they appear to have been a close and harmonious couple. In his cryptic and agonised suicide note of 1856, Miller addressed her as 'Dearest Lydia … My dear, dear wife … '[14] She was at his side in Edinburgh when he edited the new Evangelical newspaper, the *Witness*, from January 1840 through the stirring events of 1843 and beyond, and accordingly close to the leaders of the new Free Church. She clearly held her own in a demanding arena of debate.

She prepared her novel, published anonymously, with the claim that if its pages had any value, it was 'as a faithful record of personal experience'. She modified this when she added that 'In the earlier chapters I have not introduced a character which I had not familiarly known, and scarce an incident which did not occur in real life.' The later chapters were admittedly fictional[15]: so, manifestly, were the earlier, since Lydia Miller was not the descendant of a Norman Conqueror or the daughter of a wealthy English Whig landowner. Jane Hamilton Leigh inherits the property of her father, who had run his estate, Chester-Lee, and governed her education by strict principle:

> Strange as it was, he made the science of ethics the basis of all her acquirements – the centre from which all other knowledge radiated. Two questions he constantly kept in view as the grand problems of life, 'What is in itself good?' and 'What is the method of producing the greatest amount of practical good in any given circumstances?'[16]

Bereaved of this admirable parent, she goes to stay with her mother's brother, a Ross-shire 'reué' (sic), Sir Duncan Ross. 'Every inch of wall' in his house, Rosemount, is covered with paintings. His taste in these is admitted to be fine, but he has been morally corrupted by dissipation in Paris and Rome. He is 'half a Catholic on the Continent, and nothing at home'. His lairdly neighbours are less exotically delinquent. Davidson of Kilblair, their leader in 'county matters', reviles the Evangelical party in the Church. The Moderates, he avers, 'have something more of gentlemen about them'. Our grave heroine asks how they show this:

'Why', said Davidson, 'they don't meddle with what does not concern them. They can sit quietly while their superiors stow away a couple of bottles or so (though I hold that to be too much for them, as the times go at any rate); they can sing a good song, take a hand at Whist, and in short, be friendly and social in their way: and then, you know, it is natural that, after all that, they should tip the wink at certain gentlemanly follies.' He winked at Sir Duncan as he spoke. 'You have enlightened me on the subject of Moderation, and on that of *patronage* too', said Jane, her eye giving out an indignant flash, as it was wont when she detected anything radically false and hollow, but giving no other sign of emotion. 'But you will pardon me', continued she, 'if I think that those accomplishments you have mentioned are not the chief ends of a clergyman's life.'

Davidson, not wishing to alienate a wealthy heiress, backtracks at once. He suggests the clergy should be ' "moral ... in order to set a good example to the lower orders". "Ay, the rascal multitude" ', begins Sir Duncan. Jane interrupts: ' "*I* have not been accustomed to speak of the *rascal multitude*" ' – but her uncle goes on to deplore that the rascal multitude has left Scotland almost without 'decent' churches since the Reformation. Jane argues that the people were right to attack popery, that the Reformers didn't instigate iconoclasm, and that it was a pity that the images went out with the popery.

Conversation flows on to the topic of patronage. Davidson flies into a rage on the subject of non-intrusion – 'the Church may go to the ——— bottom, before I lose my patronages. Did I not pay £400 only two years ago for Cambusnethan and Kilrathy? It is downright swindling to speak of it.' When Jane argues back, he asserts that he and his kind are 'not so helpless' as she thinks. 'Excellent fellows' among the Moderates are working on their side. 'It were odd if they didn't, since we gave them their livings and have got those of their sons in our hands. What between our power and their art, we *must* gain over the young men by shoals.'

At the end of this unedifying evening, Jane returns to her room gloomily asking herself whether morality be really 'the chief end of existence'. She undergoes what might be described as a 'conversion experience'. She asks her 'little' Highland maid, May, '*What is the chief end of man's being?*' May replies '*To glorify God, and to enjoy him forever.*' Asking where May learnt that, Jane discovers it was in a 'worn and half dirty pamphlet', the Shorter Catechism:

'These are extraordinary views' said the young lady, as she finished

reading the pamphlet for the third time, 'and an extraordinary peasantry they are who hold them. They *do* love good … It is with me as
writing on a slate, which may be effaced. It is engraven somehow on
these people's hearts.'
Praying that night, she feels unprecedented awe.[17]

The next chapter connects May to the Covenanting tradition – she is seen
reading *The Cloud of Witnesses* to her dying grandfather John Morrison, who
explains Erastianism to her and blesses the Lord that he has 'lived to see the
day when the root of bitterness is about to be taken out of Zion – when
Erastian patronage shall be digged out and cast away'. He tells May how her
own mother was killed as soldiers shot at the people resisting the intrusion
of one Donaldson by a Catholic laird. Then he has a fatal stroke.[18] Lydia
Miller now introduces her own 'stroke'. She has promised in her preface

> to introduce to the reader a class of humble individuals with whom he
> [sic] has probably heretofore had but little acquaintance. They are the
> relics of a primitive age – extinct everywhere except in those parts
> where a different language has preserved the manners and customs of
> the olden time from the inroads of change. Marked by peculiarities,
> assuming in some districts, it has been said, a less agreeable aspect than
> in others, I am far from advocating their support when the necessities
> of the past have ceased to exist. Certain it is, however, that they have
> lent most material aid in evangelising the Highlands of Scotland.[19]

These 'humble individuals' are 'The Men'. Four of this 'class' gather
round old John's deathbed in his crude cottage; a catechist, two crofters, a
shopkeeper. They come from an unofficial order of Churchmen below
ministers, elders, and deacons – permitted, in Ross-shire, to take a share in
the public exercises of the Church and utter their thoughts on scriptural
texts. (Lydia Miller reassures us that this 'prophesying' is allowed for in the
Book of Common Order and the First Book of Discipline, though now
confined to the North of Scotland.) Over their dying fellow the Men now
pray, read the Bible and sing psalms. Next day, in Jane's presence, John dies
pronouncing a kind of prophetic curse on Donaldson's son George, who
has joined the villagers around him.

By far the most interesting pages of the novel explore Lydia Miller's
conception of The Men. Though she claims, as we have seen, that these
passages are documentary, her discourse, deriving more from Scott than
Galt, is ultimately Ossianic. She assimilates The Men with the Highland
romance of the Ossianic noble savage.

It is worth mentioning here Peter Womack's searching analysis of the
Highland romance as it developed after 1746 through Macpherson, Scott
and lesser writers:

> It is the ideological function of the romance that it removes the
> contradictory elements from the scope of material life altogether; that
> it marks out a kind of reservation in which the values which Improve-
> ment … suppresses can be *contained* – that is preserved, but also
> imprisoned…. Officially, Romance and Improvement were opposites:

native and imported, past and present, tradition and innovation. But in reality they were twins.[20]

That is, the sentimentalisation of the Highlands supported, ideologically, the capitalism of the Lowlands. It is, in a way, to Lydia Miller's credit that she is explicitly uneasy about this twinning. In so far as The Men are part of an 'ancient' order hostile to market forces, free trade and improvement, she is clear in her Preface that they must become extinct: 'I am far from advocating their support when the necessities of the past have ceased to exist.' Yet when she elaborates on the case of the pious shopkeeper Munro who attended Morrison's deathbed, her tone is quite different. He also owns a 'small but very excellent farm': 'He was thus a wealthy man in his way, and an excellent specimen of that worthy class which the remorseless spirit, misnamed *improvement*, has so nearly swept from the country.'[21] Though Lydia Miller wants to make them also the guardians of the Lowland Covenanting tradition, men of this 'class' are now usually Gaelic speakers. When they gather from as far as 40 miles away in the shopkeeper's house, on the occasion of a half-yearly communion at Glenmore (the parish where Rosemount is situated, and where the minister Dr Blair is famous for piety), they speak English in deference to 'one or two of the company' not fluent in Gaelic. Miller's suggestion that the Lowland Covenanting tradition found a strong fortress at last in the Gaeltacht makes historical sense. She produces, however, an idealised image of The Men and their people as essentially 'primitive' (a word flavoured in this connection by its usage in 'Primitive Church'). When Jane passes at this time a gathering of 'thousands' singing psalms, in Gaelic, in the open air, the music is 'simple in its scale, like the melodies of all primitive people, but rapid and involved in its transitions'.[22]

As the patronage issue impinges directly upon her, she recognises in this 'primitive' fervour something of far greater spiritual weight than the gentility of Moderates. Her 'madcap' young soldier cousin, Harry McLeod, divulges to her that Sir Duncan has sold the presentation of Glenmore to his father. Harry himself has made his father promise to give it to young Donaldson, a college friend, whose eye he put out with a fork in a romp. Jane is appalled – 'could she doubt that this George Donaldson was immeasurably inferior, both morally and intellectually, to many of her humble friends?' But old Dr Blair, knowing his death is near, has already pleaded with his congregation that there should be 'no riot and confusion' when his successor is installed. We learn that when Mr McLean was intruded into the adjacent parish of Dalry, the people were so law-abiding that they tholed this – 'the church remained empty, that was all'. Lydia Miller's comment is

> to submit to unrighteousness personally or locally, may be virtue; to submit to it *nationally* is either insensibility or cowardice ... When the *nation's* cry against iniquity arises, the '*power that is*' is the awakened strength and integrity of a great people, the enlightened, determined conscience of a nation – in which is the voice of God[23]

Leave it to Dr Chalmers and his colleagues ...

The Revd Dr Blair himself is allowed to expound the reasons why popular choice should prevail in the appointment of ministers. Even presbyteries are likely to act at times from 'corrupt' motives: members 'might accommodate one another'. However, the power of the Church to license ministers ensures that the people can only choose from among candidates of sound doctrine.[24]

We are now over a quarter of the way through a novel of 429 pages. So far we have been given 'scenes', not story. These scenes set up starkly the contrast between utterly admirable Gaelic Christians and generally corrupt Anglicised gentry, and we have learnt that the former represent the true Scottish nation. The beautiful Jane has acquired correct Non-Intrusionist opinions. Now, for better or worse, Lydia Miller has to cope with the promise implied when she gave her heiress youth and beauty: a novelistic development must be essayed.

At once she demonstrates that she could cope, but won't. A young English lieutenant, a comrade of Harry's, falls wordlessly in love with Jane. They go with Sir Duncan and a party of young officers to visit the Intruder, Old Donaldson. The trip takes them into fine Highland scenery, ambitiously described. Old Donaldson is a grotesque, in whose potential Walter Scott would have revelled. He dresses like a 'gardener', speaks in broad Scots, convincingly rendered, and has married his serving lass as his third wife. He is by far the most vivid – and hence, for novel-readers, the most appealing – character so far presented. But we only get one taste of him, and no more is heard of Jane's military admirer. Further frustration occurs when Jane, sallying forth to read Mrs Hemans, her favourite poet, at a favourite scenic spot, rashly loses herself in the mist after ascending a mountain for the view. She is rescued by Evan Munro, son of one of the Men, who is destined for the ministry. Surely romance must blossom? Not likely. Jane goes off to stay in Ainslie Place, with Lord and Lady Lentraethen, for whom 'good' is little more than taste. Lydia Miller's mode switches from scene-painting in a Romantic environment to the territory of 'comedy of manners'.

She shows evidence that she might have succeeded in the medium of Austen and Ferrier. We get a vivacious account of a discussion at a society dinner where Jane makes play with the fact that Jeffrey and Cockburn side with Chalmers over patronage. However, her happy fate is to be taken in hand by Lord Lentraethen's pious brother, General Maitland, who lectures her at length on Church affairs. Greatly daring, Lydia Miller gives him a past – he married at 19, in India, an extravagant 'baby-wife' now long dead. What attracts Jane to this austere character (whose physical characteristics, save his 'penetrating gaze' are not described) is, primarily, his relationship with his daughter by this marriage. A psychologist might be interested as to why Lydia Miller, herself the offspring of a failed man, should attach such extraordinary importance to the father–daughter relationship. After meeting Maitland's daughter and taking to her, Jane weeps 'bitter, orphan tears' on her pillow and 'images of General Maitland and his child' mingle 'strangely and uneasily in her dreams' with those of her own beloved father.[25]

Meanwhile, young George Donaldson has been 'intruded' by Davidson at Glenmore, following Dr Blair's demise. In an otherwise passive demonstration, a snowball knocks off Davidson's hat. This leads to a stand-off with young Kenneth Ore, previously identified as swain of Jane's servant May, when Donaldson orders him to pick it up:

> Kenneth folded his arms and stood erect. 'Pick it up for yourself, Mr Davidson', he replied quietly but haughtily, 'or order your footman to do it. *I* am no man's footman'. Davidson stepped up to him, almost beside himself. 'If I had my pistols here', he vociferated, 'by —— , I would send a bullet through you.' The low and somewhat mean figure of Davidson, and his face purple as it was with rage, presented rather a curious contrast to the manly form, the handsome features, and contemptuous lip of the young Highlander. The latter certainly looked for that moment the aristocrat.[26]

At the moment when George Davidson is to be ordained, the congregation stages a mass walk-out, but those who remain in the gallery howl out their feelings. Hence Kenneth Ore and old Samuel, one of The Men, are sent for trial in Edinburgh as representatives of the 'rioters'. Maitland brings Samuel into the Lentraethen drawing room after their acquittal, and Jane, conversing with him, is 'struck with that sense of the grave sublime, which an adequate faith in omnipotence never fails to inspire; and which she knew deeply pervaded the minds of the Christian mountaineers'.[27]

But such virtuous folk now feel impelled to emigrate. Lydia Miller had some understanding of the processes involved in the Clearances. Samuel told Jane, back in the Highlands, that 'distress and poverty are making many of us look to a foreign land', and Kenneth has spoken more forcibly about landlords who use their people 'worse than brutes'. But Miller suggests, through Samuel, that people would not bring themselves to leave the place of their fathers 'so long as the preaching of the gospel' continued there,[28] making young Donaldson's intrusion spur these men overseas. Miller implies that the Clearances involve choice by the emigrants, and that the victory of true religion would keep them in Scotland.

This is in line with the views of Thomas Chalmers on poverty, which Maitland expounds to Jane. He believes that 'spiritual philanthropy' rather than cash is the answer. Once the poor are converted, 'self-help' will raise them from pauperism. His millenial aim goes beyond Chalmers's godly Commonwealth towards the vision of a fully Christianised world – 'Why confine our wishes to Scotland?'[29]

Jane is now closely involved in Church of Scotland matters. She meets the great Chalmers himself, whose simplicity of dress betokens 'a toilet devoid of concentration'; but 'with him the sense of duty itself was absorbed in the higher principle of *love*'.[30] She sees the case of the Strathbogie ministers, heard at the 1841 General Assembly, and sits till the conclusion of debate at 3.00 a.m. Then, very abruptly, she and her General are married, and she returns with him to her English estate.

This proves to comprise a never-never portion of England, sagely governed by her late father. The land is rich. Life is idyllic. Paternalistic local manufacturers now provide employment for the surplus rural population,

Jane's father having talked them into responsible behaviour. The interests of landlord and tenant here are identical. Jane, whose mansion has a gallery of ancestral portraits of 'noble knights and ladies' suddenly becomes Countess of Lentraethen on the demise of Maitland's brother. But she grows discontented with the 'rich Epicureanism of England', as compared with the 'hut on the Highland mountain' where old John Morrison had lived and died. Furthermore, her land steward has carelessly sold the living of the Parish Church to the highest bidder and he – horror! – is a High Churchman. 'Figments of popery ... the grossness of Romanism' can be seen in the church and after attending one service there Jane and her husband decide that if the 'plague spot of Popery' spreads throughout the Church of England, they will lend aid to forming a purer 'Free Church of England', 'unfettered by State support', a 'purified' Church which might 'one day be adopted by a regenerated *State* as her true help-mate'.[31]

Here Miller entertains the remarkable idea that there is actually a 'Popish Plot' involving not only the High Church faction in England but also the Moderates in the Kirk. The Romish vicar of Jane's parish, Edward Clayton, is unmasked to her readers as a Jesuit – a tortured soul, an ex-criminal who flew to Rome for mercy. We are treated to an exchange of letters between him and the Scottish Moderate leader 'Bremner' who likewise has 'a secret in Rome's keeping', and is presumably acting under threat of blackmail. Alas, Miller does not develop this remarkable fantasy.

The tell-tale correspondence (unknown, of course, to the novel's other characters) immediately precedes a routine, hagiographical, distant description of the scenes of Disruption in Edinburgh. Now God's providence ties up the novel's loose ends. Sir Duncan Ross is 'assassinated in the streets of Rome, at midnight, by a disappointed rival'. Jane, who has brought out poor Clayton and settled a good Evangelical person on her English estate, inherits Rosemount and returns there to the plaudits of 'a picturesque population full of motion and enthusiasm'.[32]

Alas, Clearance has wreaked its havoc. The pious Mrs Munro, wife of the shopkeeper (whose son Evan is dying, partly from studying too hard, partly, it is suggested, for hopeless love of Jane) tells the Countess how lordly persecution drove the Ores, Samuel and others to emigration – 'They'll turn the land into the land of the stranger and the sheep'. But under the friendly rule of the new owners, Rosemount now prospers, with 'smiling cottages ... ease and plenty'. Only the manse, occupied by the unregenerate George Donaldson, remains un-improved – its lawn is 'rank with unsightly weeds'. Naturally, the emigrants, funded by Jane, will return to join in open-air Free Church worship under Charles Blair, son of the good old Minister ...[33]

Why, we must wonder, does Lydia Miller not end her heiress's story here? It is because her novel is directed as an appeal and an inspiration towards the *English* reading public. It was published in London. Its last fictional chapter is set in Jane's English estate at Chester-Lee, where her tenants celebrate the first public appearance of their Countess's son and heir 'Lord Arthur'. A bizarre conjuncture of discourses closes the book. While on 'far

Highland Mountains' Kenneth Ore and others light bonfires to hail the birth of the young master, that fortunate babe lies in the ancestral drawing room in a 'sculpted cradle of mother of pearl', surrounded by lamps 'fed with perfumed oil' and by 'gems of art ... costly luxuries from the courts of foreign princes', while his parents earnestly discuss the laws of property.[34]

Miller's final chapter resumes her own position. She tells her English readers: 'The progress of Popery on the one side of the kingdom – the creation and vital energy of the Free Church on the other, are the grand antagonistic movements of the powers of good and evil in our day.' The planting of ministers among the indigent and outcast will save a 'social fabric tottering at its base' by mediating between rich and poor. Meanwhile, members of the Free Church no doubt as attentive as the Lentraethens to the laws of property, have already poured £1.5 million into its coffers ...[35]

Miller, it emerges, has conscripted the noble savages and natural aristocrats of Ross-shire to serve the ends of bourgeois Evangelisation – and has not quailed from enlisting in the same cause a dream of 'Merry England' governed by wise landlords of ancient chivalric lineage. This enterprise was never likely to succeed novelistically. The great English public would prefer the more erotic imaginings of the Brontës and the better-submerged earnestness of George Eliot. And it has to be added that Miller's device of a 'Popish Plot' was many years past its sell-by date: Chalmers had spoken in favour of Catholic emancipation, Hugh Miller had favoured it, and Lydia Miller's introduction of this motif paradoxically reinforces something on which her text strives to be silent, but (with its ultimate 'mother of pearl' and 'gems of art') cannot avoid blurting out – the devilish attractiveness of Rome, its rituals, and the rich artistic production associated with them. If only, she clearly wishes, one could have the images without the popery ... But meanwhile her own fiction's lumpy eschewal of erotic plotting in favour of dry argumentation suggests that for Free Churches that happy day is far ahead. To write a fully novelistic novel would betray the cause. This fiction is designed, it seems, to reassure English persons that the Free Church is a true friend of social stability.

It has been necessary to quote and summarise Lydia Miller's novel at length because it is now almost unavailable. *Johnny Gibb* is far easier to find. This is paradoxical, since it was addressed not even to the whole Scottish reading public, but only to those who perused the *Aberdeen Free Press* and would understand the dialect spoken by most of its characters. Alexander, when he wrote it, was recalling his own early years in the parish of Garioch. He was relaxed and experienced within the conventions of producing fiction for newspaper serialisation and can be called a master of his own peculiar variant of the novel-form. Furthermore, he wrote a quarter of a century after the great Disruption crisis, and already felt no need to pillory Moderates, let alone taint them with Romish associations. Unlike Lydia Miller, he does not go in for lengthy Evangelical effusions, and he certainly does not idealise the adherents of the new Free Church in the parish of Pyketillim.

Dr Donaldson, author of a pioneering account of Alexander's career, sees him as a 'realist' working within the same literary movement as Tolstoy and Zola, but especially concerned with documentary veracity (so far as Victorian prudery allowed) in the presentation of language in all its spoken registers. *Johnny Gibb*, in Donaldson's presentation, emerges not as the one-off novel of a distinguished journalist – it was the only fiction by him of such length which Alexander allowed to appear in book form – but as merely a small part of a fiction-writing career which extended over several decades, from the mid-1850s. In particular, Donaldson places *Johnny Gibb* as the central section of an epic sequence nearly a quarter of a million words long, encompassing almost a century of change and development in the rural North-East; beginning with the novel 'Ravenshowe' (*Free Press*, 1867–8) and completed with the last of the short stories collected as *Life Among My Ain Folk* (book publication, 1875). This sequence deals with the agricultural revolution in Aberdeenshire, in which initially small tenant farmers like the author's own parents reclaimed 'acre by acre' featureless expanses of moss and moor, only to be ousted by 'muckle farmers' arising under the big landowners, and engulfed in the railway – which speeded a new world of commerce and industry. Alexander, as Donaldson shows, was deeply critical of capitalist values and emphatically on the side of the class of small tenant farmer represented by Johnny Gibb – 'the last defence of traditional decencies and a human scale of values in the rural economy'.[36]

The novel deals mostly with the estate of Sir Simon Frissal of Glensnicker and two of his tenant farmers, Johnny Gibb and his neighbour Peter Birse, the farmer of Clinkstyle. Birse, a weak man, and his feckless elder son are driven by his wife to aspire to the status of muckle farmers, and she plots to absorb Gibb's farm when his lease expires. Gibb seems to play into her hands – openly voting against the laird's candidate in elections, building a voluntary 'venture school' in opposition to the Moderate parish schoolmaster, and steering Non-Intrusionist parishioners through the Disruption into their own Free Kirk. He is, furthermore, elderly and childless. But he has lent money to the laird – not yet repaid – and the Birses are discomfited when Sir Simon not only gives the lease of Gushetneuk to Johnny's nominee – the husband of his own 'adopted' niece – but consigns a tongue of Birse's land to Gushetneuk by way of rationalisation.

Douglas Gifford has seen Johnny Gibb as typical of the 'mythic' figures in nineteenth-century Scottish fiction who 'in being themselves' are also 'being Scotland' – sound men in a sick society – and has proclaimed the novel to be a 'mythic masterpiece'.[37] This could create a false impression: Alexander is doggedly matter of fact, leaving it to his readers to find 'symbolic' value, if any, in such details as the absurd second-hand coach which the memorably grasping and snobbish Mrs Birse makes her husband buy in anticipation of a rise in status. This is a dry book about dry people, and Johnny Gibb himself is presented foursquare, 'a short, thick-set man', within obvious limitations: he is literate but reads little; devout but uninterested in proselytising for his opinions; content to do what he can in his own small parish.

Nor is the Disruption 'mythologised' in any usual sense of that word. Johnny's contempt for lairds precedes the Intrusion controversy and exists irrespective of their religious opinions:

> 'The tae half o' oor lairds is owre the lugs in a bag o' debt. I wud hae them roupit oot at the door and set to some eesfu trade ... Stechin' up a kwintra side wi them, wi' their peer stinkin' pride ... an' them nedder able to manage their awcres themsel's, nor can get ither fowke that can dee't for them.'

Though he has a 'very good balance' at his banker's, Johnny continues to live simply and at kirk or market 'will accost any dyker or ditcher in the parish on terms of perfect equality'. His politics are 'advanced Liberal', though the term is not used in the late 1830s when we first meet him.[38] His honest tongue ensures that the Revd Gregory Sleekaboot refuses him an eldership. So he is predisposed to interest when he hears – on his annual excursion to Macduff, where his wife takes the waters for her health – at first hand about the Marnoch Intrusion case from Maister Saun'ers of that parish – who inveighs against 'A man wi' nae gifts fittin' im for the work forc't upon an unwillin' people, i' the vera teeth o' the Veto Act ... after the noble *struggles* and sufferin's o' our convenantin' forbears to maintain spiritooal independence.'[39] They discuss the idea of abandoning the defiled Kirk and worshipping on the hillsides in seventeenth-century fashion.

This meeting stirs Johnny's 'zeal in the Non-Intrusion cause' far beyond his 'previous state of hazy, half-informed rebellion against Moderate domination'. He is further 'politicised' by following the progress of the Marnoch case, and by 1842 he has 'learnt clearly to distinguish between "Moderates" and "Evangelicals", and those words (are) frequently on his lips'. He feels he must stand up against Sleekaboot 'for the good cause' and with his ally Roderick M'Aul, souter in the hamlet of Smiddyward, invites an unattached Evangelical minister visiting the area to preach in the independent 'venture' school.

The brief description of this important occasion exemplifies Alexander's humorous detachment. Sleekaboot reads every week from a 'well thumbed ms', a sermon regularly repeated:

> But the Rev. Alister Macrory, albeit a little uncouth and violent in his manner, and given to shaking his fist and staring directly forward at a particular point in his audience, as if he wanted to single you out individually to be preached at, was, to all appearance, a man really in earnest ...[40]

Alexander is certainly not the man to separate Evangelical sheep from Moderate goats in any crude way. His picture of the convivial, tolerant Moderate schoolmaster, the Revd Tawse, is very sympathetic. The appalling Mrs Birse has fallen out with Tawse on account of his failure to drum education into the head of her stupid younger son Benjie, whom she wants to make a lawyer. Sending Benjie to the venture school as an alternative, she associates her family with the Evangelical side and, as an opponent of an individual Moderate, decides to go to its second unofficial prayer meeting.

In the controversy which inevitably follows these meetings, the laird's 'ground-officer' (sub-factor), Dawvid Hadden, moves to prevent an Evangelical pow-wow at the Smiddyware School, and it is transferred to Johnny's barn, where locals sign a paper adhering to Non-Intrusion principles, which seems to Johnny himself 'a process very nigh akin to signing the solemn League and Covenant'.[41] But this point is offered with gentle irony. The next chapter emphasises that the Disruption was not so very disruptive in Pyketillim.

A parishioner witnesses and reports an intrusion at nearby Culsalmon which provokes a riot. Hearing of a later intrusion into a Strathbogie parish where the Moderates called in soldiers though there was no riot, Johnny Gibb begins to talk in millenarian terms, declaring that 'things could not stop short of a rebellion which would put that of the "Forty-Five" in the shade'.[42] But after events in Edinburgh take their course, all that happens is that the new Free Church of Pyketillim begins to meet in his barn, pending erection of a kirk, while he, a 'Disruption leader' *de facto* rather than by 'intention', negotiates for a supply of preachers. Sandy Peterkin, the 'free' master, is expelled from his venture school but finds employment in the shop. And the laird, shrewdly proposing and disposing, frustrates the ambitions of Mrs Birse. Sleekaboot stays in his own kirk, keeps his manse; the representative of peasant independence, Johnny, stands at peaceful truce with his landlord, while the new Church which he more than anyone has promoted co-exists alongside the old. As Donaldson points out, Johnny's childlessness may be felt as symbolic: he represents a dying class. But we leave him in prosperous retirement on the land which he has personally improved, an elder of the Church which seems to him to represent his own, democratic ethos.

In its own mode, *Johnny Gibb* is a virtually flawless work of fiction. Extracting the 'Disruption' episodes from it misrepresents a book in which earnest religious controversy emerges from a vividly 'heard' flux of local gossip, talk of farming practicalities, alcoholic convivialities and exuberant wedding customs. Set beside Grassic Gibbon's *Sunset Song*, which deals with similar countryside, attitudes and people decades later, *Johnny Gibb*'s radical thrust seems restrained and its social criticism gentle. Mid-Victorian 'equipoise' seems to condition its virtual truce with time and change. Its slow, though not laboured, English narrative voice strongly affirms the best values of Doric-speakers who are heard in their own voice, and in its genial complicity, implies confidence that these values and that language can survive – in or out of the Free Kirk which gives them place.

Robin Jenkins, in contrast, wrote *The Awakening of George Darroch*[43] with an agonised sense that true 'Scotland' had slipped away. Reading it after *Johnny Gibb*, one might well marvel at the swift suppleness of narrative available to twentieth-century writers. Jenkins is able to present, in far fewer pages than Lydia Miller or Alexander, a great range of characters, milieux, arguments and striking events. Though he knows that he has to introduce the subject of the Disruption itself to readers who mostly know nothing about it, he is able to move with apparent ease from efficient exposition to critical ar.alysis.

George Darroch is the minister of a mediocre parish in industrial Lanarkshire. He has a large family – his wife is pregnant for the fifteenth time. Seven children survive, including mentally-retarded Sarah who will need attention all her life. His sons are contemptuous of the agonised conscience which has led him to subscribe to the Evangelical manifesto and contemplate leaving his manse. His brother-in-law, Robert Drummond, is the urbane Moderate minister of a wealthy Edinburgh parish and is able to dangle before him the promise of a rich living offered by a patron in rural Lothian. Furthermore, George is racked by private self-contradiction. In his early 40s, he is highly attractive to women. His wife has always refused to take pleasure in the sexual act; so has Drummond's, who has given him only one child. But whereas Robert relieves himself with strong drink, George fantasises about Eleanor Jarvie, the wife of a neighbouring minister, of immigrant Italian family. She is built, in his eyes, like the voluptuous goddess seen painted on a ceiling at the laird's house, 'lying on a bank of flowers and being nuzzled by fawns no more naked than she' – Eleanor, 'grave, slow-moving, brown-eyed, dark skinned and spicy breathed.... whose beauty was exotic and mysterious, redolent of frankincense, pomegranates, and the cedars of Lebanon'[44].

Jenkins has shrewdly noted the tension in Evangelicalism, which we have seen emerging in Lydia Miller's final endorsement of beautiful luxury. Much of the imagery of the Bible itself attaches spiritual significance to sensually potent things and people. While George feels impelled to dedicate himself to the poor and outcast, he is also hauled by his libido towards notions of running away to Italy with Eleanor. But when Jenkins, outside the pages of his novel, referred to George as 'a rather peculiar type of hypocrite', he was probably not thinking of these furtive sexual drives, nor of the blindness which makes him impervious to the fact that his wife is dying through the effects of yet another unwanted pregnancy. What seems to fascinate Jenkins is the spiritual arrogation of this mild, friendly, sincere man. Can his earnest desire to serve Christ and the poor be separated from a craving for distinction? His schoolboy son, James (an endearingly complex character, destined for the ministry, yet a devotee of Hume's, a Moderate in his views, yet stubbornly honest), is 'white with despair' when he sees his father walk out of St Andrew's church on 18 May 1843, the first of the 'unknowns' to follow the famous leaders ... 'Given the best opportunity of his life to show off his father had not been able to resist it. For the sake of a minute's vanity he had sentenced his family to years of hardship.' But matters are more complex than James realises. The charming neighbour, Mrs Wedderburn, who has recently married his cheerful sailor uncle, reassures him that his father will inherit Mr Jarvie's Church, larger and more convenient than his present one in Craignethan. 'Unfortunately it would allow his father to devote more time, devotion, and money, to his Pauper's mission, and to have himself appointed chaplain to the prison, where he would carry out his duties with absurd seriousness. He would become busy, ambitious and false ...'[45]

Jenkins's title must refer to the point in his novel where George, we must understand, undergoes change at the basis of his character. This is the crisis where Jenkins's method most strongly echoes late medieval Morality. Eleanor Jarvie, though vivid enough, is hardly 'plausible' in routine novelistic terms. It is not explained why this strong-charactered, voluptuous woman consented to marry the unseductive and latterly fat and impotent Revd Jarvie and live in a small provincial town. However, as clearly as Sensuality in Lindsay's great *Three Estates*, she represents Temptation. After his colleague's death, George goes to Jarvie's manse with the notion of enjoying the widow's body very much in mind, though he has been legitimately invited to make a selection from Jarvie's books. Eleanor is drunk but has no trouble putting him in his place. His own wife has died: he should marry his plain but sensible housekeeper. As for herself, she is off to Italy. In Jarvie's library, George reaches a 'turning point in his life'. He recognises that he had intended to have 'carnal relations' with Eleanor. 'Only the lack of a bed or couch had prevented him from making the abominable attempt.' But Christ is merciful, and now in his pain and confusion he hears 'the voice of God, with a message'. It tells him that he has been 'picked to turn the Kirk of Scotland away from arid theology' towards 'compassionate and responsible involvement' with the outcast poor. Since he has this divine mission, it would be bad if his lust towards Eleanor was revealed. For that reason the Lord has 'put it in her head to go to far-off Italy'. When Eleanor rejoins him, she notices his changed state and is puzzled. 'Others were going to be similarly perplexed.' Now, confident of his mission, he will set out cunningly to beat 'the hypocritical world at its own game'. When Eleanor, not without affection, calls him a 'crafty little rogue', he does not feel discomfited. 'He would never be discomfited again.'[46]

Jenkins is setting up George, in fact, as an unusually subtle version of the 'justified sinner', a type prominent in Scottish writing from Burns's Holy Willie to Spark's Jean Brodie. What he takes to be the voice of God spurs him to calculated, antinomian, deviousness. Jenkins's reader is likely to sympathise with George's ardent commitment to the poor, which draws him into earnest prayer in the Cadzow jail with a woman who has murdered her prostitute daughter and survived after cutting her own throat, and which has earned him the approval of the democratic agitator, Taylor, whom he permitted to take sanctuary in his Kirk. His mission, unlike Chalmers's, is not constrained by theology. But Jenkins knows, and reminds us, that just as Chalmers's vision of godly Commonwealth was unrealisable by the Free Church which he founded – not least because the Disruption itself deprived Presbyterians of unchallenged leadership in Scottish affairs – so George's really anticipates the work of Socialism, and the prophet of Socialism is the unbelieving Taylor. George's kindness may touch the poor, but his God will not prevail through him.

On first reading of the novel, it seems to be very much on George's side, against his brother-in-law. Yet rereading establishes that Robert Drummond, a kind man with artistic tastes, is, beneath the gaze of eternity, no more contemptible than Darroch. They have in common the burden of wives schooled to reject pleasure in sex – and at least Drummond cares deeply for his sister, whose life is blighted and at last terminated early by Darroch's imperious physical attentions. Drummond doesn't really like George but, as a Tory in the Dundas tradition, is prepared to put himself out to help his relative towards wealth and ease. Jenkins's presentation of the Disruption is finely poised between recognition that real agony, real sacrifice, real nobility were involved on the Evangelical side and judgement that its values were fatally narrow and imperfect. George himself recognises this – yet, 'ambitiously', chooses to scheme within the new Free Church. Amongst all these creatures of a bygone era, Jenkins may seem to invite us to confer fuller approval on Mrs Wedderburn, who frankly likes sex, and George's seaman brother, Henry, who is happy to go along with her: yet his trade involves him in Far Eastern transactions in the period of the Opium Wars, and the secular hedonism of this couple, tested by Jenkins in that context, would surely prove equally unacceptable as a basis for morality. However, Jenkins has revived the drama of the Disruption with an imagination well informed by reading in social history and with a serious interest in the ideas and dilemmas of Presbyterians in that period.

NOTES

1 Michael Fry, *Patronage and Principle: A Political History of Modern Scotland* (Aberdeen, 1987), p. 58.
2 George Rosie, *Hugh Miller: Outrage and Order* (Edinburgh, 1981), Editorial Note.
3 Lydia Miller, *Passages in the Life of an English Heiress or Recollection of Disruption Times in Scotland* (London, 1847).
4 William Alexander, *Johnny Gibb of Gushetneuk* (Edinburgh, 1869–70).
5 Alexander Mackie, 'Introduction and Appreciation', in Alexander, *Johnny Gibb* (1912 edn), pp. v, xxi.
6 P. Hume Brown, *History of Scotland*, 3 vols (Cambridge, 1911), vol. 3, p. 338.
7 Alexander, *Johnny Gibb* (1912 edn), p. 152 (I will continue to cite this 1912 edn for convenience).
8 Glenda Norquay, 'Four Novelists of the 1950s and 1960s', in Cairns Craig (ed.), *The History of Scottish Literature*, 4 vols (Aberdeen, 1987), vol. 4, pp. 271, 273.
9 Robin Jenkins, 'Speaking as a Scot', *The Scottish Review*, 27 Aug. 1982, pp. 18–19.
10. Ina Ferris, *The Achievement of Literary Authority: Gender, History and the Waverley Novels* (Ithaca, NY, 1991), pp. 64, 70.
11. William Donaldson, 'Popular Literature', in D. Gifford (ed.), *The History of Scottish Literature*, 4 vols (Aberdeen, 1988), vol. 3, p. 209.
12. Ibid., p. 210.
13. Peter Bayne, *The Life and Letters of Hugh Miller* (New York, 1871), vol. 1, pp. 279–94.
14 Rosie, *Hugh Miller*, pp. 15, 20.
15 Miller, *Passages in the Life of an English Heiress*.
16 Ibid., pp. 6–7.
17 Ibid., pp. 17–29.
18 Ibid., pp. 36–7.
19 Ibid., p. ii.
20 Peter Womack, *Improvement and Romance: Constructing the Myth of the Highlands* (London, 1989), p. 2.

21   Miller, *Passages in the Life of an English Heiress*, p. 60.
22   Ibid., p. 87.
23   Ibid., pp. 88–9, 102–104.
24   Ibid., pp. 109–112.
25   Ibid., pp. 235–47.
26   Ibid., p. 222.
27   Ibid., p. 283.
28   Ibid., pp. 142, 145–6.
29   Ibid., pp. 270–1.
30   Ibid., pp. 288–9.
31   Ibid., pp. 341, 353–9.
32   Ibid., pp. 365–70, 378.
33   Ibid., pp. 386–7, 390–1.
34   Ibid., pp. 411–20.
35   Ibid., pp. 421–3.
36   William Donaldson, *Popular Literature in Victorian Scotland* (Aberdeen, 1986),
     pp. 101–44.
37   Douglas Gifford, 'Myth, Parody and Dissociation … ', in Gifford, *The History
     of Scottish Literature*, vol. 3, pp. 218, 226.
38   Alexander, *Johnny Gibb*, pp. 15, 25–6.
39   Ibid., pp. 40–1, 70.
40   Ibid., p. 71.
41   Ibid., p. 150.
42   Ibid., p. 129.
43   Robin Jenkins, *The Awakening of George Darroch* (Edinburgh, 1985).
44   Ibid., pp. 9, 23.
45   Ibid., pp. 266, 268.
46   Ibid., pp. 177–9.

PART THREE

The Disruption Outside Scotland

CHAPTER EIGHT

The Disruption and the Colonies of Scottish Settlement

BARBARA C. MURISON

ACCORDING TO LORD COCKBURN, that astute contemporary commentator, the quarrels of the Ten Years' Conflict and the ensuing Disruption of the Kirk were matters 'purely and utterly Scotch': no one else, he suggested, could understand them.[1] By implication, their impact must be limited and local; and the conflicts of Scotland could and should be confined to the area in which they originated. For many, there seemed no need to transfer the religious problems of Scotland to the colonies overseas. As a parishioner remarked to the Revd William Proudfoot, missionary of the Presbyterian United Secession Church in Upper Canada, it would be best to 'bury all distinctions that prevail in Scotland... and go to work on the broad basis of the Gospel'.[2] A new environment required a fresh approach.

Indeed, any dispassionate analyst must agree with the assessment of the Colonial Committee of the Church of Scotland: whatever the problems at home, the introduction of divisions into the colonial synods and congregations was 'utterly gratuitous and uncalled for'.[3] There was little indigenous material in the colonies to cause religious strife in the Kirk. The Scottish patronage system did not exist there. There was slight connection between Church and state, if any. Moreover, the committee report continued, the colonial churches were neither subject to the authority of the Church of Scotland nor responsible for its actions. The Revd John Machar of Kingston, Canada West, put the case even more emphatically: 'our connection with the Established Church [of Scotland] implies no jurisdiction or control or interference whatever'. The Presbyterian Church of Canada, he argued, had not one reason to separate, but every reason to preserve union. His final verdict on the Disruption, in a letter to a friend in Brechin in 1846, was that 'with you, there might have been cause for division, but *here* division took place without a cause'.[4] The grievances of the Church of Scotland at home were either absent or present in very attenuated form in the colonies.

None the less, Disruption certainly reached the colonies of Scottish settlement. In British North America, the provinces of Canada (i.e., modern Ontario and Quebec) and Nova Scotia, containing the largest number of emigrant Scots, were the areas which felt the impact first. Twenty-three ministers of the Canadian Synod of the Kirk, one-quarter of the total number, left it in July 1844, to form the Free Church of Canada.[5] At the same time, the Kirk Synod of Nova Scotia (which included Prince Edward Island), repudiated the Church of Scotland and adopted the title 'Synod of Nova Scotia adhering to the Westminster Standards'. Four years later this became the Synod of the Free Church of Nova Scotia. Two Kirk ministers were all that remained in this area and there was no Church of Scotland presbytery there for the next ten years.[6] The proportions were reversed in New Brunswick, where the synod was strongly in favour of retaining the connection with the Church of Scotland and only three ministers out of thirteen withdrew to form a Free Church. Newfoundland's one organised Presbyterian congregation, in St John's, vacillated between adherence to the Kirk and to the Free Church until it finally split in two in 1849.

In Australia, too, the Disruption proved impossible to ignore, though the number of Scots was much smaller here than in British North America and they were more widely scattered. The Australian synod, after first attempting to maintain a judicious neutrality and to continue in communion with both the Established and the Free Church of Scotland, split in 1846. While sixteen ministers remained with the Establishment, three ministers, afterwards joined by a fourth, formed themselves into the 'Synod (Free) of Australia'. The following year, an additional four ministers formed a second Free Church Synod in the south: the Synod of Australia Felix (later the Synod of Victoria).[7] In New Zealand, colonisation was barely begun at the time of the Disruption. News of it certainly reached the few Scots there, as indicated by letters from Wellington, mentioned in the Free Church General Assembly minutes of 1844.[8] But there was no organised Kirk to suffer Disruption.

British North America was the favoured destination of emigrant Scots in the first half of the nineteenth century. These were long-established colonies, of major concern to Church colonial committees and similar types of organisation at home. Committee reports consistently dealt first, and at greater length, with this area. I shall follow their example and consider British North America initially and then Australia and New Zealand.

'Disruption without a cause' had been the phrase used by Machar. Why did the 'angry spirit of Churchism which ... disturbed every fireside in Scotland [thunder] at the door of every shanty in the backwoods'?[9] All the evidence suggests that a close eye was kept on Scottish affairs by expatriate Scots, particularly from across the Atlantic. A deputation from America was among those congratulating the Free Church in its first Assembly in 1843,[10] and the President of the United States, James Knox Polk, himself was shortly to find it politic to allege that (on his mother's side) he was connected with John Knox![11] Between 1841 and 1844, the Canadian synod was sending annual messages of sympathy to the mother Church in its time of trial, and recording in its resolutions its support for the principle of non-intrusion. Even the technicalities of the Ten Years' Conflict had, in some form, reached the colonies. The Revd Norman Macleod, emissary of the Kirk, found that

arguments over Lord Aberdeen's bill or the proper form of spiritual independence were common in the most isolated settlements of British North
America, whilst the Revd George Lewis, visiting Nova Scotia as a representative of the Free Church of Scotland, was very surprised when a young
gentleman quoted his own tracts back to him. Dr Robert Burns of Paisley,
most distinguished of all the Free Church visitors to British North America
in the 1840s, was struck by the strength of the attachment to Scottish
institutions which he found there;[12] it meant that there was keen interest in
the 1830s and 1840s in the question that kept all Scotland 'in a flame',[13] the
Church question. The introduction of steamship service on the North
Atlantic routes during the late thirties and early forties made it easier to
satisfy that interest as the whole pace of communication quickened.

One decisive influence on the course of events in the colonial synods was
the quality – and quantity – of ministerial leadership in each area.[14] Presbyterianism had already faced less severe secessions before 1843; the idea of
fragmentation was not a novelty. The Churches that had emerged from the
eighteenth-century secessions had seen their mission responsibilities more
quickly than the Church of Scotland and had sent ministers to the colonies;
although there was a handful of Church of Scotland ministers in British
North America in the early years of the nineteenth century, it was not until
1825 that the Glasgow Colonial Society, in connection with the Church of
Scotland, was formed specifically for the purpose of supplying the religious
needs of the Scottish settlers in British North America. In 1840 it amalga-
mated with the General Assembly's Colonial Mission, which had been
belatedly formed in 1836. Dr Robert Burns of Paisley was the driving force
here and within ten years of its formation it had sent out over forty ordained
Church of Scotland clergymen.[15] It was the 1830s, therefore, before the first
regular presbyteries and synods in connection with the Scottish national
Church were set up. From the perspective of the Disruption, the Church of
Scotland was a Church-come-lately to British North America.

It is hardly surprising, then, that virtually every Church of Scotland
minister in the colonies had been raised and trained in Scotland. There was
little hope of a native-trained ministry as yet, desirable though all agreed
that to be.[16] These Scots ministers were naturally familiar with the long-
standing tension between the Moderate and Evangelical wings of the
Church at home. In the main they were of the latter persuasion. The Glasgow
Colonial Society was a product of Evangelical zeal, and future leaders of the
Free Church, such as Burns and Welsh, were prominent in its organisation.
Frequently, too, the emigrant ministers had had personal – and unpleasant
– experience of the Scottish patronage system, a point stressed in almost
every biography of the leading colonial ministers of the day. The Revd John
Bayne, who laid the protest on the table of the Canadian synod in 1844, had
been unwilling to wait for preferment at home and was 'disgusted with the
system of lay patronage'. The Revd Mark Stark, first Moderator of the Synod
of the Free Church in the province of Canada, was similarly unable to obtain
a settlement in Scotland.[17]

The quality of these ministers is difficult to gauge, given the hagiography of some sources and the vituperative malice of others. They were not all possessed of the missionary enthusiasm of a Bayne or a Stark;[18] equally, not all were the incompetent dregs of the Establishment, 'stiff, dry, formal and worldly-minded'.[19] The great Candlish himself would have gone to Upper Canada but for a last-minute offer from St George's, Edinburgh. Whatever their quality may have been, their quantity was insufficient to supply the needs of emigrant Scots. Writing from Kingston in 1828, Machar told his sister in Scotland that he was exhausted from his journeying, there being no Presbyterian minister between Kingston and Niagara at that time. Dr Burns's observations on the districts around Pictou, Nova Scotia, could be duplicated throughout the colonies: Earlton and New Annan had made very early applications to the Glasgow Colonial Society for a pastor, but years later (this was 1844) they still had not received one. 'They have a church and desperately need a minister.'[20] This 'destitution', as contemporaries put it, became immeasurably worse after 1843 and was a key factor in the decision of so many colonial congregations to adhere to the Free Church in the years that followed.

Free Church writers took a malicious delight in describing the reaction of some colonial ministers to the Disruption in Scotland. In practical terms, it meant a revolution in the ministerial job market. Over four hundred pulpits in the Established Church at home were vacant; it was too good an opportunity to miss. 'In hot haste', according to the *Annals of the Disruption*, 'men left their Canadian congregations, and started across the sea eager to have a share of the spoil'. Satan had taken them to the top of an exceeding high mountain and showed them 'empty manses, good stipends and comfortable glebes' across the Atlantic.[21] The Free Church General Assembly was thoroughly entertained by the report regarding the six ministers who left the Pictou area for Scotland all at once, 'in the discharge of their duty – a difficult one of course – (a laugh) – of taking possession of vacant watchtowers, deserted alike by ministers and by people, and thus, in a twofold sense, vacant. (Hear, hear, and loud laughter)'.[22]

This desertion of their charges by colonial ministers (more neutrally referred to as the transference of services to the home vineyard in the General Assembly minutes of the Church of Scotland for 1844)[23] created a critical shortage of ministers, particularly in Nova Scotia where the loss was highest. It did not, very naturally, please the colonial Scots. The inhabitants of areas such as Tatmagouche and Wallace, Nova Scotia, whose long-serving Church of Scotland minister left his flock without notice of his intentions or valedictory address, and went home to Scotland 'for reasons known to himself', in Dr Burns's scornful words,[24] were thereafter highly likely to favour the Free Church. Those who believed with John Redpath, wealthy Scots merchant of Montreal, that the Church of Scotland had always tended to send over the dregs of the Scottish clergy now felt that they would 'get nothing but the dregs of the dregs' if they clung to the Establishment.[25] There was a colonial vacuum waiting to be filled and the Free Church at home was perfectly well aware of it. On its side, the Church of Scotland found it difficult and disheartening to face the dual task of filling its vacant charges at home and reorganizing all the foreign and colonial missionary agencies of the Church, which had disappeared in a single day.[26] The Kirk faced an acute crisis of personnel, and also of confidence; this was bound to affect its dealings with the colonies.

By contrast, the Free Church at its inception was buoyed up by an intense spiritual enthusiasm. All the forces of revivalism were there; Lord Cockburn thought the first Free Church General Assembly so exciting that it must stimulate the whole country.[27] But this was not simply an unfocused outpouring of emotion. The Disruption had been meticulously planned; among Dr Chalmers's watchwords was 'Organise – organise – organise!'[28] Free Church leaders felt that 'not Scotland, but the world is the field': what had begun in Scotland would not end there. The Free Church felt a responsibility to 'Take up the Saviour's commission, to preach the gospel to every creature' and to testify widely 'for Christ's Headship'. The very fact that all the missionaries of the Church of Scotland and most of the colonial committee members had adhered to the Free Church suggested to its leaders that they had crucial mission responsibilities; they must expound Free Church principles far and wide. There were universal ideas at work here; if, as one American supporter put it, the Free Church movement was the greatest event in the Church of Christ since the Reformation in Germany, then it must have equally significant results.[29] Disruption was designed for export.

Early in 1844, therefore, Dr Cunningham, a leader in the Disruption, and Dr Burns sailed for New York in order both to explain Free Church principles and to collect money for the Free Church Building Fund. Immediately there came requests from British North America, from Evangelicals such as the Revd Thomas Alexander of Cobourg and the Revd William Smart of Brockville, to extend the visit northwards. It was a prospect viewed gloomily by those like Machar in Kingston who wanted to maintain the ecclesiastical peace but well knew that 'should [they] visit us and seek our separation, there is no saying what may happen'.[30] His worst expectations were fulfilled. Dr Burns's visit to Canada and Nova Scotia turned into a triumphal progress. For twenty years he had been 'the life and soul of the Canadian mission'.[31] He was well known to all those ministers who had gone to British North America under the auspices of the Glasgow Colonial Society. He had repeatedly held the presidency of various emigration societies in the Paisley area (he was minister of the Low Church, Paisley, for thirty-four years); some of those he had helped to emigrate he now recognised on his travels.[32] His influence was immense, and the fact that lack of time prevented him from visiting New Brunswick was a key factor in the continued adherence of most New Brunswick ministers and their congregations to the Church of Scotland. Burns's visit was the first of many such by representatives of the Free Church in Scotland. In the aftermath of the Disruption, the Colonial Committee of the Free Church had recourse to what it called 'extraordinary measures', frequent short-term visits by ministers to the colonies, not designed to be permanently continued but to seize the initiative.[33]

This policy was certainly successful. It was not until 1845 that the demoralised Church of Scotland was able to send out a deputation to British North America. The time-lag was fatal.[34] By that time, all the North American colonial synods had undergone Disruption. Moreover, although this Church of Scotland deputation contained the redoubtable Revd Norman Macleod, one of the foremost preachers of his generation,[35] its impact was muted by its determination 'not to utter a disrespectful word regarding ... Free Church brethren'. No doubt this was the spiritual high ground: but making 'the question of the Church of Scotland a secondary matter' had the unfortunate result that the Kirk came second in this contest for the hearts and souls of the Scottish emigrants.[36] Dr Burns, by contrast, an equally spirited speaker and rather more choleric, had made it a major aim to press the case for the Free Church and refused to preach in pulpits offered him only on condition that he preached sermons of a wishy-washy neutrality.[37]

Furthermore, Burns and his fellow Free Kirkers attempted to expand their support in British North America by making a deliberate appeal to Secession Presbyterians, including some who up to this point had been in connection with US synods. Burns was certain that the Free Church in the colonies needed to amalgamate 'the labours of all evangelical Presbyterians as a set-off against all the foes of civil and religious freedom'.[38] There were also meetings with Baptists, Independents and Methodists; Egerton Ryerson, President of the Methodist Victoria College in Toronto, allowed Burns to address the students.[39] Free Church leaders hoped that their Church would be not merely 'another fragment; but a point of union for many churches'. The Free Church aimed to move forward on a broad Evangelical base.[40]

On their part, Protestant Dissenters admired the sacrifices of Free Church ministers and made financial contributions accordingly. Moreover, they sympathised with the Free Church's Evangelical principles. Doubtless they, too, hoped for a union of fragments – though not one where leadership would ultimately fall to the Free Church. In any event, observers such as the Revd Norman Macleod feared that both at home and in the colonies, the result would be 'a strong united combination of all Dissenters against all the Establishments of [the] country ...'.[41]

In all these endeavours, the laity had a substantial role to play. In Montreal, a movement in favour of the Free Church had, in fact, formed *before* the Disruption happened in Scotland (which shows how carefully planned the Disruption really was), with the merchant John Redpath in the forefront. Tracts had been printed and meetings held well before the invitation to come to Canada was issued to the Free Church deputies Cunningham and Burns. And it was a group of leading Presbyterian Evangelicals in the province of Canada who invited the Scottish newspaper editor Peter Brown and his son George to move from New York and to take up the struggle for Free Church principles north of the border. The Browns began the *Banner* in Toronto in August 1843, soon after the stirring events at home.

The *Banner* placed the Disruption firmly on the agenda in British North America. 'The battle must be fought by the people of Canada', it told its readers.[42] It was all too obvious to observers that 'the Banner people … desire disunion'; indeed, they worked for it so energetically that even one of the Free Church deputies to North America, the Revd George Lewis, felt early in 1844 that a few 'cooling drops' could be infused into their zeal.[43] Although relations between the Presbyterian Church and the state were quite different in the colonies from those in Scotland, the *Banner* strained to make connections, helping to create a furore, for example, over the Presbyterian Church Temporalities bill in Canada West and stirring up the Scots laity against their more moderate ministers. The temporalities scheme, dealing with the management of congregational property, had received unanimous assent from the Canadian Kirk Synod before being introduced to the legislature in 1843. However, the bill emphasised the power of Church courts rather than those of congregations. The *Banner* presented it as an Erastian plot, a sinister invasion by the state of the ecclesiastical sphere. Dr Burns, too, insisted that it was a 'fatal delusion' to regard the question of spiritual independence as exclusively Scottish.[44] Thus, matters such as the Church of Scotland attitude to the clergy reserves in Canada West (land set aside for the support of a 'Protestant' clergy), or the special arrangements regarding Presbyterian Churches and glebes which obtained in New Brunswick, would now be linked to the Disruption question. The Church of Scotland had fought hard for a share of the clergy reserves in a colony where congregational financial support for ministers was minimal; the Free Church did not immediately become voluntarist, but within a few months those who wished to retain a share were portrayed by Free Church supporters as seekers after Mammon. These were political as well as religious issues and of deep concern to leading Scots colonists such as the Evangelical sympathisers John Redpath of Montreal and Isaac Buchanan of Toronto and the equally determined supporter of the Moderates, William Morris of Brockville, who had played a key role in the campaign for a Kirk share of the clergy reserves and who remained a 'zealous and influential friend' of the Kirk.[45]

Interest in religious matters was not confined to middle and upper-class settlers. Highland peasants, who tended to settle in groups, were likely to take with them significant religious experiences and traditions from Scotland to the colonies. A 'blessed revival of religion' in Cape Breton was noted by the Colonial Committee at the first General Assembly of the Free Church; obviously it owed something to the settlers' experiences of the Highland revivals in the early nineteenth century.[46] Memories of the Highland Clearances may also have had their effects; resentment of landlords, lingering in the minds of Highland emigrants, was doubtless exacerbated by news of landlord refusals to grant sites for new Free Churches in Scotland and by the high-handed exercise of landlord religious patronage. Perhaps it was this which led the Highlanders of Zorra, Canada West, to send £130 to the Free Church Sustentation Fund in 1846: a substantial sum from a very poor congregation.[47]

Resentment of landlords was not confined to Highlanders. Some of the reactions to Norman Macleod on his 1845 visit to British North America were coloured by the suspicion that 'better things could have been expected of him had he not [as minister of Dalkeith] been placed in proximity to that *notorious oppressor* of his tenantry, the Duke of Buccleuch'.[48] There were Lowland religious revivals, also, which had affected emigrants from these areas: the Kilsyth and Dundee revivals of 1839–42 and, in a more general sense, the whole movement of Evangelical Revival which quickened the Scottish Kirk in the early part of the nineteenth century. Equally, these years were a period of substantial Scots emigration, especially by poor textile workers from the Lowlands. The connection between revivalism and the Free Church has already been alluded to; the Scots settlers who came from revival areas in this period would find, in the appeals of the Free Church to the colonies, much that touched their own experiences.

There was also an undoubted connection between the Free Church and the old Covenanting strongholds of western Scotland, from which had come many of the Scots emigrants of the period. Even the leading Establishment minister Norman Macleod admitted that 'the Free Kirk are the descendants of the Covenanters'.[49] It was a point emphasised in the Free Church Memorial Exhibition in 1893, which was crowded with Covenanting memorabilia. The Covenanters' flag for the parish of Fenwick was one of the many displayed at the Exhibition.[50] Fenwick was also the location of one of the west of Scotland emigration societies which flourished in the 1830s. The geographical impact of the Disruption in Canada West substantiates these ideas. The settlers of the 1820s and 1830s, who in numbers swamped the earlier Scots population, were largely opening up the western areas of the province and it was primarily these areas, the presbyteries of Toronto, Hamilton and London, which went over to the Free Church in 1844. Earlier settlers, in contrast, who had gone out at a time when, and from areas where, Moderatism was in the ascendant, were less likely to be sympathetic to Free Church notions. Geographical origin and time of emigration seem to have been more important than social origins of settlers in influencing behaviour.[51]

Dr Burns had argued that, in terms of wealth and numbers, Presbyterians ought to be at the head of the religious community in most of the provinces of British North America. In his view, Presbyterianism was of all others the system best adapted to popular institutions in the colonies, holding a due medium between the hierarchical English system and the 'democratic laymanism and anarchy' of the United States.

Whatever the truth in Burns's arguments regarding the appeal of Presbyterianism, for a generation the impact of the Disruption much diminished Presbyterian chances of assuming the religious leadership for which he had hoped. Census returns and other statistics are difficult to interpret, given a certain bafflement by compilers regarding the many shades of Presbyterianism; however, division obviously weakened the whole. The Free Church continued to demonstrate more dynamism than the body it had left; and for some time the Kirk in the colonies seemed to look passively on, without, as one disgusted member put it, 'raising a finger in its own defence'.[52] Burns and others had noted that a large proportion of the Scots Presbyterian clergymen in all the North American provinces were hostile to the Free Church cause[53] but that proportion diminished every year in the decades following 1843. Key figures left for home, among them Dr Liddell, Principal of Queen's College in Kingston and leader of those desiring to retain the Canadian synod's connection with the Kirk in Scotland in the crucial months of 1843 and 1844. The *Historical and Statistical Report* of the Church of Scotland in Canada, published in 1866, painted a picture which could be replicated in the other provinces.[54] Time and time again the surveys of each congregation show that, in those many cases where, in 1844, a minister left for the Free Church or returned to Scotland, a lengthy period of 'destitution' followed. In these crucial years of neglect, membership plummeted, and the losses were not made good. Unions of Free and Secessionist Presbyterian Churches took place in the Maritimes in 1860 and in the province of Canada in 1861, further tilting the balance against the Church of Scotland. It had refused to contemplate a union with the other Presbyterians at that time, leading the *Presbyterian Witness*, from a Canadian perspective, to aver that it was surely 'contrary to the genius of Presbyterianism to be hanging on to the skirts of the transatlantic churches'.[55] Hanging on to transatlantic (i.e. Scottish) skirts had been precisely the colonial position in the years of the Disruption and those immediately following; it was not until 1875 that the Kirk in Canada decided that the issues of the 1840s in Scotland were no longer relevant to its situation.[56] A union of all Presbyterians in the recently created Dominion was achieved at that date, more than half a century before the rifts were partially healed in Scotland.

In many ways, the effects of the Disruption in Australia were similar to those in British North America, although the numbers of ministers and settlers involved were far smaller. The distance from the battle zone was, of course, greater, as was the time that information took to arrive. However, the struggle at home was watched with intense interest by Presbyterians in Australia, the majority of whom were recent arrivals from Scotland. New South Wales, the oldest colony, opened to free settlement only in 1821; the first Presbyterian minister, the redoubtable Revd John Dunmore Lang of the Church of Scotland, arrived two years later. There was a Secessionist Presbyterian minister in Van Diemen's Land from 1822, but no representative of the Kirk until the early 1830s.[57]

In the last half dozen years before the Disruption, there was a surge of immigration to Australia, encouraged by a government bounty system and by the fact that British North America, for a time, was rendered less attractive because of economic depression and the rebellions in Upper and Lower Canada. The population of New South Wales rose rapidly and Scots shared in the increase, providing about one-sixth of the total arriving in that period.[58] Such immigrants, whether Highland labourers, Lowland craftsmen, or investors in commercial and pastoral enterprises could hardly fail to be well-versed in the issues of the Ten Years' Conflict. So, too, were their ministers, who largely arrived as a result of the proselytising zeal of Lang. If the Revd Robert Burns is regarded as the Apostle of Canada, the Revd John Dunmore Lang is the Apostle of Australia. During visits home in the 1820s and 1830s, Lang preached the needs of religion in Australia, and persuaded ministers, teachers and other settlers to go out. It was an uphill struggle to procure ministers, for the Church of Scotland, as we have already seen, was lamentably slow to recognise its colonial responsibilities. 'Cold-blooded and unnatural indifference' was the phrase Lang used to describe the Church of Scotland attitude,[59] an attitude which persisted, as regards the Australian colonies, until the formation of the General Assembly's Colonial Committee in 1836. The committee was motivated, not just by the desire to promote the religious interests of Scottish Presbyterians in the colonies, as its title suggests, but also by the need to assert the right to 'perfect equality with the Church of England'.[60] Further worries were the standard of education in the young Australian colonies and whether the recently formed Australian presbyteries should have the right to license probationers. The latter reflects doubts over the quality of the few ministers in the area. There was a fear, even stronger than in the North American case, that 'comparatively few went out who could find important work at home'.[61] Even Lang admitted that in the early days (and the 1830s were still early days for Australia), anything was considered good enough for the colonies.[62]

The fact that the Kirk ministers were few in numbers and, in many cases, mediocre in ability, did not mean that they were unanimous in viewpoint. On the contrary, they were rent by divisions even before 1843. Lang, a man of undoubted gifts and conscious of every one of them, assumed a domineering attitude towards his fellow ministers, whose patron he was and whose passage out he had provided in some cases.[63] Combative and opinionated, he withdrew from the presbytery of New South Wales in 1837 because of difficulties over the admission of the ministers he had brought out from Scotland. With supreme self-confidence, he formed his own synod; although synod and presbytery reunited briefly in 1840 under the name of the Synod of Australia, the elements of discord were still present. They surfaced over the issue of Church – state relations. At this time, small state salaries were paid to all Presbyterian ministers in New South Wales. Lang became convinced of the merits of voluntarism, particularly after a visit to the United States in 1839. As a result, he renounced all connection with the state and the state Churches of the colony in 1842; in response, an enraged Kirk deposed him from its ministry.[64]

It was shortly after these troublesome events that the Australian Kirk faced the news of the Disruption. Perhaps conscious of the recent divisions among its own members, the Synod of Australia resolved at its first meeting after the Disruption that its primary duty was to maintain unity and to avoid any act of 'adherence' to the Church of Scotland or the Free Church. Although there was general support for Free Church principles, the synod aimed to maintain friendly relations with both sides.

It was not an attitude which commended itself to those at home. The Church of Scotland thundered and threatened. Despite its own Declaratory Act of 1840, which disclaimed any authority over the Kirk in the colonies, it still believed that 'encouragement and reproof' were justified.[65] It now stated that all adhering to the resolutions of the Australian synod were no longer to be regarded as ministers and elders in connection with the Church of Scotland or as entitled to the privileges ensured by law to such; it had the look of a threat to deprive ministers of their state salaries, especially since the Colonial Committee sent off all the relevant documents to the Secretary of State for the Colonies, so that he would have the facts at his disposal when he came to consider any amendments to the Australian Temporalities bill.[66]

The Free Church ridiculed and mocked. The 'milk and water' resolutions of the Australian synod sat ill with a Church sustained by a sense of messianic fervour and proud of the self-sacrifice of its members. Dr Candlish felt that the General Assembly of the Free Church must take the same attitude as that of the Church of Scotland: the Australian synod 'must be either off or on – either in the Establishment or out of it (laughter)'.[67] Lang later reflected (and not in tranquillity) on his emotions at the time, remarking that Dante represented Satan himself as a respectable character in comparison with those angels who attempted neutrality.

Disruption in Australia was therefore forced from home. In 1846 the synod, having to make a choice, decided to remain in connection with the Church of Scotland. Australian newspaper reports that most ministers were prepared to adhere had already reached the mother Church; sixteen did so, while four ministers protested and withdrew to form a Free Church. By 1851, there were 6 Free Church ministers in New South Wales, 5 in Victoria (formed out of New South Wales in that year), 2 in South Australia, where settlement had begun in the late 1830s, and 2 in Van Diemen's Land. Perhaps, as Lang suggested, the delay in taking a stand harmed the growth of a Free Church; he was convinced that ministers were hanging on as long as possible to 'the pelf' of the Kirk connection, their state salaries and subventions from the mother Church.[68]

The home Churches, preoccupied by events in the colonies in North America, whose size of population and accessibility seemed to demand more immediate action than Australia, took some time to send out deputations. It was not until 1847 that the Free Church even discussed sending a deputation (of one!)[69] and by that stage its attention in the area was largely taken up by its grand scheme for New Zealand. The imperial government was experimenting with a system of 'class colonies' and the whole province of Otago had been put into the hands of the Free Church. A special Free Church colony, complete with minister, schoolmaster, families and trades, was organised and sent out.[70]

The Church of Scotland, struggling to fill the gaps at home and convinced that the crisis in Australia and New Zealand was not as severe as in British North America, was also slow to send deputies, and even slower to send out permanent ministers. There must have been many congregations like the one at Auckland, which, when services by a Church of Scotland minister were not continued in the early 1840s (perhaps he had returned to Scotland), resolved to appeal to the Free Church Colonial Committee – and failing success there, to any other Presbyterian Church in Scotland.[71] A Presbyterian minister of whatever stripe was preferable to none. Statistics for the southern section of New South Wales (the future Victoria) show the Church of Scotland trailing in the effort to deal with 'destitution'; in the eight years following the Disruption, 9 ministers came out from the Presbyterian Relief Church, 3 from the Free Church, and none at all from the Church of Scotland. In the Queensland area of New South Wales, the Free Church sent out a larger number of ministers to the colony than any other Presbyterian Church in the twenty years or so after the Disruption.[72]

By the late 1850s, Australian and New Zealand presbyteries and synods had blossomed in luxuriant confusion, all of them anxious to minister to the increased population of the gold-rush days. In 1859, at the meeting to discuss the projected union between the United Presbyterian Church (Secessionist) of Victoria and the Free Church of Victoria, the Revd Irving Hetherington remarked that he had been twenty-two years in Australia and had witnessed six disruptions; every little fragment, he went on, called itself a synod, 'thus making the term Synod a very by-word in the country ... '.[73] Common sense alone seemed to suggest that this constant fragmentation did no service to Presbyterianism in Australia. As the issues of the 1840s became more remote, and the state withdrew from the ecclesiastical sphere altogether,[74] negotiations for union proceeded. All the Presbyterian Churches in New South Wales united in 1865. Consolidation proceeded at different rates in different states, with discussions about unifying all Presbyterian Churches throughout Australia under way by the end of the nineteenth century and reaching a successful conclusion in 1901, some twenty-six years after a single Presbyterian Church was formed for the Dominion of Canada.

The effects of the Disruption in British North America, Australia and New Zealand indicate the accuracy of contemporary comments regarding the fierce loyalty of emigrant Scots to the homeland and their devotion to the national Church. As the dispirited Church of England missionary (and sole minister) in the Red River Settlement of British North America reported in the 1820s, the Scottish settlers there 'brought their religion along with them, and are conscientiously wedded to the rites and discipline of the Presbyterian form of worship, and nothing will make them forsake the church of their forefathers'.[75] When a Presbyterian minister belatedly arrived there in 1851, the Scots left the English Church in a body, to the number of over three hundred, to place themselves under his ministry. This tenacious attachment to Scots institutions was strengthened in the years of the Disruption by improvements in communication. It was the more striking because of the statistics of Scots emigration: there was a particular surge in the 1830s, virtually inundating an earlier emigrant population which had struck deeper local roots.[76] The large number of recently arrived Scots emigrants in the colonies, and even more their Scots-born and Scots-trained ministers, were fresh from the scene of conflict and followed its stages closely from afar. Some came from the old Covenanting areas, others from areas where religious revivals had recently occurred. All were marked by their experiences and indifference was unlikely in these circumstances. This was a period when Church leaders had a central role in public life and religion was a focus of national interest in Scotland.[77]

Studied neutrality, reached after careful consideration of the issues, *might* have been a possibility, given that the Church/state problems of Scotland were largely absent from the colonies. However, this option was made unworkable in British North America by local lay and ministerial pressure and by the propagandising efforts of the home Churches, particularly the Free Church. Great efforts were made to present the Disruption as something relevant to emigrant Scots.

In Australia, where a majority of the synod would have preferred neutrality, such an approach was rendered impractical by the refusal of the home Churches to accept it. Instead, a decision to be 'off' or 'on' was demanded. Thus, the Church of Scotland's statement in 1846 that the introduction of divisions into colonial synods and congregations was 'gratuitous and uncalled for'[78] did not mean to suggest that the colonies should stand aloof from the fray. It aimed, rather, to apportion blame – to hold the Free Church up as a troublemaker and to urge that colonial synods should unequivocally and unanimously have thrown in their lot with the Established Kirk.

Many anodyne statements were made at the time about the independence of the colonial Churches. This was technically true; but we should remember that, in practical terms, they still relied on help from Scotland – to some extent financially and above all in personnel. Thus they were not self-supporting in any real sense and their organisation, although it had progressed rapidly in British North America in the 1830s, was still very rudimentary in Australia and virtually non-existent in New Zealand.

The Disruption was deliberately exported from Scotland to the colonies of Scottish settlement and as deliberately received there. Its impact testified to the fact that, whatever the geographical horizons of the emigrants, their mental horizons remained emphatically Scottish. It constituted the triumph of denomination over environment.

NOTES

1   Henry, Lord Cockburn, *Journal of Lord Cockburn, being a Continuation of the Memorials of his Time*, 2 vols (London, 1974), vol. ii, p. 9.
2   *Proudfoot Diary*, 9 Sept. 1833, University of Western Ontario Library, Regional Collection. The name Upper Canada was changed to Canada West in 1841 on the union of the Canadas; it became Ontario in 1867.
3   Report of the Colonial Committee to the General Assembly of the Church of Scotland (1846), p. 27.
4   A. M. Machar, *Memorials of the Life and Ministry of the Reverend John Machar, D.D., Late Minister of St. Andrew's Church, Kingston* (Toronto, 1873), pp. 82, 83, 94.
5   Known as the Synod of the Presbyterian Church of Canada. In Canada West (Ontario), the Church of Scotland had been the second largest

denomination, with 16 per cent of the population adhering compared to the Anglican Church's 20 per cent. J. S. Moir, *Church and State in Canada West* (Toronto, 1959), Appendix 1.

6   J. S. Moir, *Enduring Witness: A History of the Presbyterian Church in Canada* (Toronto, 1974), p. 104.

7   Revd Thomas Brown, *Annals of the Disruption* (Edinburgh, 1877), pp. 566–7.

8   Report of the Colonial Committee to the General Assembly of the Free Church (Edinburgh, 1844), p. 126.

9   Revd Norman Macleod, writing of his visit to British North America in 1845; Revd Donald Macleod, *Memoir of Norman Macleod, D.D.* (London, 1876), vol. 1, pp. 247–8.

10 Cockburn, *Journal of Lord Cockburn*, vol. ii, p. 28.

11 Report of the Colonial Committee to the General Assembly of the Free Church (Edinburgh, 1846), p. 127. The Free Church claimed to be the true inheritor of Knox's principles.

12 Report by Revd Norman Macleod to the General Assembly of the Church of Scotland (Edinburgh, 1846); Revd George Lewis, *Impressions of America and the American Colonies* (Edinburgh, 1845), p. 17; *Report presented to the Free Church Colonial Committee, on Canada and Nova Scotia by Reverend Dr Burns, Paisley* (Edinburgh, 1844), p. 21.

13 The phrase is Lord Palmerston's.

14 The point is emphasised in Neil G. Smith, 'By Schism Rent Asunder: A Study of the Disruption of the Presbyterian Church in Canada in 1844', *Canadian Journal of Theology*, i (1955), 175–183.

15 William Gregg, *History of the Presbyterian Church in the Dominion of Canada from its Earliest Times to 1834* (Toronto, 1885), p. 283.

16 Queen's College in Kingston, designed to train Church of Scotland ministers, did not acquire its charter until 1841.

17 Revd G. Smellie, *Memoir of the Reverend John Bayne, D.D, of Galt* (Toronto, 1871), p. 16. *Sermons by the late Reverend Mark Y. Stark, A.M., with Memoir by the Reverend William Reid, A.M.,* (Toronto, 1871), p. 3.

18 The Revd John Bayne, sent out by the Glasgow Colonial Society to Upper Canada in 1834, first supplied St Andrew's, Toronto and then settled in Galt; the Revd Mark Stark went out in 1833 and was called to Ancaster and Dundas, Upper Canada.

19 An Evangelical's view of the Moderates: *Burns Report*, p. 34.

20 Ibid., p. 28. The general picture of 'destitution' is undoubtedly correct but a caveat is in order. Sometimes the term was used by commentators to describe the lack of a minister of their particular type of Presbyterianism – not the lack of *any* Presbyterian minister.

21 Brown, *Annals of the Disruption*, p. 560.

22 *Proceedings of the General Assembly of the Free Church, May 1846* (Edinburgh, 1846), p. 125.

23 *Proceedings of the General Assembly of the Church of Scotland, May 1844* (Edinburgh, 1844), p. 6.

24 *Burns Report*, p. 28.

25 Lewis, *Impressions of America*, p. 361.

26 Every Church of Scotland foreign missionary left the Establishment at the Disruption; so did the bulk of the ministers involved in the Kirk's Colonial Committee.

27 Cockburn, *Journal of Lord Cockburn*, vol. ii, p. 49; and see Brown, *Annals of the Disruption*, vol. ii, 'Religious Revival a Preparation for the Conflict'.

28 Brown, *Annals of the Disruption*, p. 82.

29 Lewis, *Impressions of America*, pp. 4, 99, 348; Brown, *Annals of the Disruption*, p. 622. Note also the emphasis in *Disruption Worthies*, both in the historical sketch of the Free Church and in individual entries, on the universal applicability of the spiritual forces liberated by the Disruption: James A. Wylie (ed.) *Disruption Worthies: A Memorial of 1843* (Edinburgh, 1881), p. lxxxviii – historical sketch by James A. Wylie, and entry on Dr William A. Hetherington

on p. 305. The hope of receiving financial aid from outside Scotland was doubtless an additional factor.

30 Machar, *Memorials*, p. 82.

31 Colonial Committee Report to the General Assembly of the Free Church (Edinburgh, 1845), p. 166.

32 Robert Ferrier Burns, *The Life and Times of the Reverend Robert Burns* (Toronto, 1873), pp. 95, 152; and see id., *Burns Report, passim.*

33 Colonial Committee Report to the General Assembly of the Free Church (Edinburgh, 1846), pp. 119, 120. This report lists eighteen deputies sent out in 1844 and 1845.

34 A point not appreciated by J. S. Moir, who mistakenly dates the Church of Scotland deputation to 1844, the same year as that of the Free Church: *Enduring Witness*, pp. 103–4.

35 Macleod was not yet the household name he was later to become, but he had already gained a substantial reputation, in part because of a series of pamphlets written in 'pithy Scotch' for ordinary folk. The most famous, *A Crack aboot the Kirk for Kintra Folk* (1843), went through eight editions. See Maclcod, *Memoir of Norman Macleod*, vol. i, p. 124 and Appendix B.

36 Ibid., vol. i, pp. 234, 248–9.

37 *Burns Report*, p. 9.

38 Ibid., p. 30. In 1840, the bulk of the Secessionist Presbyterians in the province of Canada had entered into a union with the Kirk. No such union had been achieved in the Lower Provinces (the Maritimes), where competition between Secessionist and Church of Scotland ministers had been much more acrimonious and where the gains for the Free Church in co-operating with Secessionists were likely to be greater.

39 *Burns Report*, pp. 5, 6, 7, 30.

40 Lewis, *Impressions of America*, pp. 377, 351. Lewis appreciated the energy of the Methodists and others in providing the Gospel to areas where no other denomination had penetrated. There was, of course, an implied criticism of the inertia of the Church of Scotland here.

41 For Addresses to the Free Church deputation by Congregational Unions, Methodists and others, see *Burns Report*, Appendix no. 1. Macleod's gloomy prophecy is contained in a letter to his sister, Jane, 25 May 1843, cited in Macleod, *Memoir of Norman Macleod*, vol. i, p. 199.

42 *Banner*, 8 Mar. 1844.

43 Oliver Mowat to John Mowat, 12 June 1844, in Peter Neary (ed.), 'Neither Radical nor Tory nor Whig: Letters by Oliver Mowat to John Mowat 1843–1844', *Ontario History*, 71 (1979), 105; Lewis, *Impressions of America*, p. 347.

44 On the technicalities of the Temporalities bill, see Richard W. Vaudry, *The Free Church in Victorian Canada, 1844–1861* (Waterloo, Ontario, 1989), pp. 22–4, and Moir, *Enduring Witness*, p. 103. For Burns's comment see *Burns Report*, p. 35.

45 Report from the Colonial Committee to the General Assembly of the Church of Scotland, (1846), p. 20. Buchanan, from a strongly Evangelical background in Glasgow, had actually been paying an extended visit to Scotland at the time of the Disruption. Other influential Toronto Presbyterians had been members of Dr Chalmers's congregation in Glasgow; some had been elders there: *Proceedings of the General Assembly of the Free Church, May 1845* (Edinburgh, 1845), p. 20.

46 *Proceedings of the General Assembly of the Free Church, May 1844* (Edinburgh, 1844), p. 126. It owed something also to the efforts of strongly Evangelical Scottish ladies such as Mrs Mackay of Rockville in donating and raising funds to send equally Evangelical ministers to the Cape Breton Highlanders. See R. Gordon Balfour, *Presbyterianism in the Colonies* (Edinburgh, 1900), p. 33.

47 *Proceedings of the General Assembly of the Free Church, May 1846* (Edinburgh, 1846), p. 137. For the great support in the Highlands for the Free Church, see Andrew L. Drummond and James Bulloch, *The Scottish Church 1688–1843: The Age of the Moderates* (Edinburgh, 1973), p. 249.

48 *Proceedings of the General Assembly of the Church of Scotland, May 1846* (Edinburgh, 1846), p. 41.
49 Brown, *Annals of the Disruption*, pp. 450, 617. The tenacity of Covenanting passions is worth noting. Even in the twentieth century they are not dead: in the late 1960s the Labour politician Tam Dalyell, descendant and namesake of Sir Tam Dalyell of the Binns, scourge of the Covenanters, was campaigning on behalf of a parliamentary candidate in Ayrshire. The local party agent told him not to go to certain villages – these events were still remembered.
50 Item 283 in the Exhibition Catalogue.
51 See Vaudry's comments on the dubiety of linking social origin or occupation to behaviour in religion: *Free Church in Canada*, p. 29.
52 Neary, 'Mowat Letters', p. 110.
53 *Burns Report*, p. 35.
54 *A Historical and Statistical Report of the Presbyterian Church of Canada in Association with the Church of Scotland for the year 1866* (Montreal, 1867).
55 Cited in Moir, *Enduring Witness*, p. 135.
56 For example, such small Church endowments as existed in the colonies had long since been secularised by that date.
57 Two-thirds of the leading merchants of Van Diemen's Land were Scots in this period: David S. Macmillan, *Scotland and Australia, 1788–1850: Emigration, Commerce and Investment* (Oxford, 1967), pp. 111–12, 173.
58 Ibid., p. 303.
59 Revd John Dunmore Lang, *Historical and Statistical Account of New South Wales* (London, 1875) vol. ii, p. 404.
60 Report by Principal McFarlan of Glasgow to the General Assembly of the Church (1836), cited in Macmillan, *Scotland and Australia*, p. 307.
61 *Proceedings of the General Assembly of the Free Church, May 1847* (Edinburgh, 1847), p. 102.
62 Lang, *Historical and Statistical Account*, vol. ii, p. 432.
63 He was not slow to point this out: see Ibid., p. 432.
64 He was later reinstated after an appeal to the General Assembly in Scotland. For the details of his chequered career, see the editor's introduction to Lang's highly coloured reminiscences: D. W. Baker (ed.), *Reminiscences of My Life and Times* (Melbourne, 1972).
65 Letter from the General Assembly to the Presbyterian Churches in the British Colonies in connection with the Church of Scotland (1840), Presbyterian Church Synod Papers, 1839–1842, Queen's University Archives, Kingston, Ontario.
66 *Proceedings of the General Assembly of the Church of Scotland, May 1845* (Edinburgh, 1845), pp. 11–14.
67 *Proceedings of the General Assembly of the Free Church, May 1845* (Edinburgh, 1845), p. 167.
68 Lang, *Historical and Statistical Account*, vol. ii, p. 443.
69 *Proceedings of the General Assembly of the Free Church, May 1847* (Edinburgh, 1847), pp. 103, 110–11.
70 For an account of the setting-up of the colony, see Brown, *Annals of the Disruption*, pp. 569–71.
71 Balfour, *Presbyterianism in the Colonies*, p. 231.
72 Ibid., pp. 118, 169.
73 Ibid., p. 133.
74 State aid to religion was discontinued in South Australia in the 1850s; all grants for Church purposes were abolished in New South Wales in 1862.
75 Gregg, *History of the Presbyterian Church*, pp. 567, 573.
76 See the comments of J. M. S. Careless, 'Mid-Victorian Liberalism in Central Canadian Newspapers', *Canadian Historical Review*, xxxi (1950), 234–5.
77 T. C. Smout, *A Century of the Scottish People, 1830–1950* (London, 1986), p. 181.
78 See n. 3.

CHAPTER NINE

The Dutch Reformed Church of South Africa
A Product of the Disruption?

A. C. ROSS

THE DUTCH REFORMED CHURCH OF SOUTH AFRICA is a Church which was created in the nineteenth century by a group of Scottish ministers of the 'Popular' or Evangelical party in the Church of Scotland, the same party whose dedicated stand on deeply held principles led inexorably to the Disruption of 1843. These ministers warmly applauded it when it came, and their work was later consolidated and developed by Scots and Afrikaners trained in the leading theological college produced by the Disruption, New College. It was the piety generated by the Disruption and nurtured in the Free Kirk that created the Dutch Reformed Church. This had gained the loyalty and shaped the world view of the vast majority of the Afrikaner people by the time they were fully incorporated in the new Union of South Africa in 1910. Then in the next twenty years, within this Church, the theology of apartheid was formed.

Some historical background is necessary to understand this process. While it was to be fundamentally transformed during the nineteenth century by the theology and piety of the Scottish Disruption, the Nederduitse Gereformeerde Kerk van Suid Afrika (NGK) had its origin in the decision of the classis (presbytery) of Amsterdam in 1665 to send pastors to serve the small Dutch East India Company settlement at the Cape. The settlement was founded by Jan van Riebeck on behalf of the Company in 1652. The first minister, Jan van Arkel, was based in Cape Town, the only parish. It was not until 1685 that Stellenbosch became the second parish. A third was added at Paarl soon after the arrival of the Huguenot refugees at the Cape in 1688. These were readily absorbed by the Dutch Burghers and time-served German servants and soldiers of the Company, who together made up the farming community of the Cape, the Boers. Many began to call themselves Afrikaners in the last decades of the eighteenth century.

Two different styles of Boer life developed: the first was of those who farmed in the area of Mediterranean climate close to Cape Town, producing wheat, vegetables, wine and brandy for its market; the other was of the cattle-rearing trekboer. The area occupied by these graziers was constantly

expanding as they moved northwards and eastwards. These families came
to have only minimum contact with Cape Town. They sought their 'lekker
lewe', their 'sweet life', the freedom to live in their own way on their huge
ten-to twenty-thousand-acre 'farms'. On each farm there could be a considerable community, made up of some of the grown-up children of the grazier
with their spouses and children, the Coloured servants and herders and, in
the richer families, slaves.

Despite popular ideas to the contrary, these trekboers were not a devout
Calvinist people. In 1753, the Governor, Baron van Imhoff, did a tour of
some of the distant farms. This was unusual, for the East India Company
cared little about South Africa as long as Cape Town was safe and could
supply its ships. On his return, Imhoff reported

> that he had observed, with amazement and sorrow, how little interest
> was taken in the public services of religion, and in what a depth of
> indifference and ignorance in this respect a great part of the country
> people were living so that they seemed more like a gathering of blinded
> heathen than a colony of European Christians.[1]

As a result of what he had learned on the tour, two new parishes were created:
Roodezand (Tulbagh) and Zwartland (Malmesbury). But even this provision was totally inadequate. Each parish encompassed an enormous area of
rough terrain without roads and containing several hundred ranches.

Trekboers did try to come to the church for the baptism of their children
and to receive Holy Communion, but this was at most once a year and very
often at even less frequent intervals. Sometimes a family-group would wait
till there were several children to be baptised in order to justify the difficult
journey which could be as much as seven or eight days each way. The practice
of ministers going out on a tour to visit all the far-flung families and holding
open-air communions like the old Scots Covenanters, an image much loved
in the romanticised picture of trekboer life in some twentieth-century
writing on South Africa, began in the 1790s and only became a regular
practice after the Scottish take-over of the NGK in the nineteenth century.
Certainly, the families within a day's journey of the parish churches – seven
by 1799 – did try to attend the quarterly Communion service (Nagmaal).

> Once a quarter the Holy Communion was celebrated, when the farm-
> ers came in their wagons from far and wide. The square in front of the
> church was a lively scene of people and wagons and here the sale and
> bartering of goods went on. The farmers generally arrived in the village
> the Tuesday night before the celebration as on the Friday afternoon a
> preparatory service was held … The visit was the occasion to bring
> produce to the market and to lay in a stock of groceries and other
> household requirements.[2]

However, for most trekboer families, attendance at the Nagmaal was a
once-a-year event at best.

One can hardly conceive of a pattern of Church life farther from what
was traditional in Reformed Churches. From the beginning, they demanded
the regular hearing of the Word preached by an academically trained

preacher and the close supervision of each family's life by the whole congregation through the work of the elders. The Calvinist Churches thrived in towns or areas where the density of population allowed for that style of congregational life: Geneva, The Netherlands, Provence, Lowland Scotland and New England. It is worth noting that New England Calvinism was simply unable to cope when, after the American Revolution, a massive population crossed the mountains and began moving the frontier farther and farther westwards.

The picture often drawn of the Boer population in the eighteenth century is of a devout Christian people, stubbornly clinging to their Calvinism, cut off from the intellectual advances of Europe of the time. It is inaccurate in almost every way, as we have begun to suggest. Even in the few areas where there was regular attendance at Church, the ethos was not one of deeply pious Calvinism. Professor du Plessis describes it thus:

> The Mother Church in the Netherlands supplied them with ministers, while the salaries of these officers were paid by a paternal Government. At the Cape there was no local effort, very little local interest, and, of course, no local control. Religion was severely unemotional and chiefly a matter of form, and it exercised but little influence over the everyday life of the population.[3]

This was the situation in Cape Town, Stellenbosch and the few other places where any kind of regular Church life was possible. The trekboer graziers' contact with organised Church life was minimal.

It is important to understand that although some families drifted away from any kind of Christian connection at all, most developed a pattern of Christian life that suited their needs. Since, as most historians of South Africa are agreed, the designation 'Christian' was the key badge of identity of the White Boer over against Khoi, or Xhosa or any other African, family worship came to be the outward symbol of this identity. This worship was led by the head of the family, morning and evening. A portion was read from the Dutch Bible and then prayers were offered and sometimes a psalm sung. In many families the Khoi house servants and slaves, if there were any, attended, sitting on the floor or standing near the door.[4]

Just how far the secular and religious life of the trekboer had become detached from the world of Cape Town and any form of Calvinist Church authority became tragically clear in the 1790s. During this period Cape Town had its two most devout and dedicated ministers in all of its history hitherto, Helperus Ritzema van Lier (1786–93) and Michael Vos (1794–1819). These dedicated men were aided in their attempt to bring Evangelical life to the NGK by the arrival of two other Evangelical and missionary-minded ministers, J. H. van Manger and Henrik W. Ballot. In 1795, reaction to these young men and their concerns showed up with startling clarity when, during the Patriots' rising of the frontier Boers against Cape authority, Manger was expelled by the rebels from Graaff-Reinet along with Maynier, the landdrost (Government administrator and magistrate). The rejection of the Church was repeated when Ballot was expelled in the second Boer rising of 1799. As J. Alton Templin has noted

It is interesting to compare the Boers' attitude with their actions. Although they begged for more educational [sic] leadership, such leaders were not welcome unless they re-inforced the presuppositions of the Boer superiority over the Africans and Boers insistence on their own rights in the face of the law and order of the central government.[5]

The trekboers were insistent that they were the 'Christians' but theirs was a popular folk-religion that had only tenuous connections with classical Calvinism. We have no major source that gives any insight into the fundamental theological concepts of this folk-religion. But Cape records[6] show the consistent use of the word 'Christian' for a White person whatever his or her relationship to the Church, while all Africans of any background were being denied that name. 'The children of Hottentot women, in whose veins *Christian blood* often flowed, were educated in Christianity; they learned to sing psalms and to read.'[7]

When one-third of the Boer people quitted the colony during the period of the Great Trek, 1834–40, these voortrekkers left writings which are very informative: they reflect a sense that the voortrekkers were replicating Israel's travels in the wilderness and that the African people they met played the role of the Amalekites, etc.[8] There was also a sense of a special calling in God's plan for Africa. These ideas were apparent by the late forties and what little information we have about the earlier period appears to confirm that the seed of this growth lay in the folk-religion of the trekboer.

When we return to look at the formal history of the NGK we have to consider what happened under the British. When they reoccupied the Cape Colony in 1806, an occupation which became permanent and legitimate by the Treaty of Vienna (1815), they recognised the NGK as the state Church of the colony and continued to pay the stipends of the parish ministers. In return, the Governor kept the authority to appoint the ministers to their charges and maintain strict control over the Church's affairs, as had been laid down by the Batavian Governor, de Mist, in his Church regulations. Despite this, one might ask, however, how far there was a Church at all at the Cape in 1806. J. C. McCarter, the young NGK minister from Scotland, who wrote the first history of the NGK, said of the situation

Up to the point that our sketch has reached, it could scarcely be said with correctness that a Dutch Reformed church existed at the Cape at all. There were seven isolated congregations receiving emoluments from the Government but fettered, trammelled and deprived of all freedom of action.[9]

His emphasis on the helplessness of these congregations came from his distress at the tightness of state control. There was no presbytery or synod, the congregations were separate, each with its own session (consistory) on which sat a political commissioner appointed by the Governor, usually the local landdrost. Under Dutch rule, these congregations had belonged, theoretically, to the classis of Amsterdam. This link was now broken and so by any standard the situation was unsatisfactory. However, the British

Governor asserted that, when there were enough ministers and parishes to justify it, a synod could be set up, as had also been allowed, but never carried out, under de Mist's regulations.

The British initially tried to improve matters by finding additional ministers for the Church. The first recruits were the Revd George Thom and the Revd John Taylor, two Scots Presbyterian ministers who left the service of the London Missionary Society and in 1818 were placed in NGK parishes by the Governor.

By 1821, five of the existing twelve ministers were Scots. In that year, in order to move towards synodical status, Thom was sent to Scotland to find recruits for the ministry of the NGK, as well as teachers for the system of schools the Governor hoped to develop. He was very successful, and recruited twelve ministers from the Evangelical wing of the Church of Scotland, then a thirteenth. Thus the ministerial strength of the NGK was doubled at one move. With it the Scots majority among the ministers, seventeen out of twenty-four, became very large indeed. By 1830, Scots had really taken over the NGK.

Of this first group of recruits, the most important were Andrew Murray sen., Colin Fraser, Alexander Smith and William Robertson. As a result of their deep Evangelical commitment these young Scots began a new style of ministry in the NGK. In particular, Murray, Fraser and Smith, together with Robertson when he returned to the Cape as a minister, spent a great deal of their time and energy itinerating around their vast parishes. These Scots so cared for and stimulated the Christian life of the people that they created in effect a new Church with a new spirit. For example, Murray, who remained forty years in Graaff-Reinet, set up seven new parishes; within the old bounds of Swellendam, Robertson, who also stayed for forty years, created six; and Fraser created five new parishes.

This growth was the product of exhaustive and exhausting itineration. Of the work done by his father, Colin Fraser's son later wrote,

> that usually he and one of the elders went out together, mounted with an 'achterryder' or groom, leading a packhorse on which there was a packsaddle to carry their bedding, changes of clothing, gowns and communion plate, also articles of food for the road. The parish had been marked off in districts which were visited in turn and at the most populous or rather occupied parts, services would be held; baptisms administered, catechumens instructed and examined or admitted into membership, marriages performed and the outlying families visited.[10]

Their achievement was also the creation of a new ethos. Now in the Cape Churches there developed a warm Evangelical piety. Hundreds of families were brought to an acceptance of this Evangelical piety that allowed the new parishes to be created. For many, Christianity ceased to be simply their badge of identity but became a personal Evangelical faith. This, which van Lier and Vos had striven unsuccessfully to inculcate, was now being successfully propagated by the Scots. In the more populous parishes, regular mid-week prayer meetings were held and Sunday schools were begun. These latter were not primarily to teach reading and writing, which had been an essential element in the Sunday school movement when it began in Britain, but the Sunday schools in the Cape Church were specifically for religious instruction – indeed, they were aimed at bringing young people to the point of a personal conversion experience.

Andrew Murray, Colin Fraser, William Robertson, Alexander Smith and the other Scots were responsible for this turn-around in the ethos of the Reformed congregations, as they were also for the institutional shape of the NGK. The regulations laid down by the last Dutch administration at the Cape were continued by the British. With the coming of the Scots recruited by Thom, it was felt that there was a case for the creation of the synod, allowed in the regulations, since there were now fourteen parishes and twelve ministers. The consistory of Cape Town formally appealed to the Governor, who granted its plea. The first meeting of the synod took place in the Groote Kerk[11] on 2 November 1824. The plan was for a synod to be held every five years. But as what was being attempted was the creation of a new Church with its own rules, regulations and procedures, it was decided to hold a second synod in 1826 and only thereafter apply the five-year interval rule. Just as each of the original consistories had the local landdrost as a member, so the synod had two political commissioners appointed by the Governor, and the presence of the two commissioners was essential for a session of the synod to be properly constituted. This unambiguous control of the Church by the state was embarrassing to the Scottish ministers. The clear majority they had in the synod meant, however, that there was no need of a Disruption at the Cape, even though they all asserted their sympathy for the Free Church in Scotland. They began a steady pressure on the Governor for change, and when, at the 1842 synod, one of the political commissioners grossly misused his powers, they seized the opportunity to press their case. The Governor, Sir Robert Napier, gave in gracefully and said he would

> 'free the church from the trammels of secular interference in all
> spiritual or purely ecclesiastical matters and substituting in all other
> matters, the authority of the highest civil tribunal'.[12]

The next year, 1843, he issued the Church Ordinance, which put this into law, and the era of the political commissioner was over. However, not long afterwards, the synod was to learn that what the state has the right to grant, it also has the right to take away.[13]

Andrew Murray (sen.) had five sons and four daughters. His five sons all became ministers of the NGK. The two elder sons, John and Andrew jun., were sent to Scotland to be educated. They attended Aberdeen Grammar School and University, staying with their uncle, John Murray, who had a profound influence upon them. He was one of the leaders of the Disruption that took place two years before they graduated at Aberdeen. Indeed, he led a formal withdrawal by a number of ministers and congregations from the Church of Scotland at the meeting of the synod of Aberdeen, prior to the fateful meeting of the General Assembly in 1843.

The two young South Africans subsequently went for theological training at Utrecht but spent most of their time there with fellow students affected by the Réveil movement[14] and rejecting the teaching of their professors, whom they deemed cold and indifferent when not infidel rationalists. It was the Revivalist piety, which characterised the new Free Kirk as well as the Réveil, that their father, Andrew sen., desperately desired for the congregations of the NGK. His daughter, in her reminiscences of the old man says

> As sacred as the memories of the Sunday evenings are those of the Friday evenings, which our father regularly devoted to praying for a revival. He would shut himself up in the study, and read accounts of former revivals in Scotland and other countries.[15]

In 1849, back in South Africa, John was settled at Burgersdorp while Andrew jun. was sent to be the first minister of the NGK permanently settled north of the Orange among the voortrekkers. There had previously been three extended visits by special delegates, one in 1848, by Andrew Murray sen. and P. K. Albertyn, who had preached, baptised and distributed Bibles but were always suspect as possible British agents; so was another delegation of P. E. Faure and William Robertson. Andrew jun., however, was extraordinarily successful in the Orange Free State. But he also travelled widely in the territories beyond the Vaal where the voortrekkers were much more bitterly anti-British and suspicious of the synod, which had condemned the Great Trek. Even here he was well received. Indeed, the extremist leaders in the north, Andries Pretorius and A. H. Potgieter, each urged him to stay north of the Vaal and be their minister.[16] This shows how much the Murrays, like most of the other Scottish families, had become Afrikaners.[17] As old Andrew used to say, 'ik woon in het midden mijns volks' (I live in the midst of my people).[18]

In 1859, the NGK set up its theological school at Stellenbosch, the nucleus from which the present university grew. The first three professors were John Murray, his brother-in-law J. H. Neethling, and his friend from the Reveil circles in Utrecht, N. J. Hofmeyr. So the new seminary was staffed by three close friends, all of whom were devout members of this Scottish Evangelical tradition. It was clear, however, that the seminary would not be able for some time to supply the Church's needs for ministers, so the synod sent Robertson to the Netherlands and Scotland to recruit anew. He found only two suitable candidates in the Netherlands, but in Scotland he was much more successful. He recruited eight Free Church licentiates who had just completed their course at New College. After studying Dutch in the Netherlands, they arrived in South Africa in 1861.

Meanwhile in 1860, Andrew jun. returned to the Cape from the Free State to be minister of Worcester. There, the same year, a great conference of the NGK was held, which is seen as the beginning of the Revival that Andrew sen. had so long desired.

This connection with Free Church piety was further reinforced by the fact that in the following thirty-five years, forty-four young Afrikaners went to Scotland for their theological training, all but four of them to New College. From 1860 until the first decade of the twentieth century, the piety epitomised by the Murray family dominated and shaped the NGK. In the sixties there was a brief attempt by a handful of ministers, trained at Utrecht, to challenge this domination. But they were defeated and, under the influence of the Murrays and their allies, deemed to be 'heretics'.[19] Subsequently, the tradition, dubbed by du Plessis as 'Liberalism', disappeared from NGK Church life.

The Scots of the Free Kirk tradition gained this domination not simply because of their devoted pastoral work and their regular Evangelistic campaigns but above all because of the massive amount of literature they produced. It became the staple reading in thousands of Afrikaner homes. John Murray wrote thirteen books, many of which went into multiple editions: his *Kinderbybel* went through eighteen, the last in 1900; his *Catechisatieboek* through thirty-seven editions, the last in 1925! Andrew Macgregor also produced a number of very popular books. But it was Andrew Murray jun. who was the supreme publicist of this style of Evangelical piety. He published 240 books or tracts, many of which went into multiple editions. They were held to be so good by the wider Evangelical world of the time that many were translated into other languages – French, German, Danish, Spanish, Urdu and Chinese among them. A number of his most popular works began as series of articles in *Die Kerkbode*, the Church magazine that was often the only periodical in many Afrikaner homes.

Despite the creation in 1868 in the Transvaal of a separate official state Church, the Hervormde Kerk, the NGK survived and flourished increasingly there. The Gereformeerde Kerk (the Doppers)[20] also existed among the Afrikaner people in all four territories. Yet it was the evangelistically active and deeply pious NGK which was the link for all Afrikaners throughout South Africa. The parishes were bound together not simply by formal ecclesiastical structure but by the Sunday school movement, the Bible and Prayer Union, and men and women's organisations, like the Layman's Missionary Union, though the separate provincial synods were autonomous judicatures until well into the twentieth century.

This unity of the people can be seen as early as the First Boer War (1880–81), when Andrew Murray jun. wrote a widely supported appeal for British and international sympathy for the Transvaal cause though he was a citizen of the British Cape Colony. Again the NGK, of which he was the unrivalled leader, played the key role in having Dutch recognised formally in the Cape Colony as an official language, reversing various half-hearted efforts by the colonial authorities at Anglicisation that had been going on since around 1812.

The Free Church of Scotland tradition, whether through the channel of Scots brought up in that tradition or of Afrikaners educated at Stellenbosch and New College, was one which, by shaping the NGK, helped shape the self-consciousness of the Afrikaner people in all the four territories. This tradition is called by contemporary South African scholars like Durand, Bosch and du Toit, 'Scots Pietism'. It helped to make the Day of the Covenant[21] a religious as well as a nationalist festival. On the eve of the

Second Boer War (1899–1902), Andrew Murray expressed the feelings of the NGK, in the British as well as the independent territories, when he appealed for peace and argued the justice of the Transvaal and Free State cause. In the bitter aftermath of that war, in which 25,000 Afrikaner women and children died in the infamous 'concentration camps' while only 4,000 Boer soldiers died, the erection of the Vrouemonument to these women was one of the great moments of Afrikaner self-consciousness. Here is a significant excerpt from an eyewitness account of the ceremony.

> After General Botha, General Hertzog, Senator Reitz, and several ministers and other personages had seated themselves at the foot of the monument, President Steyn was led in, accompanied by his wife … Immediately after him came Dr Andrew Murray, leaning on the arm of Mr Gordon Fraser. Shall we say what feelings stirred within us as we looked upon these two figures? We cannot. This only lets us down – Our two great men, each the first in his own sphere! … It was General de Wet, no other, who extended an umbrella over the head of the revered octogenarian.[22]

In 1910, when the Union of South Africa was created by the British government, the Afrikaner people were more united than they had ever been and the NGK was one of the key elements which held them together.

How far then does this go towards understanding the theological endorsement by the NGK of Apartheid and the authoritarian nationalist regime of 1948–1988? An editorial in *Die Kerkbode*, so long the vehicle for the spread of Scottish Evangelicalism and piety, declared in 1948: 'As a Church, we have always worked purposefully for the separation of the races. In this regard apartheid can rightfully be called a Church policy.'[23] Despite this, one is inclined to contradict the claim. After all, it was the NGK in the period of Scots' domination that developed a massive missionary concern for Africans both inside and outside what is now the Republic of South Africa. Indeed, various members of the Murray clan personally took the lead in opening up the missionary efforts of the NGK among the African people of the Transvaal, Zimbabwe and Malawi. In the last country, the NGK mission entered at the invitation of the Free Church of Scotland and initially worked as their auxiliary.

Again, although in 1857 the first move was made in the Cape synod to have separate worship for Black and White Christians, the decision was so expressed as to make it clear that the synod believed all humanity to be one in Christ. The converts at that time were people of Khoi, slave and mixed descent who lived among the Afrikaner people as servants, shepherds and herders, and sometimes as squatters; and in the few towns as craftsmen. They spoke the local, simplified form of Dutch with African loan words, which many Boers spoke also, the origin of modern Afrikaans. Many of these people had become Christians and worshipped together with the Whites. However, because of pressure building up in some parishes in the Cape, the synod of 1857 had to rule on the issue of separate, racially defined worship services. The synod ruled thus:

Synod considers it to be desirable and in accordance with Scripture
that our converts from paganism be received and incorporated into
existing congregations, wherever possible; however, where this practice, because of the weakness of some, constitutes an obstacle to the
advancement of Christ's cause among pagans, congregations formed
or still to be formed from converts from paganism should be given the
opportunity to enjoy their Christian privileges in a separate place of
worship.[24]

It is important to notice that the synod did not for a moment contemplate
the setting-up of a separate denomination for the 'Coloureds', which it did
in 1881, the Nederduitse Gereformeerde Sending Kerk, – then a Black, and
later still an Indian Reformed Church in the twentieth century. The synod
was thinking in terms of separate services for the two groups, not necessarily
in separate buildings, although the text does not make that clear.

However, this was a turning-point of enormous significance and set a
fundamental precedent. The leaders of the Church did not believe this
separation to be right, but their Evangelical vision was of bringing as many
people into the Church and so to salvation as possible. This vision, as is clear
from their literature,[25] focused on the one-to-one relation of sinner and God.
The essential thing was the sinner being established in a right relation with
God. The lateral relationship of person to other persons was on a second
level.

Anything that would get in the way of personal conversions had to be
avoided or changed. This is seen clearly in the 1857 decision. (Whites object
to Blacks in church. The Blacks feel rejected and hurt. Separate services solve
the tension and in any case, like always enjoy being with like. The growth of
the Church is not hindered.) This disturbed what they agreed was the New
Testament understanding of the nature of the Church. That worries them
a little, but not enough to deter them from this course of action.

Even of less concern are the formal structure of the state and structures
of society. The NGK lived very happily in the Cape Colony in the period
1852–1910, when there was absolute equality before the law for all people
of whatever ethnic origin, but also equally happily in the Free State and the
Transvaal, where there was no equality in Church or state between the races,
as in Natal with its nominal adherence to ideals of equality and its *de facto*
rigorous segregation.

All of this fits the spirit of the synod decision of 1857. It shows that the
Evangelicalism that the Scottish Free Church tradition gave to the NGK was
not that of Wilberforce or John Philip on the British side of the greater
Evangelical movements, – or that of Charles Finney and Theodore Weld on
the American. That brand of Evangelicalism believed passionately in gaining
personal conversions but also in the demand of the Gospel for social justice.
This explains Wilberforce's work for abolition of slavery, and the stance
upon abolition and Black equality of the Finney–Weld alliance in the United
States, as well as John Philip's plea for equal civil rights 'for all His Majesty's
subjects' in the Cape Colony in 1828.

The Evangelical piety that the Scots developed in the NGK was rather that of Lyman Beecher, the Evangelical opponent of Finney and Weld. He believed that slavery was wrong but making too much of a fuss was going to endanger the primary Evangelistic task of the Church, the unity of Christians. The nature of slavery itself was not for him a central Gospel issue. This parallels the thinking of Thomas Chalmers, the father of the Free Church.

Soon after the Disruption, a delegation was sent to the United States to raise funds for the Free Church. They returned with a large sum of money, some of which had been given by slave-holders in the slave states. Immediately there was a cry in Scotland of 'Give back the money' from the small dedicated band of abolitionists in close touch with those in the United States. Chalmers's attitude was clearly of vital importance here. Although appealed to directly by American abolitionists, Chalmers defended the retention of the money. He did so on firm theological grounds which ruled out as unscriptural the unchurching of slave-holders, advocated by the abolitionists in the United States. He insisted that

> Distinction ought to be made between the character of a system, and the character of the persons whom circumstances have implicated therewith ... We hope that our Free Church will never deviate to the right or to the left from the path of undoubted principle. But we hope, on the other hand, she will not be frightened from her propriety, or forced by clamour of any sort, to outrun her own convictions, so as to adopt, at the bidding of other parties, a new and factitious principle of administration, for which she can see no authority in Scripture, and of which she can gather no traces in the history or practice of the Churches in Apostolic times.[26]

His attitude was a great embarrassment to the Evangelical abolitionists in the USA for his arguments were precisely those of the great Southern Presbyterian intellectuals Drs Robert Dabney and J. H. Thornwell in their defence of slavery as compatible with Christianity.[27]

To the NGK of the period and the main tradition in the Free Church of the period, the organisation of society or the state so long as it did not interfere with the preaching of the Word was not a fundamental concern to the Church. Not only was the NGK lacking in a theology of social justice, it also was deficient in its ecclesiology. In 1881, at the initiation of its massive outreach to the non-Christians inside and outside South Africa, it set up a completely separate Church for the Cape Coloureds, the Sending Kerk. This was a new denomination, not cut off from the NGK over issues of Scripture or dogma, but simply because of colour. It was not even a matter of language because the Cape folk, as the so-called 'Coloureds' prefer to be called, spoke the same language as the Whites, Afrikaans. Again this fits the philosophy behind the synodical decision of 1857. It also fitted a new theory of Christian mission that began to be developed in this period in the German universities and missionary societies, and reached its apogee with the writings of Gustav Warneck. This was the concept of Christianising people in their natural units; culture and ethnicity were seen as the key elements in the creation of new Churches. As a modern exponent of the idea says, 'Men like to become Christians without crossing racial, linguistic or class barriers'.[28]

Another new influence began to make itself felt, when in the 1890s Transvaalers looked to The Netherlands for sympathy and they encountered the brilliant theologian and politician Abram Kuyper. Increasingly after the Second Boer War, NGK students began to go to the Free University of Amsterdam, Kuyper's university, and gradually Kuyperian thought, filtered through Afrikaner minds, came to influence the NGK. The traditional NGK attitude to mission easily welcomed the new theories of Warneck. But its proponents were unhappy about the advent of neo-Kuyperian thought. However, it had no ammunition in its theological locker to combat the threat of this powerful new theology which insisted on its Calvinism, its scriptural authority. Its wide range covered thoroughly the very issues of ecclesiology and of society absent from the Evangelical tradition which the Scots-Afrikaners owed to Free Kirk-style piety. Unhappy though many of them were about the new political theology coming in from The Netherlands, they had no intellectual defences against it. They could do nothing to prevent the neo-Kuyperian insistence on God's creation of mankind divided into peoples as part of the 'given' of Creation, or a merger with the Warneckian ideas of folk Churches. In the 1920s and 1930s, within the NGK these ideas came together in a new theology of nature and society which, when translated into the specifically political sphere, created the ideology of Apartheid.[29]

As D. P. Botha said in a speech to the South African Council of Churches in May 1980

> The role of organisations like the FAK and the Broederbond fade into insignificance compared with the overwhelming role of the Church (the NGK) in preparing the Afrikaner to accept and vote for a socio-political programme that would revolutionize South Africa.[30]

This is exactly what they did do in 1948, sweeping the Nationalist party to power. Under Dr D. F. Malan, a minister of the NGK, the structure of apartheid was set up.

It was three waves of deeply devout, inexhaustibly active ministers rooted in an Evangelical piety drawn from the Free Church of Scotland tradition that created the NGK of the twentieth century. It encompassed the great majority of the Afrikaner people, whose piety defined, at least partly, what it was to be an Afrikaner. This piety, epitomised by the Murrays, was deeply felt by many and outwardly conformed to by most. It was, however, inadequate intellectually and theologically to provide any effective resistance to the take-over of the Church in the first thirty years of the new century by a potent mixture of German missiology and neo-Kuyperian theology. 'Scots Pietism' had created a popular and deeply devout Church of the people, often affectionately referred to as 'die Boer Kerk'; they had created a ready-made tool for the Christian Nationalism of Malan.

It is interesting that in 1913, the aged Andrew Murray jun., only a few months after the moving scenes at the opening of the Vrouemonument, clashed with the young D. F. Malan. It was a symbolic clash, for Malan and those whom he represented were now going to take over the Church that the Evangelicals, whom Murray supremely represented, had created.

NOTES

1 Quoted in J. McCarter, *The Dutch Reformed Church in South Africa* (Edinburgh, 1869), p. 11.
2 Ibid., p. 22.
3 J. du Plessis, *The Life of Andrew Murray* (London, 1920), pp. 78–79.
4 M. K. H. Lichtenstein, *Travels in South Africa* (Cape Town, 1928) (rep. of 1812 ed, vol. II, p. 447.
5 J. Alton Templin,*Ideology on a Frontier* (London, 1984), p. 73.
6 See D. Moodie, *The Record* (Cape Town, 1834), p I, *passim.*
7 Lichtenstein, *Travels*, p. 303.
8 F. A. van Jaarsveld, *The Afrikaner's Interpretation of South African History* (Cape Town, 1964), Ch. I, *passim.*
9 McCarter, *The Dutch Reformed Church*, p. 34.
10 J. G. Fraser, *Episodes in my Life* (Cape Town, 1922), pp. 11–12.
11 This is the large NGK church in Adderley Street in Cape Town, regarded as the 'Mother' church of the NGK.
12 McCarter, *The Dutch Reformed Church*, pp. 37 8.
13 In the 1860s, Utrecht-trained liberals took the synod to the civil courts and were granted the right by the courts to disregard the Church's Confession and Catechism. The synod led by Murray jun. appealed all the way to the Privy Council in London and lost! However, the 'Scots Pietist' majority dominated the life of the Church so successfully that the 'liberals' disappeared from the scene and that theological tradition sunk no roots in NGK soil.
14 The Reveil was a movement of Evangelical revivalism, started by Scots in Geneva, which spread to The Netherlands. Its principal leaders were in close touch with the 'Popular' party in the Church of Scotland and later regular visitors at the Free Church General Assembly.
15 du Plessis, *The Life of Andrew Murray*, p. 27.
16 Ibid., p. 126.
17 Several young men of these families, notably the Frasers, fought in the Free State army in the Second Boer War.
18 du Plessis, *The Life of Andrew Murray*, p. 25.
19 See McCarter, *The Dutch Reformed Church*, ch. and du Plessis, *The Life of Andrew Murray*, ch. 10 for a full study of these cases and Murray's final triumph despite losing in the courts.
20 Dopper is a popular name for an extremely strict Calvinist tradition among Afrikaners, which finally became a separate Church – the Gereformeerde Kerk – in 1858, which exists in all four provinces today.
21 This is Dingaan's Day, 16 December, when the decisive battle in the voortrekkers' war with the Zulu of Dingaan took place. Pretorius made a Covenant with God on behalf of the volk, and God, in response to this, gave them the victory.
22 du Plessis, *The Life of Andrew Murray*, p. 430. Steyn was the president of the Free State at the beginning of the War of 1899–1902. De Wet, a leading 'bitter-ender', was the leader of the last commando to surrender. Thus Murray is being recognised as a true Afrikaner in a setting that excluded Moderates like Smuts.
23 *Die Kerkbode*, 22 Sept. 1948, quoted in J. de Gruchy and C. Villa-Vicencio, *Apartheid is a Heresy* (Cape Town, 1983), p. 6.
24 Ibid., p. 32.
25 The books of all the Murrays, of Robertson, of MacGregor and the columns of *Die Kerkbode*are all about personal salvation, personal spirituality, personal ethics, evangelism, temperance, almost to the exclusion of all else.
26 Chalmers in a letter to the *Witness*, 12 May 1845. The text is in W. Hanna,

Memoirs of Dr Chalmers, 4 vols (Edinburgh, 1849–52) vol. iv, pp. 582–91.

27 J. H. Thornwell, 'Report to the Synod of North Carolina on the Subject Slavery' (Columbia, SC 1851) (Pamphlet in New College Library), *passim.*

28 D. A. McGavran, *Understanding Church Growth* (Grand Rapids, 1970), p. 223.

29 David Bosch, 'The Roots and Fruits of Afrikaner Civil Religion', in J. W. Hofmeyr and W. S. Vorster (eds), *New Faces of Africa* (Pretoria, 1984), pp. 25–32.

30 Quoted in Alan Boesak, 'He made us all, but ...', in Gruchy and Villa-Vicencio, *Apartheid*, p. 6.

CHAPTER TEN

The Disruption and Church Life on the Mainland of Europe

FRIEDHELM VOGES

IN THE SCOTTISH DISRUPTION OF 1843, two developments came to a head: the Evangelical revival showed its power – and, perhaps, its limits – and the relationship of Church and state quite literally reached a point of no return. In both areas, there are a number of parallels and connections with the life of Continental Churches, and this chapter will therefore have those two lines of attack. We will have a brief look at various European revival movements, and then go on to deal with the Church–state problem in the respective countries.

This remit is wider than merely focusing on direct reactions to the Scottish events. With few exceptions these remained on a fairly superficial level. Many Continentals seem to have had problems similar to those of the British government. They found it hard to look beyond London and England. If foreign observers were interested in British Church affairs, their concern was more with Irvingism and Puseyism, i.e. with questions of doctrine. Both these movements had a number of sympathisers as well as critics on the Continent, and their debate claims some space in the ecclesiastical journals. The Scottish troubles emphasised questions of Church discipline, which were more difficult to relate to one's own situation. Of course the relationship of Church and state became an issue in many places on the Continent too, but local conditions were very different.

Few foreign observers seem to have had a sufficient understanding of the events that so much troubled Europe's north-western corner. Reports in the ecclesiastical magazines are generally friendly to the Free Church, but short; they take notice, but remain at a distance. There is admiration for the energy and moral backbone of the Free Church people, and when they had to suffer from the refusal of sites for their churches, sympathetic notices appeared. But this is on a moral rather than an analytical level. Two German authors, Sack and Sydow, who had spent some time in Scotland, tried hard to explain the situation more thoroughly, but although their accounts are well done, the echo was limited. Perhaps they tried rather too hard: Sydow in particular was completely on the Free Church side and could easily be dismissed as partisan. When he contended that the Presbyterian constitution of the Church 'is going to be a determining factor in the future of the Protestant world',[1] his critics lost no time in pointing out that he was going over the score: could the Scottish experience really be applied elsewhere? His description of events is gratefully acknowledged by all the reviewers, and one can suspect that they had no criteria for being critical on details. But they were not going to keep quiet if Sydow wanted to transplant 'the Presbyterian constitution not just in its good sides, but also with its dangerous idiosyncrasies'.[2]

Mostly, the Scottish events just provide Continental authors with material to emphasize a point they wish to make anyway. Thus, a German Establishment essayist finds warm words for the pure and sincere motives behind the Disruption – but his main concern is to alert his readers to the dangers of separation.[3] The Swiss theologian, Alexandre Vinet, when speaking of the Vaudois Free Church, compares the popular support for the Scottish Disruption with popular enmity towards the Vaudois ministers, and then says of his countrymen: 'Their sacrifice is thus more complete, and the divine promises are their grand, but their only compensation.'[4] Swedish observers like Torén and Lundborg were also impressed by the religious fervour they had found in the Free Church of Scotland. For them the Scottish example was a stimulus to work for a revival in their own country. But under Swedish conditions there was never any question of following the Free Church lead to the extent of founding a new Church.[5]

Other reactions are of similar calibre. Usually, these comments remain fairly superficial. But in Germany it is quite possible to find contemporary journals supporting the demands for a more Presbyterial form of Church government and not making any mention of lessons to be learned from the Scottish events. Rather than list such direct reactions or their absence, it would seem more fruitful to ask how the Disruption and its background relate to the general trends of contemporary European Church history. We will do this under two headings: first, there will be a look at other revival movements – Evangelical or otherwise – and then follows a slightly shorter discussion of the relationship of Church and state. This two-pronged approach is not without problems: the rise of the different revival movements and the stance taken by Church people towards the state are interrelated. To treat the two areas separately may, however, give a clearer line of argument.

EUROPEAN REVIVAL MOVEMENTS

After 1815, Europe presented a picture of outward peace. But the European mind was still struggling with the impulses of the age. On the Continent, the political system had been violently shaken up, and at the same time the onset of a more industrial age was felt everywhere. Old ideas had become discredited; new ones were being tried out. Politically, the Vienna treaties tried to recreate the old order in a new guise, but under the surface thoughts and emotions were stirring. In religion, three kinds of reactions can be distinguished.

First, there is the new approach that Schleiermacher pioneered with his *Speeches* in 1799 and later developed from his chair at Germany's youngest university in Berlin. For him, religion belonged to the realm of taste and feeling, and his definition of religion as a 'feeling of absolute dependence' made the educated classes listen in a way not often achieved by European theologians since. More orthodox – or should one say more conventional? – minds had lots of objections but the movement gained a fair amount of influence.

Secondly, we have a going-back to the certainties of ages past – the revival especially of Lutheranism. This movement shows that received convictions were still strong. The right preacher at the right time could make a powerful appeal to them, and few people noticed that this was not merely a restating of the old, but also involved slight changes of emphasis.

The third kind of revival drew on the ground laid by pietism a century earlier. It was a kind of grassroots movement and, like the Schleiermacher school, emphasised the religious needs and feelings of people. But unlike the romantics and the idealists it spurned new doctrinal departures and instead restated traditional theology with a greater emphasis on feeling. The Evangelical revival in Scotland probably stood somewhere between the second and the third type – partly a backlash against Moderatism and partly a need for more emotion. But one must be careful of drawing the parallels too closely, since events in Scotland followed their own course. It should also be noted that between the three types of revival there were interconnections. Even Schleiermacher as the head of one movement had partly had a Moravian upbringing, which did leave a mark on him.

The influence of Schleiermacher and his school was more or less restricted to the Continent, and here it centred on Germany and Switzerland. It was something like a theological counterpart to the romantic movement and its appeal is therefore not surprising. At the same time, Schleiermacher was much more than a romantic. His was one of the most astute theological brains of the century, and he became the founder of systematic rather than dogmatic theology. Some critics, then as now, had their questions: how was he going to reconcile a general definition of religion as a matter of feeling with the particular teachings of Christianity? But Schleiermacher was much more positive in affirming the central points of Christian doctrine than most rationalists had been. The young ministers who were trained in this kind of theology opened a way into faith for many who might otherwise have remained sceptical outsiders. People were taken seriously with their questions and their feelings and at the same time shown a Christian response. After Schleiermacher, there was more freedom in theological thinking, even if this freedom was sometimes abused by the left wing of the movement. In one sense we are not really talking about a revival, rather about a new departure, but the Christian faith and the Christian Church were certainly revitalised and became a talking point among the educated classes again. As an influential movement on the Continent, we certainly have to take account of this revival.

Scotland, even more than England, was practically immune to these tendencies. Partly, people saw the aberrations of some of the more extreme German or Swiss theologians and felt no inclination to enquire any further. But that alone does not sufficiently explain the resistance to this sort of thinking. The romantic spirit as such made itself felt very much – even to the naming of the main Edinburgh railway station after a romantic novel. But in theology, the Scots kept to their own ways.

I would like to make three suggestions why this might have been so. In the first place, Scottish Presbyterianism still had a practical vigour that gave it enough self-confidence to view such outside developments very critically. It was also at this time steeped in a philosophical tradition of its own, Thomas Reid's school of common sense, which certainly didn't encourage 'lofty speculation' and kept its hold on Scottish universities until at least the 1820s. Both these factors might not have precluded individuals from taking up outside influences, but this would have been difficult for another reason: every minister's and professor's doctrine was open to scrutiny and challenge in presbytery, and, unlike on the Continent, no tolerant state authority could hold its hand over any deviant. The structure of the Church thus acted as a safeguard of orthodoxy, though at the same time it was a barrier against independent theological thinking. For the moment, in any case, the Church was probably saved a lot of doctrinal argument, and the Evangelical revival could concentrate on practical matters.

The second way in which Protestant Christianity was revived in the early nineteenth century was a going-back to the fountainhead of the Reformation period. Scotland shared in this development mainly through the biographies of Knox and Melville by McCrie and later through the works of Merle d'Aubigné. But Scotland was a Reformation country of the second generation. Germany and Switzerland were by now starting to celebrate the tricentenary of various Reformation events, and these festivities gave a strong impetus to a more traditional kind of religion. Names like Luther and Zwingli still carried an aura of their own, and the rise of Church history as a theological discipline helped to strengthen their reputations. An event like the Zwingli jubilee of 1828 took on national importance for cantons like Berne and Zurich and, for a moment, almost recreated the old notion of a Christian community.

It might still not be necessary to classify this kind of historic revival separately, if it were not for the particular turn that events took in Germany. For a while – and before all those Reformation anniversaries – it had looked as if parts of the Reformation heritage were actually going to be forgotten or overcome. But there was then a decided backlash. Before dealing with the revival movement itself, we will first have to describe the counterforces that made the traditionalists rally.

In the period of rationalism and 'neology', the old differences between the Lutheran tradition and the Calvinist – or as it is known on the Continent, the Reformed – tradition had lost much of their importance. This has parallels in the thought of the Scottish Moderates or Irish non-subscribing

Presbyterians. When it was time to celebrate Luther's ninety-five theses in 1817, people not only remembered his vigour; they also thought of occasions like Marburg, where Lutheran and Reformed theologians had tried so hard to bridge the gap on the Communion question. Therefore, an initiative by the King of Prussia to forge a union was willingly received by many.

It was only natural that Prussia should take the lead. Since 1613, the Hohenzollerns had themselves been Reformed (Calvinist), though rulers of a Lutheran country. This made for a tolerant attitude anyway, and now there was also a political consideration. Through the Napoleonic upheavals, Prussia had gained large areas in the West with a mostly Reformed population, and it was going to be easier to have only one Protestant Church to deal with. But the importance of the political factors should not be overrated. To many the time seemed just right for a 'truly religious union' of both Churches. The Prussian King was a leading influence in these matters and gave them a great deal of personal attention, but he spoke for large parts of both clergy and laity.

It was a fairly superficial union. There was no attempt formally to state a new doctrinal accord. The theological basis seems to have been a hope that, with time and close contact within the one Church, the differences would gradually fade away. To some extent, this is what happened, but there was also a strong Lutheran backlash. The tricentenary of the Augsburg Confession helped to concentrate on the doctrinal issues. Significantly, though, the first open conflict focused on the question of a new joint liturgy: when the state – on the King's personal initiative – tried to change the form of service, congregations took note and defended their time-honoured usages. The government's intransigence did not help. In a Silesian parish, the Lutheran pastor was suspended and the induction of his successor could only take place under military cover – echoes of the Ten Years' Conflict in Strathbogie. The Prussian government, unlike the British, eventually relented on the liturgy question, but by then minds had been stirred and another powerful stimulus given to the reconstruction of a decidedly Lutheran theology. The conflict had also brought forth the first small Lutheran Free Church.

In some territories, like Mecklenburg or Bavaria, this kind of tendency was strengthened both by the theological faculties and by the Church authorities, which acted under the influence of their civil governments. Lutheranism appeared as a solid rock against the critical voices that were raised in the failed revolutions of 1830 and even more of 1848. If the move towards the union had been intended as a step into the future, one of its side-effects was a revival of denominationalism that had consequences well into the present century.

Neo-Lutheranism was a movement not unlike English tractarianism: a reaction against the prevalence of a subjective, individual piety and a return to what seemed the more objective body of tradition. In 1857, the Prussian judge Ludwig von Gerlach summed up the change in tone: forty years ago,

the basic mood... was a consciousness of being a child of God, of being awakened and belonging to the Lord... . The difference between clergy and laity receded into the background. Christianity was mainly understood in relation to the individual, working on the heart of each person.

Now, von Gerlach says,

> God's glory and honour come before the individual…. Now our main concern is with the kingdom of heaven, not merely in the abstract, but as a living institution, as the body of which Christ is the head … From which follows a strong emphasis on holy orders (*Amtsbewusstsein*), on distinguishing the particular ministry of the clergy from what all children of God share.[6]

On such a basis, there could be no sympathy for what some wits had called a 'bookbinders' union' that merely put Reformed and Lutheran symbolic writings between the covers of the same volume. It took more than a century before the 1973 Leuenberg Concord dealt with the doctrinal differences in a theologically reflective and mature way.

The third kind of revival has much in common with the Evangelical movement in Scotland before the tone of the latter was so strongly influenced by the patronage question. We are simply talking about more emphasis being given to the heart rather than the mind in matters of faith. Compared with Scotland, however, the Continental meetings and groups of readers were often distinguished by a greater involvement of lay people. Indeed, in Norway and Finland, the leading figures of the revival, Hans Nielsen Hauge and Paavo Ruotsalainen, were peasants, and all over Scandinavia the 'readers' (of the Bible and older devotional literature) could be rather at odds with the official Church. Again these stirrings at grassroots level can be seen as something of a backlash against the prevailing religious atmosphere, though this should not be the only key when trying to understand them.

In the previous generation or two, the Enlightenment throughout Europe had done much to create a freer atmosphere in the Churches and encourage a critical approach to tradition. Many pulpits and chairs of theology had been opened to the voice of what was understood by 'reason'. But the movement had not been all that successful in building up its own forms of doctrine or giving rise to a deeper kind of piety. By the early nineteenth century, theological rationalism was still a powerful force in a fair number of universities, but many people were looking for other sources to satisfy their spiritual appetites. Depending on where – which period, which author, which preacher – they happened to find a stimulus, the individual revival movements took on a different shape. But they all have a conservative theological outlook, and they all breathe a new urgency that translated itself into action.

In Switzerland the Réveil started in Geneva. The early converts were Reformed theology students and pastors, and their conversions took place under the influence of such diverse people as the Lutheran Baroness Krudener, the Scottish Congregationalist Robert Haldane and the Methodist Henry Drummond. The Réveil soon encountered a difficulty that was typical of Continental affairs, where governments still regarded people as subjects and tried to control their religious beliefs and practices: religious meetings in private houses met with great suspicion and were sometimes even banned. But the idea behind this policy fast became obsolete: state and Church were no longer identical. The automatic assumption that everybody was a Christian no longer held true, and canton after canton had to allow varying degrees of freedom. In view of its various contacts with Free Churches in Britain, it is not surprising that the Réveil led to the foundation of a number of independent congregations. But its more important influence probably lay in changing the religious tone within the Established Churches.

In contrast, the Finnish revival stayed firmly within the National Church. In the different areas of the country, four different revival movements encountered strong initial opposition under government leadership. Ruotsalainen and other leaders found themselves in court for holding illegal meetings. But eventually they overcame these obstacles, not without assistance from some of the clergy, and between them the revival movements became the leading force in the Finnish Church. In Lapland, the revival had enthusiastic or charismatic overtones, but elsewhere in Finland – and indeed most places on the Continent – the leaders were careful to stay within certain limits. Ruotsalainen not only viewed any enthusiasm with suspicion, but was also careful to guard against too much emotion. The conversion had to be a definite experience, but after that the believer should focus on his or her unworthiness rather than glory in the new-found grace. 'There is honey at the beginning of the way, but then you get pitch and tar for your food', was his description of the Christian life.[7] On this point, the other factions of the Finnish revival were less strict. What they all share is a strong practical sense, even if no schemes like poor-relief or Church Extension were started. But their effect on the moral tone of the nation was considerable.

The German revival movement of the early eighteenth century was a complex affair. Germany was divided into a number of practically sovereign territories, and although there was something like a joint German culture, the differences between Saxony and Baden, Hanover and Bavaria, Württemberg and Prussia – to name but a few – were considerable. In some areas – notably Württemberg – the older pietism was still alive and proved a stepping-stone for the revival. Two organisations transcended regional boundaries: the Moravians influenced many people by their *Daily Bread* publication and through personal contact. Meanwhile the Christentumsgesellschaft, a society centred on Basle, was in correspondence with many pious minds and spawned some forty local groups in Germany and Holland. Another influence was the new Bible Society movement which owed a lot to contact with the British and Foreign Bible Society. In the south of the country there was also close contact with a revival movement in the Roman Catholic Church, which gave the Protestant Church one prominent preacher and founder of a missionary society in the convert Gossner. But all these stimuli only became effective because of general dissatisfaction with the spent forces of rationalism and neology. Those of a more speculative bent turned to Schleiermacher and his school, but many preferred a more conventional theological approach, though one with more substance and especially more feeling.

Conditions were not equally favourable everywhere, and there were of course strongholds of the older schools. The actual course of the revival in the different areas depended strongly on the work of individuals. At this point any general historical theory that would explain the course of the revival by systematic categories reaches its limitations. In the Lüneburg Heath parish of Hermannsburg, for example, the preaching of Louis Harms started to move hearts and minds in an unprecedented way and soon swept the whole neighbourhood. Harms became assistant to his ageing father in 1844, and by 1849, he was able to establish his own training college for missionaries to Africa. The movement had far-reaching effects: to this day, Hermannsburg is an important centre for foreign missions still supported by the area. But there is no sufficient explanation why the revival should have reached certain parishes and stopped at the boundary of others. According to persuasion, people will have to content themselves with talking of the influence of individuals or of the Holy Spirit.

Other areas had similar developments. In Bavaria, Wilhelm Löhe transformed his parish of Neuendettelsau near Nuremberg and became one of the founders of the deaconess movement. In due course, the small village also became the home of a theological college. In their theology, both Löhe and Harms were strong Lutherans, but if one looks at the effect of their preaching, the revivalist aspect must stand in the foreground.

To Scottish eyes, the Württemberg minister Ludwig Hofacker may be of particular interest, since both in the appeal of his preaching and in his early death he closely resembles Robert Murray McCheyne. Hofacker died in 1828 and thus belongs to an earlier phase of the revival than Harms and Löhe. The fiftieth edition of his sermons was published in 1963 and he is not the only revivalist of his time whose influence still carries on.

A complete description of the German revival movement would have to describe its strong influence on the social conscience of the Churches, although usually the 'rescue houses', hospitals and other institutions were started on the basis of Christian societies. But in time, the official Churches acknowledged this kind of work and took it under their wing. Given more space, we would also have to detail many bitter local conflicts, since at least in the larger towns it was not possible to carry a majority in the way Löhe, Harms and some others did in their rural spheres. And it would be necessary to talk about the role of the gentry, who furthered the revival considerably in many areas and in Pomerania practically founded it against the resistance of a rationalist clergy.

One final aspect must, however, be mentioned that should be particularly pleasing to Scottish eyes. This is the influence that Reformed ministers had in the early stages of the revival even on Lutherans. Names like Menken and Krummacher may stand for several others. The re-emergence of Lutheranism was only one side of the coin, and even among its strong proponents there could be respect for the Christian spirit in other Churches. The Evangelical Alliance with its emphasis on a united Protestant front is a fruit of this development, even though some of the more extreme Lutherans stood aloof when the Alliance held its 1857 conference in Berlin. A more typically German example is the Gustav-Adolf-Verein, which was founded to commemorate the bicentenary of that Swedish hero of Lutheranism, the King who led his armies in the religious battles of the Thirty Years' War. But it soon grew into a society to help small and beleaguered congregations of all Protestant descriptions, and attracted wide support.

Of course, the Evangelical revival in Scotland has a character of its own. It is distinguished, for instance, by its emphasis on observing the Sabbath and by the role large communion services could play at least in country areas. But in many other points it displays the same characteristics as the Réveil or Erweckung on the mainland. Here also, the Evangelicals at least made a start in tackling the social questions of the age, even if their response was often not satisfactory, because people like Chalmers were too backward-looking. And both on the European mainland and in Scotland there was often a playing-down of theology and an emphasis on experience. The German revival theologian, Neander, would have found ready agreement from people like Thomas Chalmers when he said that 'the most learned theologians are not always the most pious' and when he quoted Augustine with 'fides praecedit intellectum'.[8] The differences in denominational standards and local conditions remained in force, but when the Evangelical Alliance was founded in 1846 it proved that revivalists from various countries recognised each other as kindred spirits.

QUESTIONS OF CHURCH AND STATE

All the European churches – even the Roman Catholic one with its new concordats – had to grapple with changes in the relationship of Church and state. This chapter can only deal with one aspect of this very complex field: if we are talking about possible comparisons with the Disruption, our main concern has to be with the Evangelicals. On both sides of the Channel they were perhaps less ready than other Christians to accept state authority in Church questions and to settle for some form of compromise. But this should not be taken to infer that other schools were without courage or convictions. At any rate there were few breakaways and nowhere on such a scale as in Scotland.

In regard to constitutional questions the British Churches had had a quiet time compared with their Continental counterparts. Apart from the advent of toleration for Dissenters and Roman Catholics the situation had remained stable for a long time. This was particularly true for Scotland, where the Church enjoyed securities going back to the Act of Union. Until the Ten Years' Conflict, the situation between Church and state had evolved in a quiet, unspectacular way.

By contrast, the European mainland had seen great changes through the

French Revolution and the Napoleonic wars. Now it took some time for the
various nations to adjust to the new situation. In France itself, in Holland
and in Switzerland, the Churches had undergone very radical, though
short-lived, transformations at the hands of the Revolution. Then, Napoleon
had steered a more moderate course, and after his demise, yet another
system had to evolve – now under the conservative auspices of the Holy
Alliance between Russia, Austria and Prussia. For Germany, the changes had
been very far-reaching too. The old Holy Roman Empire had crumbled, and
dozens of small territories – as well as the not so small Roman Catholic
dioceses – had been swallowed up by their greedy neighbours. The Vienna
treaties of 1815 finalised a new-look map with states where everybody –
including the Churches – had to find their places in a new equilibrium.

It is hardly surprising that in this state of affairs, the early initiative usually
lay with the civil authorities. In Holland, for instance, the Church was so
paralysed that the Crown was able to depart from the country's Reformed
tradition – and unilaterally – to give the Church a new constitution. The new
constitutions, which some German territories now got, similarly maintained
the prerogative of the state. The Württemberg constitution of 1819, for
instance, talked of a 'constitutional autonomy' for the churches (para. 71).
But the next paragraph said:

> The supreme right of protection and supervision of the churches lies
> with the king. Therefore any ordinances of the ecclesiastical authority
> can neither be published nor put into practice without the head of
> state having seen and approved of them.[9]

Other territories found similar solutions, even if autonomy in spiritual
matters was often granted. But 'in case of doubt the civil government will
decide whether a matter is purely spiritual',[10] as the 1832 Ordinance for the
Duchy of Brunswick put it. The whole question that soon was to agitate
Scotland so much was here solved very clearly, if unsatisfactorily.

Some states allowed a little more freedom than others, but all were united
in still claiming authority over their Churches. In the Protestant states of
Germany, they could point to their rights as going back to the Reformation,
when local sovereigns had been made *summus episcopus* to safeguard Lutheran and Reformed Churches against a Catholic Emperor. The absolutist
theories of the eighteenth century had tried to extend the claims of the state
as far as possible, and even if absolutism was no longer fashionable, governments were slow to go back in practice. As we have seen from the Prussian
union of 1817, the spiritual sphere was not safe from their interference, and
quite certainly they claimed jurisdiction over the 'temporalia' – even over
denominations other than their own. Both Protestants in Bavaria and
Roman Catholics in Prussia fully expected their Kings to be involved with
the affairs of their Churches.

By the early nineteenth century, however, a number of difficulties arose.
The old Church constitutions worked on the assumption of a Christian
government ruling over a Christian people of the same ilk – and things had
changed in several ways. Up to now, a lot of territories had been

'monodenominational', i.e. it was normal that a Lutheran, Catholic or Reformed sovereign had only Lutheran, Catholic or Reformed subjects. But in both Germany and Switzerland there were now many mixed territories. To cope with this situation, a greater measure of toleration became the order of the day. It could be slow in arriving: a lot of ink was spilt in the 1840s, when Bavaria required its Protestant soldiers to attend mass and to genuflect before the holy elements. Prussia, on the other hand, took on the Catholic Church and for a while even imprisoned the Archbishop of Cologne. Eventually, however, toleration was won, and wherever that happened it tended to make for more distance between state and Church.

But the idea of a Christian ruler for a Christian people was wearing thin for another reason also: increasingly one met with free-thinkers or people who were Christian only in name, and many of them soon held responsible government positions. In this respect, the Continental experience closely resembles that in Britain. The understanding of the civil authority for religious needs could leave a lot to be desired. According to an – admittedly extreme – critic, the Prussian secretary for Church questions, Count Schwerin, brought to his office no other qualification than 'a reputation for free thinking and some meagre fragments of theological and ecclesiastical ideas, which he had acquired from some of his relations'.[11] And in 1851, the Bavarian president of the supreme consistory, a lawyer, seemed 'in no way up to dealing with ecclesiastical questions'. at least in the opinion of the theologian Adolf von Harless.[12]

Among Churchmen there was now a greater spirit of independence. The French Revolution and its aftermath had made a difference even to the most conservative elements. People were readier to speak their minds. This tendency was given some backbone by the theology of the revival movement. The 'awakened' in various places stuck out for their right to private meetings and representation in the Church, much like the Scottish Evangelicals stood up against the state over the question of patronage. The conviction, grounded in religious experience, that Jesus Christ was Lord and had claims prior to those of the state greatly strengthened their resolve. Theodor Fliedner, later to become a social pioneer, sounded almost like a Chalmers or Candlish, when he said: 'This concerns the welfare of the church, even the welfare of the state, and I count it a small thing, if I am to be judged by a human court.'[13]

The general problem may have been the same and the theological ideas very similar, but here comparison between Scotland and the European mainland ends. The Scottish way of working out the relationship between Church and state in the Ten Years' Conflict proved to be rather unique. Even the establishment of the Free Church in Swiss canton Vaud is not necessarily a parallel, since in Scotland the first initiative – the Veto Act – had come from the Church, whereas the Swiss troubles originated with the civil government. Nowhere else did the Evangelicals have a stable majority in the same way as in Scotland, and even if that had been the case, synods and other ecclesiastical bodies did not nearly have the same measure of independence. The Church of Scotland in the nineteenth century reaped the benefits of the victories won by her Reformation fathers. To establish Protestantism against a hostile Crown and with little outside help had been an unparalleled achievement, and as a consequence the Church owed nothing to other authorities. It could – then as now – raise its voice in a way no Continental Church could as yet approach.

The closest approximation to the Disruption were the events in Vaud, which had only recently become a canton in its own right, having belonged to Berne before. For both state and Church there were thus few traditions to fall back on. Spiritually and theologically the Church was in a poor state, and it was not surprising if it wielded little public influence. Governments were usually indifferent, if not hostile. During a first conflict in 1824, a state order went so far as to forbid religious meetings in private houses even if chaired by ministers. The awakened, called 'mômiers' (bigots), were declared to be a new sect. In 1845 a radical revolution had installed a new government, which treated ministers in their capacity as state officials and required them to read a political proclamation from the pulpit. When the ministers refused, their only recourse was to leave the Church. Among the clergy they had by far the majority, but public support was limited. People saw the resignations as a measure of opposition to the new regime, and this motive did play a role with some. But in the main, the ministers wanted to assert the independence of the Church, and when people saw that they were serious and ready to undergo considerable hardship, the new Evangelical Free Church of Canton Vaud slowly started to prosper. (It also slowly started to adopt the ideas of fellow Vaudois, Alexandre Vinet, who was the Continent's leading spokesman for voluntarism. But this was only a second phase, and his thoughts had played little or no role initially.)

In this case the civil government had been even more intransigent than the British one during the Ten Years' Conflict. The Church was caught far less prepared, and so the new Free Church had a harder start. Indeed, collections were taken for it in the Scottish sister Church. But there is an ultimate parallel to the development in Scotland: in the meantime, there has been a reunion as well.

The Réveil had brought forth other free congregations in Switzerland, but these were of a different kind. Not surprisingly, in view of their contacts with British Dissenters, these Evangelicals were voluntaries. The same can be said about the Dutch 'afscheiding' of 1834, one of whose leaders, Scholte, was directly influenced by the Swiss Réveil. Contact with the Swiss Evangelicals was even closer for Frédéric Monod, the founder of the French Union des Églises Évangéliques Libres in 1849. Some small Scandinavian initiatives were influenced by direct contact with English and Scottish Churches.

The foundation of these smaller independent Churches is just as much a side-issue as the emergence of small groups of independent Lutherans in Germany, mentioned before. Impressive though their stand often was, they must not obscure the main question: the general constitutional relationship between Church and state. It was not only the Scottish Church – and the

British politicians – that suffered from a lack of clarity in this field. And if in Scotland the consequences of the muddle were the most spectacular, one can ask whether in the long run they were not just as disastrous elsewhere. At a time of fast-changing social conditions, the Church had to spend much of its energy on questions of its own independence. And even if this struggle could not be avoided, it did not help that many Churchmen still hankered after the idea of a homogeneous Christian society. But this was a lack of insight they shared with many politicians.

It is surely no coincidence that the great new ventures of this age – in foreign missions and in social concern at home – were all started by spirited individuals or by private religious societies. Compared with the end of the eighteenth century, the various kinds of revival had given a more self-confident stance to many Christians, but the organised Churches were slow to convert the new mood into tangible changes. Even if this had been different, it is still very much a question, whether enough social and political realism would have been available.

NOTES

1   A. Sydow, *Die schottische Kirchenfrage mit den darauf bezüglichen Dokumenten* (Potsdam, 1845), p. xix.
2   Anon., *Vierteljahresschrift für Theologie und Kirche*, i (1845), p. 141.
3   *Evangelische Kirchenzeitung*, (Berlin, 1849) p. 489.
4   E. Staehelin, *Alexandre Vinets ausgewählte Werke*, 4 vols (Zurich, 1844–5), vol. 4, p. 93.
5   E. E. Eklund, 'The Scottish Free Church and its Relation to Nineteenth-Century Swedish and Swedish-American Lutheranism', *Church History*, 51 (4 Dec. 1982), pp. 405 –18.
6   J. Joerg, *Geschichte des Protestantismus in seiner neuesten Entwicklung*, 2 vols (Freiburg, 1858), vol. i, p. 1f.
7   G. Sentzke, *Die Kirche Finnlands* (Göttingen, 1963), p. 105.
8   A. Neander, *Dogmatik* (Brunswick and Leipzig, 1898), pp. 11 and 25.
9   E. R. Huber and W. Huber, *Staat und Kirche im 19. und 20. Jahrhundert*, 1 vol. (Berlin, 1973), vol. i, p. 142.
10   Huber, *Staat und Kirche*, vol. i, p. 161.
11   *Hengstenbergs Evangelische Kirchenzeitung*, (Berlin, 1849), p. 28 f.
12   J. Deinzer (ed.), *Wilhelm Löhes Leben* 3 vols (Nuremberg, 1877), vol. ii, p. 413.
13   M. Gerhardt, *Theodor Fliedner*, 2 vols (Kaiserswerth, 1933), vol. i, p. 398.

Index